Else Hamayan / **Fred Ge**

Foreword by **Kathryn Li**

MW00997479

DUAL LANGUAGE INSTRUCTION

from *A* to *Z*

Practical Guidance for
Teachers and Administrators

HEINEMANN
Portsmouth, NH

Heinemann

145 Maplewood Ave., Suite 300

Portsmouth, NH 03801

www.heinemann.com

Offices and agents throughout the world

© 2013 by Else Hamayan, Fred Genesee, and Nancy Cloud

All rights reserved. No part of this book may be reproduced in any form or by any electronic or mechanical means, including information storage and retrieval systems, without permission in writing from the publisher, except by a reviewer, who may quote brief passages in a review, and with the exception of reproducible pages (identified by the *Dual Language Instruction from A to Z* copyright line), which may be photocopied for classroom use only.

"Dedicated to Teachers" is a trademark of Greenwood Publishing Group, Inc.

Library of Congress Cataloging-in-Publication Data

Hamayan, Else V.

   Dual language instruction from A to Z : practical guidance for teachers and
   administrators / Else Hamayan, Fred Genesee, Nancy Cloud.

      pages   cm

   Includes bibliographical references and index.

   ISBN-13: 978-0-325-04238-1

   ISBN-10: 0-325-04238-1

   1. Immersion method (Language teaching).   2. Second language acquisition—Study and teaching.   3. Education, Bilingual.   I. Genesee, Fred.   II. Cloud, Nancy. III. Title.

   P53.44.H26   2013

   418.0071—dc23   2013004562

Editor: Tobey Antao

Production management: Diane Freed

Production: Patty Adams

Cover and interior designs: Lisa A. Fowler

Typesetter: Cape Cod Compositors, Inc.

Manufacturing: Steve Bernier

Printed in the United States of America on acid-free paper

9 8 7   VP   21 22 23 24

To Wallace Lambert for his vision of bilingual education, and to
the teachers and administrators who share this vision and ensure
bilingualism, biliteracy, and cross-cultural competence for their students

Contents

Foreword

Dual language programs can be highly effective in helping to ensure school success in diverse learners. This reputation, along with a sizable body of research, has enabled dual language programs to increase in popularity in the U.S., Canada, and other countries. Such significant growth in dual language programs over the past thirty years raises many questions about how to develop, implement, and improve these programs. In this book, dual language and second language education experts Else Hamayan, Fred Genesee, and Nancy Cloud bring together a compendium of the most helpful research findings, best practices, and effective approaches and strategies, all of which will assist educators in developing and implementing high-quality programs.

While the authors present important background information and bring clarity to the different models for and research into language education, it is my opinion that the real usefulness of this book is in its user-friendly approach—it explains, clearly and completely, how to truly develop or improve a successful program. There are numerous helpful guidelines describing how to develop such a program, how to work within the community to gain support, how to develop goals and choose a program model, and how to prepare for curriculum and articulation across grade levels. These sections include many of the often-asked questions that new program designers struggle with. In addition, the authors have added sidebars—Resource boxes, Teacher Tips, Quotes, Research Notes, and others—highlighting content, practices, and examples that further clarify information in the text.

Most dual language programs could benefit from Chapters 3, 4, and 5 on planning for instruction and, in particular, from Chapters 4 and 5 which delve into on academic content and language instruction specifically. If there is a lack of clarity in dual language programs, it is in these two areas. Many programs could be improved by a careful study of these two chapters, which delve into specifics about establishing different kinds of objectives, appropriate teaching strategies for active learning, planning for assessment, and collaboration. For example, a Unit Planning tool uses the topic of science instruction with extensions to math and other content areas, and then discusses the range of planning issues that need to be considered for the whole class—including guiding questions, content and ELA standards, and sample teaching activities—in literature circles, in partners, individually, and with the whole class. There are performance indicators for evaluating student progress, with example rubrics for listening, speaking, reading, and writing. This model could be adapted to other content areas as well, and it exemplifies the range of planning considerations that should be considered in a dual language program. A checklist for planning new programs and reviewing existing programs along with a checklist for planning instruction are provided in the last chapter. These provide a wealth of useful practical information, as do Resource lists that provide helpful websites and other teaching resources.

Furthermore, what we have learned from thirty to forty years of involvement in dual language programs is that many students do not develop full bilingual proficiency; thus, it is exciting to see that this book includes the theory, research, guidelines, and practices for how to promote higher-level bilingual and biliteracy proficiency. Many newbies, as well as those who work in longer-term dual language programs, will find considerable help here—the book provides such information as the latest research and principles on (second) language development, cross-linguistic transfer of information, equalizing the status of the two languages, and balanced literacy.

While schools continue to experience an increase in the number of English language learners, and will for the foreseeable future, educators continue to struggle with the achievement gap that separates students according to ethnic/racial, linguistic, economic, and special needs backgrounds. *Dual Language Instruction from A to Z* competently addresses how to develop, implement, and improve programs that can effectively contribute to the educational success of students from a variety of ethnic, linguistic, economic, and special needs groups. The research and practical guidelines that are presented address how to meet the many diverse needs of various student groups, such as special education students.

This book will be very useful for program developers and implementers; for teachers, principals, and administrators; and for students and parents. It is a real gem that could help all programs effectively sparkle with highly successful students.

Kathryn Lindholm-Leary, Ph.D.
Professor Emerita
Child and Adolescent Development
San Jose State University

March 2013

Acknowledgments

Preparation of this book was facilitated by the assistance of many people.

We would like to thank Naomi Holobow for her careful editing and revisions; her expertise was invaluable in bringing this book to completion.

We also would like to thank the very committed and competent people at Heinemann who helped with the preparation and production of the manuscript at all stages. This includes Kate Montgomery, publisher, for supporting us in the conceptualization of this book and the initial steps in preparing it; Tobey Antao, editor, for her close scrutiny of the manuscript, as well as her useful, insightful feedback and guidance on all aspects of the book; Kerry Herlihy, reviewer; Lisa Fowler, vice-president, design and production, for the wonderful photographs that embellish each chapter as well as the design features of the book; Patty Adams, production manager, for shepherding the book through the production process; Sarah Fournier, associate editor, for her expert coordination of our book project; and Val McNally, associate professional book product manager, for her attractive promotional materials. A special note of thanks goes to Diane Freed for her very careful, thoughtful editing of the manuscript and project oversight.

We also want to give a special thanks to the administrators, teachers, students, and their families from the International Charter School for allowing us to take photographs in their school. In particular, we would like to thank Julie Nora, the school's director, for her hospitality in inviting us to film at this truly excellent TWI school—an inspiration for us as we worked on the book.

We also thank everyone who contributed their voices to this manuscript, and for the insights and wisdom they have shared with us and our readers:

Vivian Bueno, assistant principal
The Rafael Hernandez Dual Language School PS/MS 218
Now Principal PS 73
Bronx, New York

France Bourassa, kindergarten/elementary cycle 1 French immersion teacher
St. John Fisher Elementary Schools, Junior Campus
Pointe Claire, Quebec

Rebecca Center, literacy coordinator
Barbieri Elementary School
Framingham, MA

Patricia Corduban, second-grade Spanish teacher
Dual Immersion Academy
Grand Junction, CO

Marcos Gomez, dual language kindergarten teacher
Verda Dierzen Early Learning Center
Woodstock, IL

Kimberly Hansen, dual language kindergarten teacher
Verda Dierzen Early Learning Center
Woodstock, IL

Mishelle L. Jurado, Spanish language arts II tenth-grade teacher and
    bilingual coordinator
Albuquerque High School
Albuquerque, NM

Suzanne M. Lasser, director, ELL programs K–12
White Plains Public Schools
White Plains, NY

Francisca Silvia Lima, second- and third-grade Portuguese dual language teacher
International Charter School
Pawtucket, RI

Diana L. Madrigal-Hopes, bilingual/ESL dual language program
    development consultant
Region 10 Education Service Center
Richardson, TX

Myriam Met, immersion educational consultant to dual language programs
Former district supervisor, Montgomery County Public Schools (MD)

Dr. Marjorie L. Myers, principal
Key School ~ Escuela Key
Arlington, VA

Julie Nora, Ph.D., director
International Charter School
Pawtucket, RI

Alejandra Ortiz, bilingual/ESL and migrant program consultant
Region 10 Education Service Center
Richardson, TX

David Rogers, executive director
Dual Language Education of New Mexico
Albuquerque, NM

Cynthia Simé, second- and third-grade English dual language teacher
International Charter School
Pawtucket, RI

Dr. Dania Vázquez, headmaster
Margarita Muñiz Academy
Boston Public Schools
Jamaica Plain, MA

CHAPTER ONE

▶ Foundations of Dual Language Education

THIS BOOK IS FOR TEACHERS, school administrators, education specialists, and district personnel who are interested in or currently involved in dual language (DL) education. By dual language education, we mean elementary- and secondary-level school programs that provide instruction through two or more languages with the goal of promoting full proficiency in oral and written aspects of two or more languages, along with cross-cultural understanding and high levels of academic achievement. This book is also for parents who are interested in educating their children bilingually as well as for teacher educators who are involved in the professional development of teachers working in such programs. It is relevant for those who are already involved in some way in dual language education as well as people who are beginning to think about or to plan a new program. Our goal is to provide practical advice on all aspects of planning, implementing, evaluating, and maintaining effective dual language programs. We suggest additional resources on dual language education throughout the book in special **Resource** boxes.

We focus on DL programs in Spanish and English because these are the languages most frequently used in DL programs in the U.S. When special considerations need to be made about other language combinations, such as Chinese and English, we discuss these issues in the text or in pull-out tables and boxes called **Special Notes**. We talk about DL programs for both students who come to school already proficient in English—the majority language of the wider community—and students who come to school with no or limited proficiency in English. We refer to the first group of students as English-speaking students, and, sometimes, as mainstream or majority language learners. We refer to the latter group of students as English language learners (or ELLs for short) and, sometimes, as minority language learners.

Compared to the remaining chapters in this book, the material in this chapter might seem very general and somewhat academic. This is because the material in this chapter lays the foundations for our thinking about DL education in general and because much of it is based on findings from research. We begin this chapter by discussing the importance of bilingual and cross-cultural competence for students being educated in the twenty-first century. While many readers may not need to be convinced of the importance of bilingualism, others may need to understand that educating children in more than one language is a good idea and, moreover, that it works. We hope that our discussion of these issues helps to convince you of the value of dual language education if you are not already convinced, and that it gives you ideas you can use to help others realize that it is a good thing. We go on to describe the program models that we focus on throughout the book, followed by a discussion of the rationale for each model. This material is important because it gives us a common frame of reference.

The terms *dual language education* and *bilingual education* are often used in different ways by different people. It is important that you the reader understand what we mean by dual language education. The definitions we use are those used in the professional and scientific community, and the research we discuss and the professional advice that we give are based on these definitions. The final section of this chapter summarizes key findings from scientific studies on the effectiveness of dual language education. Schools are increasingly being asked to justify what they do on the basis of valid empirical evidence. That evidence is provided in this chapter. We have tried to present this evidence in useful ways by summarizing it according to important educational questions, such as: "Do students in DL programs really learn as much English as students in English-only programs?," "Is DL education appropriate and effective for students with learning disabilities?," and "Do students in DL programs demonstrate the same mastery and understanding of academic subjects if they are taught through their second language?"

We use special **Research Notes** and **Quotes** from researchers to highlight especially important research findings and to make research findings more understandable to non-researchers. Fears and myths abound regarding DL education and bilingualism in general, and these can influence people's decisions as to whether to offer a DL program and how to implement it. However, many of these fears lack scientific support. In this chapter, and throughout the book, we discuss research that refutes some of the common concerns that educators, parents, and policymakers have about educating children through two languages; these appear in special **Myth** boxes. We also include **Checklists** and **Dual Language Voice** features in each chapter. These provide additional guidance from practitioners in the field to help when devising and revising DL programs.

Dual Language Learning in the Twenty-First Century

There are many advantages to being competent in two or more languages. It is these advantages that provide the core motivation for DL education. Understanding these advantages is at the center of advocacy efforts on behalf of DL education both in communities that are planning to set up new programs and in communities that already have a DL program. Being able to make a strong case for the advantages of dual language/cultural competence is particularly important in English-dominant communities where it is often thought that knowing English is sufficient since it is a global language.

Globalization

Few would deny that the world is experiencing unprecedented globalization. It is evident in multiple spheres of activity: economic and business, communications, travel, culture, and immigration. Globalization has brought opportunities, advantages, and challenges. Linguistic and cultural competence are key in affording students the tools they need to take advantage of the opportunities that globalization presents. In this regard, it has been estimated that there are more second language speakers of English than native speakers (Crystal, 2003). This is an important statistic because it tells us that while English is undoubtedly a global language and, therefore, important to know, knowing *only* English is not enough because many people who speak English also speak other world languages such as Spanish, Arabic, and Chinese. Thus, students who leave school competent in languages in addition to English will have a competitive edge in the global marketplace. Familiarity with other cultures and being able to function effectively in them are similarly important because the ability to use other languages effectively depends on knowing the cultures in which those other languages are used. In essence, knowing other languages in addition to English affords students the full range of benefits that globalization offers after they leave school, including the invaluable personal benefits gained through international travel and communication using the Internet.

Cultural Inclusiveness and Understanding

Schooling involves more than reading, writing, and arithmetic. Schools also socialize students to embrace broader sociocultural values and norms. Important sociocultural values of public education in the Western world are appreciation and understanding of linguistic and cultural diversity and reduction of intolerance and prejudice toward others who are different from oneself. These are important goals for students in most schools because they encounter linguistic and cultural differences in their own classrooms. As a result, getting to know and understand other languages and cultures is important for students to be able to empathize with and appreciate many of their classmates.

DL programs provide many conditions that are essential for the reduction of prejudice and discrimination and the enhancement of understanding and inclusiveness (see Genesee & Gándara, 1999, for a detailed discussion). They also clearly provide students with the communication skills and cultural awareness that facilitate intergroup contact and communication. These possibilities are most likely in TWI

(Two-Way Immersion) programs that include students from both language groups and DBE (Developmental Bilingual Education) programs since these programs provide opportunities for sustained, personalized contact with members of another group in a supportive, structured environment. However, they are also present in IMM (foreign/second-language immersion) programs for mainstream students through vicarious contact with members of the target language culture in the materials they use and through their teachers. Direct contact outside school with members of the other group (Spanish speakers in the case of English-speaking students in Spanish IMM programs, for example) is also possible when students' language proficiency is sufficiently advanced. DL programs provide mainstream students with opportunities to better understand their peers who speak other languages and belong to a variety of cultural groups, and to enjoy the diversity of their backgrounds. As well, they enhance mainstream students' and teachers' opportunities to extend their personal and social lives to include members of their community who might remain "foreign" and "hidden" because of linguistic and cultural barriers. Moreover, there are many varieties of Spanish—for example, Dominican, Puerto Rican, Mexican, and Colombian. The same is true of Chinese and most other languages. Prejudices exist among students who speak different varieties of the same language, and DL classrooms provide a supportive environment in which students can learn about dialect variation and get to know speakers of different varieties of their own language, thereby reducing prejudices toward people who speak differently. In short, using the rich linguistic and cultural diversity found in DL programs, teachers can enrich all students' metalinguistic awareness of the diversity of language and the value of such diversity.

Research Notes

Conditions for Fostering Intergroup Appreciation

Research on Intergroup Contact Theory (Genesee & Gándara, 1999) has found that positive relations between members of different social or cultural groups are fostered when the following conditions are met:

- **Equal status:** Both groups enjoy equal status.
- **Common goals:** Both groups work on a problem/task and share a common goal.
- **Acquaintance potential:** Members of each group have the opportunity to get to know each other as friends, not merely as actors playing out social roles or as representatives of their social groups.
- **Support of authorities:** Authority figures support and encourage positive intergroup relations, attitudes, and cooperation, and they create the conditions and norms that support positive contact and interaction between different groups and their members.

Pedagogical Advantages

DL programs have many pedagogical advantages. For children from the mainstream language group, there is, generally speaking, a good match between the cultural norms of the home and of the school. However, for children from other language groups, there is often a poor match. This is because what is considered appropriate in their homes may be inappropriate, or what is appropriate in school may be unfamiliar to ELLs in their homes (Greenfield, Quiroz, & Raeff, 2000). All students possess what Luis Moll has referred to as "funds of knowledge" that shape their behavior and learning in school (Gonzalez, Moll, & Amanti, 2005). Funds of knowledge are acquired in the home and community before children come to school and include the skills, knowledge, expectations, and understanding that children have about the world and their place in it. The funds of knowledge that mainstream students possess are used by mainstream classroom teachers to make students feel like they fit in and as resources for linking new knowledge and skills to students' prior learning and life experiences (e.g., Snow, Burns, & Griffin, 1998). This is done, for example, when teachers preview new learning objectives with their students by encouraging them to discuss and think about prior knowledge and experiences that are related to these objectives. Students from different cultural backgrounds have different funds of knowledge that have grown out of their unique cultural experiences. They can have difficulty fitting into the classroom and benefitting from classroom instruction because teachers assume they have the same funds of knowledge as mainstream students; this makes it difficult for many ELLs to link new learning to their prior experiences.

A particularly important aspect of the funds of knowledge that children bring to school involves norms concerning the use of language and how children and adults should interact with one another. In many English-speaking homes, it is considered normal for child to talk extensively with adults. In mainstream middle-class families in most North American families, for example, children are encouraged and expected to initiate conversations with adults, and even with strangers in the company of their parents, and to demonstrate individually what they know and want, be it at home or in the classroom

(Rogoff, 2003). Teachers take these kinds of behaviors as signs that students are engaged and focused. In contrast, children from some other cultures are socialized to not initiate conversations with adults, "to speak only when spoken to" (Greenfield, Quiroz, & Raeff, 2000); to not look directly at adults when they talk to them as a sign of respect (Richards, Brown, & Forde, 2006); and to work together with their peers to support the group rather than to work individually (Au & Jordan, 1981). These kinds of behaviors could be interpreted as signs of lack of motivation, distraction, or even of learning problems by classroom teachers who have a mainstream Eurocentric point of view because they run counter to cultural expectations associated with their own socialization patterns.

DL teachers who teach using non-English languages along with English are better prepared to accommodate diverse sociocultural backgrounds and different expectations concerning language use because they have usually had appropriate training on the importance of these issues. Many teachers in DL programs may themselves belong to non-mainstream cultural groups and thus understand their ELLs' backgrounds firsthand, or at least understand what it means to be different (Howard & Loeb, 1998; Lindholm-Leary, 2001). For mainstream students, participation in a DL program provides them with experiences where different cultural norms and expectations are respected and practiced, and this, in turn, broadens their cultural competence.

Neurocognitive Advantages

Research conducted during the past two decades has found that advanced levels of bilingual competence are associated with significant cognitive advantages (e.g., Bialystok, 2007). Bialystok has argued that the DL learners' experiences in controlling attention to two languages to keep them separate and to use them appropriately enhances the development of executive control functions. These neurocognitive advantages are evident in childhood and in later adulthood as well. The bilingual advantage found by Bialystok is most evident in bilingual people who acquire relatively advanced levels of proficiency in two languages and use their two languages actively on a regular basis.

Research Notes

Cognitive Advantages of Bilingualism

Research over the past two decades has found that advanced levels of bilingual proficiency are associated with several significant language and cognitive advantages (e.g., Marian & Shook [2012]; Bialystok [2007]). The advantages of bilingualism have been demonstrated in cognitive domains related to attention, inhibition, monitoring, and switching focus of attention. These processes are required during problem solving, for example, when students must focus their attention if potentially conflicting information needs to be considered; in order to select relevant information and inhibit processing of irrelevant information; and when they must switch attention to consider alternative information when a solution is not forthcoming. Collectively, these cognitive skills comprise what are referred to as *executive control functions* and are located in the frontal lobe regions of the brain.

These findings have significant implications for educators—implications that complement the economic and personal advantages associated with bilingual competence in a globalized world. Specifically, these findings argue that DL education is a form of cognitive enrichment. At the same time, these findings argue for programs that provide substantive and continuous opportunities for students to develop bilingual competence so that they achieve the relatively high levels of bilingualism that confer these cognitive advantages.

Models of Dual Language Education

We focus on three forms of DL education in this book. They are:

1. Foreign/Second Language Immersion programs (IMM) for English-speaking students,

2. Developmental Bilingual Education (DBE) programs for students with no or limited proficiency in English upon school entry, and

3. Two-Way Immersion (TWI) programs for both English-speaking students and students with no or limited proficiency in English upon school entry.

These are enriched forms of DL education because they aim for full competence in two (or more) languages along with high levels of academic achievement and cross-cultural understanding and appreciation (Cloud, Genesee, & Hamayan, 2000).

In this section, we discuss the most salient and important features of IMM, DBE, and TWI programs. We begin with a brief summary of important characteristics that all models share. We then discuss each model separately, starting with IMM and then DBE programs because these models were introduced earlier than TWI and, more importantly, because these program models form the basis for TWI. TWI is, in fact, the most common form of DL education in the U.S. and encompasses features and advantages associated with both IMM and DBE. After we discuss salient features of each DL model, we discuss the rationale for each. It is important to understand the rationale for the program model you are planning or implementing so that you are better able to ensure the conditions for success.

IMM, DBE, and TWI programs all share some important features.

1. They all share the same general goals, namely:
   ▸ high levels of academic achievement,
   ▸ oral and written proficiency in two languages, and
   ▸ appreciation and understanding of the home language culture and that of the other language.
2. Academic subjects are taught to students through both English and another language, during designated times of the day, week, or month for several years.
3. In all of these programs, students are also expected to interact socially with one another and with their teachers using each language during designated times.

Through social interaction and academic instruction in two languages students in DL programs acquire bilingual competence as well

Social interaction promotes learning across languages.

SPECIAL NOTE

Setting Guidelines or Grade-Level Expectations for Languages Other than English and Spanish

Various agencies and organizations provide support to programs in languages other than English. For example, here is a document published by the Asia Society for educators working in Chinese/English Immersion Programs:

Chinese Language Learning in the Early Grades: A Handbook of Resources and Best Practices for Mandarin Immersion (2012, Asia Society; edited by Mimi Met and Vivien Stewart). Download at: http://asiasociety.org/files/chinese-early language.pdf

You might also consult directories available through the Center for Applied Linguistics to find current programs operating in various non-English languages. These programs may have developed standards or expectations for their program or know

(continues)

what agencies have done for the non-English language in which they provide instruction. See:

Directory of Two-Way Bilingual Immersion Programs in the U.S. (2011, Center for Applied Linguistics): http://www.cal.org/twi/directory

Directory of Foreign Language Immersion Programs in U.S. Schools (2011): http://www.cal.org/resources/immersion/

as high levels of academic achievement and cross-cultural understanding. By using both languages throughout the elementary grades and beyond, in some cases, DL programs can create an additive bilingual environment for students where their home language is maintained and developed at the same time that they acquire competence in a second language.

MYTH: *Young children are linguistic sponges—they can acquire a second language easily and quickly with little formal instruction.*

FACT: Second language learning is a challenging and lengthy process for children. Studies indicate that it can take children a minimum of two and up to five or seven years to achieve advanced proficiency in academic English (see Genesee & Lindholm-Leary, 2012, for a review). Even mastery of basic grammar and phonology can take ELLs living in monolingual English communities more than two years (Paradis, 2006).

Foreign/Second Language Immersion

Foreign or second language immersion (IMM) programs are intended for students who come to school speaking the majority language of the wider community—English in the case of the U.S. In fact, IMM programs in French-as-a-second language for native English-speaking students in Canada were the first IMM programs in North America; they were started in 1965. The success of the Canadian programs led to their being adopted in the U.S; the first IMM program that appeared in the U.S. was in Culver City, California, in the early 1970s. We refer to research findings from both Canadian and American U.S. programs to reinforce critical recommendations that we make. In fact, IMM programs can be found around the world and, thus, the majority language differs from community to community—Japanese in Japan (see Bostwick, 2001), Estonian in Estonia (Mehisto & Asser, 2007), and Spanish in Spain (Cenoz, 2009). IMM programs are chosen by English-speaking parents in the U.S. (and other English-speaking countries) because they see competence in other languages along with English as an advantage for their children for personal reasons, such as travel, and/or because of globalization and the enhanced employment opportunities afforded people who speak more than one language. Some parents choose IMM so that their children can acquire competence in a heritage language (such as Hawaiian) or in a language of local importance, such as Spanish in California, Rhode Island, or Florida. At the end of this section, we discuss why so-called Structured English Immersion (SEI) programs for ELLs are not true immersion programs.

 DUAL LANGUAGE VOICE: CHOOSING A PROGRAM MODEL

Barbieri Elementary School's dual language model has evolved during the fifteen years I have been a teacher there. Our original model started with each language group learning to read and write first in their dominant language, thus learning separately in different classrooms during the literacy block. The two language groups were integrated for content areas in Spanish. In third through fifth grade the two groups were integrated for the whole day with 50 percent of instruction in English and 50 percent in Spanish.

We began to see many challenges in this model. Test scores were low, and the achievement gap between native English speakers and native Spanish speakers remained strong. Native English speakers were not able to access grade-level content in Spanish in the higher grades. In addition, students did not interact much with the opposite language group at recess time or outside of school.

It was time to take a good look at the program model. In the spring of 2005 and during the following twelve months, we evaluated our program using the Center for Applied Linguistics' Guiding Principles and developed action plans. After this year of study, we chose to change to an 80/20 model, with kindergarten and first grade spending 80 percent of their time in Spanish and 20 percent in English. Second grade would be 70/30 and grades 3–5 would be 50/50. After five years with the new model, we have seen some very positive shifts:

❏ By the end of kindergarten, the majority of the English dominant children are at ease learning and responding in Spanish. In the upper elementary grades their Spanish is strong enough to engage in grade-level activities. *(continues)*

- ❏ ELLs are reaching kindergarten benchmarks more effectively than under the old model due to scaffolding provided to English dominant children that is now helping the ELLs.

- ❏ The K–2 students are in self-contained classrooms with fewer transitions, allowing the teachers to attend to each student's specific needs.

- ❏ The demand for the program grew and we had to add a fifth kindergarten class.

- ❏ Now both Latino and non-Latino students are forming stronger friendships across socioeconomic and ethnic lines (as witnessed at recess and at out-of-school functions, such as birthday parties).

We can now say that we are meeting our goals for students to develop high proficiency in L1 and L2 and positive cross-cultural attitudes, while making significant progress in helping our students to perform at or above grade-level expectations.

—Rebecca Center, Literacy Coordinator
Barbieri Elementary School, Framingham, MA
Two-Way Bilingual Program; 80/20

There are a number of alternative forms of IMM programs for English-speaking students. Programs differ with respect to when the non-English language begins to be used as a medium of academic instruction. There are three common models that differ in this respect:

1. *Early immersion* starts in kindergarten or grade 1.

2. *Delayed immersion* begins in grade 4 or 5.

3. *Late immersion* begins in grade 7.

Programs also differ in how much English and the non-English languages are used for instructional purposes. Here are some common variations:

1. *Early total IMM:* These programs provide 100 percent of instruction in the non-English language in kindergarten to grade 2 or 3, depending on the school district; instruction in English, the students' home language, does not begin until grade 3 or 4. Once English is introduced, it increases each year as additional subjects are taught in English so that about 50 percent of instruction is in

the non-English language and 50 percent in English by the end of elementary school. This is a common model in Canada.

2. *"90/10" IMM:* This is a common form of early IMM in the U.S. In these programs, 90 percent of instruction is in the non-English language starting in kindergarten and 10 percent is in English. Instruction in English increases, often starting in grade 2, until approximately 50 percent of instruction is in English and 50 percent is in the non-English language by the end of elementary school (see Figure 1.1).

3. *"50/50" early IMM* (sometimes called *partial immersion*): This is also a common program in the U.S. This model provides 50 percent of instruction in the non-English language and 50 percent in English from kindergarten, and this ratio is maintained throughout the elementary grades (see Figure 1.1).

4. *One-year and two-year late IMM:* In these programs, between 50 percent and 80 percent of instruction in grade 7 only (one-year late IMM) or in both grades 7 and 8 (two-year late IMM) is taught in the non-English language and the remainder is in English. Late IMM students have traditional L2 instruction during the elementary grades to prepare them for academic instruction in the L2 starting in grade 7. Immersion teachers in late IMM programs focus on L2 development during the first two or three months of the program to prepare students for academic instruction through the L2 that is at the appropriate grade level (see Genesee, 2004, for a more detailed description of these programs). Students in these programs take selected subjects (e.g., geography, history, mathematics) in the non-English language after grade 7 or 8 to maintain their competence in that language.

Programs with a delayed or late start provide traditional instruction in the non-English language (often referred to as "core L2 instruction") in those grades that precede the beginning of immersion (from kindergarten to grade 6 in the case of a grade 7 late immersion program, for example). This means that students in delayed or late IMM programs are not taught academic subjects through their L2 without having had some prior instruction in the target language. Delayed IMM programs are not very common in the U.S., but are more common in Canada, and late IMM programs exist in Canada but not in the U.S.

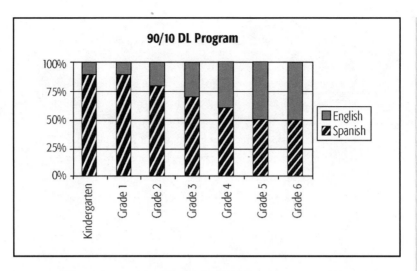

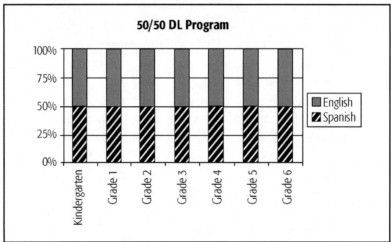

Figure 1.1 Schematic Representation of Both 90/10 and 50/50 IMM and DBE Programs

To be considered a bona fide IMM program, there must be a minimum of 50 percent instruction in the non-English language for at least one school year; in fact, most IMM programs provide this level of immersion for several years. Programs with less instruction in the non-English language are generally referred to as "enriched foreign language" instruction.

Programs vary considerably in how they distribute each language during those grades when instruction is given in both languages. The classic IMM program divides up the languages by subject matter with specific subjects being taught in a specific language; for example, mathematics in English and science in Spanish. The language of instruction for a specific subject, like mathematics, might change from one grade to the next, but generally the same language would be used during a whole school year to teach a specific subject. Many IMM programs seek to provide instruction in each language every day during those grades when both languages are used for academic instruction. For example, during those grades when each language is used 50 percent of the time, the favored model is using the non-English language to teach in the mornings and English in the afternoons. Table 1.1 summarizes the rationale for IMM.

Table 1.1

Rationale for IMM Programs
1. Second-language learning is relatively easy for young school-age learners compared to older learners and adults, although we shall see later that it is nevertheless a complex and time-consuming task. Early IMM programs take advantage of young learners' facility at learning language.
2. Young school-age children are especially open to new linguistic and cultural experiences and thus are open to learning new languages in the early grades of schooling.
3. Children learn a second language most effectively when it is used for meaningful, authentic, and sustained communication, contexts that are like those when children learn their L1. For school-age learners, teaching academic content and literacy through an L2 is such a learning context, provided it takes the students' learning needs into account.
4. Literacy and academic skills and knowledge acquired in one language facilitate the acquisition of related knowledge and skills in another language (August & Shanahan, 2006; Genesee, Lindholm-Leary, Saunders, & Christian, 2006). For English-speaking students in IMM programs, literacy and academic instruction in Spanish, for example, facilitates the acquisition of literacy and academic skills in English. Even in IMM programs with languages that are typologically very different from English, such as Chinese or Japanese, transfer of language skills takes place. As a result of cross-linguistic transfer, English-speaking students in IMM programs need less time to attain grade-appropriate levels of competence in English literacy and academic domains than students educated entirely in English, and they do not experience long-term deficits in these domains of English achievement despite the fact that they have less instruction in and through English.
5. English-speaking students in IMM have extensive exposure to oral and written English outside school, and this exposure offsets any possible negative effects that reduced exposure to English in school might have.

▶ Structured English Immersion for ELLs Is Not Additive DL Education

It is important to clarify the distinction between additive forms of IMM for students who speak English, as we describe here, and English-only programs for ELLs, which are often referred to in the U.S. as Structured English Immersion (or SEI) by some educators. The definition of IMM that we use is the definition used in the research community. There are a number of important differences between these forms of immersion education:

1. IMM programs, as defined in this book and by researchers, are programs for students who speak the majority language of the larger community (English in the case of the U.S. and Canada); in fact, virtually all students in IMM classrooms are native speakers of the majority language. In contrast, SEI programs are intended for ELLs.

2. IMM programs are additive forms of DL education because they promote full proficiency in English and the non-English language. In contrast, SEI programs for ELLs make no provision to support the development of ELLs' home language. In fact, ELLs are generally expected to give up their home language and culture for the sake of acquiring English; these programs are regarded as subtractive forms of bilingual education because they often result in loss of the home language as students become more proficient in English.

3. IMM programs provide continuous academic and language instruction through the non-English language and English for several years. Fifty percent of instruction in the non-English language is regarded as a bare minimum for a program to qualify as IMM. SEI programs provide support in ELLs' home language for only one or two school years, at most, and often do not satisfy the 50 percent rule.

4. Classroom teachers in IMM programs for native English-speaking students modify instruction in the L2, taking into account that their students are learning through an L2. More specifically, they adjust their use of language, their instructional activities, and the materials they use in ways that ensure that students acquire academic content at grade level even though they are learning through their L2. They do this throughout the day, as they teach

mathematics, science, or other academic subjects (see Cloud, Genesee, & Hamayan, 2000, and Met, 1998, for descriptions of these accommodations), and they do this for the duration of the program—six years and more in the case of early IMM. At the same time, students get instruction in their native language. We talk about the accommodations and adaptations that are made in additive IMM programs in general in Chapters 4 and 5. In contrast, SEI programs in the U.S. provide instructional accommodations for ELLs' particular linguistic and cultural needs for only one or two years usually. Some English-only programs provide instructional accommodations for ELLs for more than one year. This form of instruction is sometimes referred to as "sheltered instruction." However, these students do not get sustained support to maintain and advance their competence in their home language.

Developmental Bilingual Education

Developmental Bilingual Education (DBE), also referred to as *maintenance bilingual education* and *late-exit bilingual education*, is intended for students who come to school speaking a non-English language and have no or limited proficiency in English. DBE programs are offered in a variety of minority languages in the U.S., including Chinese, Vietnamese, Russian, Japanese, French, German, and Spanish, with the vast majority of programs serving Spanish-speaking students. DBE programs are intended to serve speakers of the same non-English language in the same classroom. Even when students all speak the same language, such as Spanish, they might speak different varieties of the language. In the case of Spanish-speaking ELLs, they might speak Spanish that is typically spoken in Mexico, Cuba, Puerto Rico, or Colombia. These children will also have very different cultural backgrounds and different funds of knowledge, as we discussed before. Students in DBE programs can also vary considerably with respect to their level of proficiency in the non-English language and English— some DBE students may be born and raised in the U.S. but speak no, or only limited, English when they first enroll; some DBE students may already be proficiently bilingual; and recent Spanish-speaking immigrants from other counties may know no English at all. These are all learner characteristics that need to be considered when planning instruction. We discuss these differences, how to identify them, and what to do about them elsewhere in the book.

Most DBE programs begin in kindergarten and extend until the end of elementary school. It is strongly recommended that efforts be made to extend students' opportunities to participate in DBE programs through high school to maximize their bilingual competence and to minimize the risk of students losing competence in the non-English language which, in general, gets relatively little support outside school. There are two common models of DBE—90/10 and 50/50:

1. *90/10:* Beginning in kindergarten and extending to the end of grade 2, 90 percent of instruction is taught in the non-English language and the remaining 10 percent is in English. Instruction in English increases, usually beginning in grade 3, until about 50 percent of instruction is in English and 50 percent is in the non-English language; refer back to Figure 1.1 for a schematic representation of this.

2. *50/50:* In this model, 50 percent of curriculum instruction is taught using each language from the beginning and throughout the elementary grades (refer back to Figure 1.1).

There are variations of these two common models: The non-English language might be taught for 70 to 80 percent, for example, and English for the balance. At least 50 percent of instruction should be given in the non-English language for more than one year; otherwise, the program cannot support full development of the home language and thus the program would not be a true additive DL program. Research findings that we present in this and other chapters are based on programs with a minimum of 50 percent instruction in the non-English language. Thus, it is critical that new and existing DBE programs conform to these models if the research results we review are to apply to them. As in the case of IMM programs, the distribution of the languages for instructional purposes in DBE programs varies and, as before, we recommend that programs distribute the languages in ways that give students regular (preferably daily) exposure to each language and that do not require extensive switching from language to language for the same subjects. See Table 1.2 for a summary of the rationale for DBE.

Table 1.2

Rationale for DBE Programs
1. Research shows that strong native language skills provide a solid foundation for the acquisition of an L2. Minority languages, such as Spanish, in the U.S. have low social status and, as a result, ELLs often have little incentive to learn and use the home language. This puts ELLs at risk for difficulty acquiring literacy and academic language skills in English in school because development of the home language is relatively unsupported in the wider community. In contrast, students who speak English as a native language usually acquire a solid foundation in English because it is well supported in the community at large. Thus, students who speak the mainstream language can be immersed in a second language in school without jeopardizing their native language development. Instruction in the home language of ELLs in DBE programs provides them with a solid linguistic foundation for the acquisition of English as a second language.
2. ELLs who are taught academic subjects through the home language are better able to keep up in academic domains than ELLs taught in English only because they are learning through a language they already know.
3. ELLs who are taught academic language, literacy, and academic subjects through the home language during the primary grades are better able to close the achievement gap with mainstream students in the long run because they are better able to make significant gains in the primary grades; and they can transfer skills they acquire in the home language to English once instruction in English begins.
4. ELLs in DBE programs have superior levels of proficiency in the home language and attain the same levels of proficiency in English, or better, than ELLs in English-only programs. Advanced levels of bilingual proficiency result in enhanced academic achievement and general cognitive ability (Bialystok, 2006; Lindholm & Aclan, 1991).
5. The advanced levels of bilingual competence achieved by ELLs in DBE programs is advantageous for reasons linked to globalization, cognitive development, and cultural tolerance.

Two-Way Immersion

Two-way immersion (TWI) programs (also known as *two-way bilingual education* and *dual-language immersion*) include both ELLs and English-speaking students in the same classrooms. In fact, TWI programs are an amalgam of both IMM programs for English-speaking students and DBE programs for ELLs (see Figure 1.2). By including both ELLs and English-speaking students in the same classrooms, TWI programs create unique language and cultural learning environments in which students from both the majority language group and the minority language group can become bilingual by learning from one another. Because there are native speakers of both languages in TWI classrooms, all students are both first language models for other students and

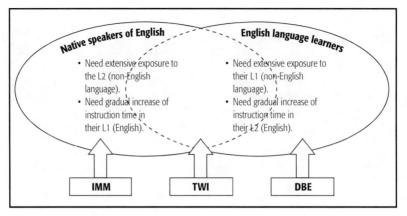

Figure 1.2 TWI Is an Amalgam of IMM and DBE

second language learners; for example, in a Spanish-English TWI program, native Spanish-speaking students serve as models of Spanish for
native English-speaking students during classes when Spanish is used
for instruction and, vice versa, English-speaking students serve as models for ELLs when English is the language of instruction. Students in
TWI programs also have the advantage of learning about the culture of
the other language group and making friends with members of that
group. This is a unique advantage of TWI that sets it apart from DBE
and IMM programs. In these programs students usually have minimal
contact in class with native speakers of the L2 because these programs
include only ELLs in the case of DBE programs and only English-
speaking students in the case of IMM. Because TWI is a unique learning
environment, it has its unique rationale. See Table 1.3.

It is recommended that there be 50 percent English speakers and
50 percent ELLs in every TWI class and that this balance be maintained at all grade levels as much as possible. Languages other than
English tend to have less status in U.S. schools and, thus, every effort
must be made in DL schools to support and enhance the status of that
language and its associated culture. If too many native English-
speaking students are included, there is the risk that English will take
on more status than the non-English language and that it will dominate in both curriculum instruction and student language use.

Most TWI programs start in kindergarten or grade 1 and continue until the end of elementary school; preferably, they continue into
middle and high school. It is highly recommended that efforts be made

Table 1.3

Rationale for TWI Programs
1. Because TWI is an amalgam of IMM and DBE, the rationale for each of these program models (refer back to Tables 1.1 and 1.2) also applies to TWI. At the same time, TWI programs are unique learning environments and, thus, there are unique aspects of the rationale for TWI.
2. The systematic linguistic and cultural integration of native speakers of English and ELLs in TWI classes facilitates acquisition of both English and the non-English language because it promotes authentic, meaningful interaction with native-speaking models of each language.
3. Integrating both ELLs and native speakers of English in TWI classrooms promotes the value of and respect for both English and the other language and of the culture of the speakers of those languages. This promotes positive intergroup attitudes and relations that can have a particularly positive impact on ELLs' self-esteem and, in turn, on their engagement in learning in school (González, Moll, & Amanti, 2005; Lantolf, 2005). It also provides mainstream students with a unique opportunity to learn about other cultures.

to extend the program through middle and high school so that students do not lose proficiency in the non-English language. Again, this is important because the non-English language is less likely to be used and reinforced outside school. There are two common models of TWI, and these follow the same format as in DBE: 90/10 and 50/50; these models were defined in the previous section on DBE.

A summary of the primary characteristics of all three models is presented in Table 1.4.

What Does Research Tell Us About DL Programs?

In this section, we answer some commonly asked questions about DL programs by drawing on research findings. There has been extensive research on each program model and, thus, educators planning a new program or reviewing an existing one have a great deal of scientific information to inform their decisions about new programs and their evaluations of existing programs. It is highly recommended that schools setting up a new program include plans for assessing the program and that existing programs engage in regular

On the Importance of School-Based Assessments

"It is important for educators to develop an evaluation plan to determine whether the DLI program is meeting the needs of the students. Evaluation data can be helpful in pinpointing additional instructional needs and in assuring parents and educators that the program is helping students to develop bilingual and biliterate proficiencies."

—Professor Kathryn Lindholm-Leary
Professor Emeritus,
San Jose State University

Table 1.4

Primary Characteristics of Dual Language Program Models			
	Foreign/Second-Language Immersion (IMM)	**Developmental Bilingual Education (DBE)**	**Two-Way Immersion (TWI)**
Student characteristics	• Speak majority language of community at home—English in the U.S	• No/limited proficiency in English • Same home language, but perhaps different dialects of that language • Mixed cultural background	• Both native speakers of English and students with no/limited proficiency in English (ELLs) • Different cultural backgrounds • ELLs may speak different dialects of non-English language
Language goals	• Native levels of oral and written competence in English • Advanced functional competence in the L2 (i.e., the non-English language)*	• Native levels of oral and written competence in English • Native levels of oral and written competence in the non-English language (i.e., Spanish)*	• English-speaking students: native levels of oral and written competence in English and advanced functional competence in the non-English* • ELLs: native levels of oral and written competence in the home language and in English
Cultural goals	• Understanding and appreciation of the L2 culture • Full development of home culture	• Acculturation of ELLs to majority culture • Full development of and appreciation of the home culture	• For ELLs: acculturation to majority culture while maintaining and appreciating the home culture • For English-speaking students: understanding of the L2 culture and maintenance and appreciation of the home culture
Academic goals	School, District, and State Goals and Standards		
Grade levels served	• Elementary and preferably middle and secondary	• Elementary and preferably middle and secondary	• Elementary and preferably middle and secondary
Entry levels	• K or primary; late elementary or middle school; early secondary	• K, grade 1, or grade 2	• K or grade 1

Primary Characteristics of Dual Language Program Models (continued)			
	Foreign/Second-Language Immersion (IMM)	Developmental Bilingual Education (DBE)	Two-Way Immersion (TWI)
Length of participation	• Minimum of 6 years, preferably 12 years	• Usually 6 years (+K), preferably 12 years (+K)	• Usually 6 years (+K), preferably 12 years (+K)
Role of teachers	• Non-English-speaking/bilingual teacher is class teacher • Monolingual English-speaking teacher may teach English portion of the curriculum • Monolingual English-speaking and non-English-speaking/bilingual teacher collaborate to teach curriculum	• Non-English-speaking/bilingual teacher is class teacher • Monolingual English-speaking-only teacher may teach English portion of the curriculum • English-speaking-only and non-English-speaking/bilingual collaborate during bilingual phase of program to teach curriculum	• Non-English-speaking/bilingual teacher teaches non-English portion of the curriculum • Monolingual English-speaking teacher may teach English portion of curriculum • Monolingual English-speaking and non-English-speaking/bilingual teacher collaborate to teach curriculum
Teacher qualifications	• Native speaker or near-native speaker competence in non-English language • Preferably certificate in immersion education	• Native speaker or near-native speaker competence in non-English language • Bilingual-multicultural certificate	• Bilingual/immersion certification • Bilingual proficiency • Multicultural training
Instructional materials, texts, visual aids, etc.	• Adapted for non-native speakers of non-English language in primary grades • Appropriate for native speakers of non-English language in higher grades	• Materials in non-English language: appropriate for native speakers of non-English language • Materials in English: adapted for L2 learners of English in primary grades; and appropriate for native speakers of English in the higher grades	• Materials in non-English language: appropriate for native speakers of non-English language • Materials in English: adapted for L2 learners of English in primary grades; and appropriate for native speakers of English in the higher grades

* Different levels of proficiency in the L2 are expected for English-speaking and ELL students because the latter have lots of exposure to their L2 (English) in the community and in school, whereas English-speaking students often do not have such exposure to their L2.

assessments of student progress as they advance through the grades. In-school assessments are invaluable for making adjustments to programs in order to maximize student outcomes. Planning in-school assessments has the added benefit of motivating schools to clearly define learning objectives. Without clear objectives, it is difficult to gauge student progress and to know whether the program is succeeding. Without clear objectives, it is also difficult to develop appropriate curriculum, lesson plans, and learning materials. Assessment can drive these critical activities. We discuss how to do this in greater detail in the following chapters. Many schools, school districts, and states have their own benchmarks, and these can be used to establish goals for students in DL programs, at least when it comes to English. A useful resource for planning your own evaluation is the Evaluator's Toolkit for Dual Language Programs, which is available at http://www.cal.org/twi/EvalToolkit/ (Lindholm-Leary & Hargett, 2007).

Question: Can students really learn as much English in DL programs as students in English-only programs?

A primary concern among parents, educators, and policy makers is whether students who participate in DL programs attain the same levels of competence in English as students in English-only programs. Common sense might argue that students in DL programs will attain lower levels of proficiency in English because they have less exposure to English in school than students in English-only programs. DL education would not be viable or desirable if it were to result in loss of English language competence among either English-speaking students or ELLs. It is important to consider this question from the perspective of each group of learners because it implicates somewhat different issues. With respect to English-speaking students, the issue is whether they can maintain and continue to develop skills in the native language that are typical for their age group. With respect to ELLs, the issue is what level of competence they can acquire in English-as-a-second language, a language that is critical for their academic success and long-term career success because it is the majority language of the community. Fortunately, there is a wealth of evidence on these issues and, thus, we can be confident in our answers to these questions. Let's

Language minority children succeed when their native language is valued and developed.

start off by talking about ELLs in DL programs (see reviews by Genesee & Lindholm-Leary, 2012, and Lindholm-Leary & Genesee, 2010).

▶ ENGLISH OUTCOMES OF ELLs

Numerous studies have found that by late elementary or middle school ELLs in DL programs score significantly higher than ELLs in general on norm-referenced standardized tests and criterion-referenced state tests of reading in English. They also perform on par with English-speaking students in English-only classrooms (e.g., Block, 2007; Christian, Genesee, Lindholm-Leary, & Howard, 2008; Howard & Sugarman, 2007; Thomas & Collier, 2002). These results extend to studies of Chinese- and Korean-speaking DL students (Garcia, 2003; Ha, 2001; Lindholm-Leary, 2011). The English language outcomes of ELLs in DL programs sometimes lag behind those of students in English-only programs during the primary grades when the focus is on using the non-English language. However, evaluations that are carried out in grades 4 and higher indicate that ELLs in DL programs achieve parity with ELLs in English-only programs and often score at state-mandated levels by grade 4, or later. Here are some additional important findings about the English language outcomes of ELLs in DL programs:

- Lindholm-Leary (2008) found that redesignation rates of ELLs from "limited English proficient" to "fully English proficient" tend to be higher for ELLs in TWI programs than in all-English programs.

- In a review of research on the English literacy development of ELLs in DL and all-English programs, Francis and his colleagues noted that, "Overall, where differences between two instructional conditions were found in the studies reviewed, these differences typically favored the bilingual instruction condition" (Francis, Lesaux, & August, 2006; p. 398).

- Howard and her colleagues conducted a number of studies of the reading and writing development of ELLs and native English-speaking students in TWI programs and found they met or exceeded grade-level norms at least by grade 5 (e.g., Howard & Sugarman, 2007; Lindholm-Leary & Howard, 2008).

Howard's results, above, are important because they underline the importance of a long-term commitment to participation in DL programs if students are to benefit fully. They also highlight the importance of a long-term school plan to ensure the conditions for program success. The short-term lags in English outcomes that DL students sometimes exhibit during the primary grades, as noted by Howard and her colleagues, disappear with more instruction in English. If decisions about program success are made too early, the wrong choices would be made.

▶ ENGLISH OUTCOMES OF ENGLISH-SPEAKING STUDENTS

Extensive research in the U.S., Canada, and elsewhere has shown consistently that English-speaking students in DL programs achieve the same or higher levels of proficiency in English as students in English-only programs. This is true even when researchers control for socioeconomic status and academic ability, factors that often favor students in DL programs and are often associated with differences in school achievement (Genesee, 2004; Paradis, Genesee, & Crago, 2010). English-speaking students in early DL programs often do not score on par with other English-speaking students on standardized tests of reading and writing in English during the first two or three grades of a DL program—when all or most instruction and, in particular, literacy instruction is in the non-English language. This makes sense because the emphasis during the primary grades is on developing students' oral language and literacy abilities in the non-English language. English-speaking students in DL programs achieve parity with students in English-only programs in reading and writing once instruction in English is introduced into the program—for example, by the end of grade 2 or 3 in early total IMM or 90/10 TWI programs.

Both Genesee and Lindholm-Leary have found that, for English-speaking students in DL programs, there is little correlation between how much exposure they have to English in school and the level of proficiency they attain in English by the end of elementary school. For example, students in total immersion or in 90/10 programs achieve the same level of competence in English as students in partial immersion or 50/50 programs even though the former have less exposure to English. However, and in contrast, they found that students who had more exposure to the non-English language in school achieved higher levels

> ### On the Importance of Long-Term Commitment
>
> *"When considering the implementation of a dual language program, it is critical for administrators, teachers, and parents to understand that they require long-term planning and commitment in order to be successful. While new programs typically start with just kindergarten and first-grade classes, there is a clear understanding that the program will grow to encompass at least the full elementary sequence, and provisions are made to identify and train teachers and obtain or develop appropriate curricular materials before the first cohort of students advances to the next grade level. Furthermore, there must be an unwavering commitment to the long-term goals of academic achievement, highly developed bilingualism and biliteracy, and strong cross-cultural competence so that program integrity is upheld despite external pressures, such as the current atmosphere of high stakes testing."*
>
> —Liz Howard, Assistant Professor of Bilingual Education, Neag School of Education, University of Connecticut

of proficiency in that language than students with less exposure. This makes sense insofar as students' exposure to English outside school is extensive, so the reduced exposure to English in school is relatively inconsequential; however, exposure to the non-English language is less extensive outside school and, thus, more exposure in school benefits their proficiency in that language.

MYTH: *More time in English in school results in higher levels of achievement in English.*

FACT: Contrary to popular belief, beginning instruction in English earlier in elementary school and providing more instruction in English during the elementary school grades do not result in better outcomes in English for either native speakers of English or ELLs. For example, English-speaking students in early total IMM and ELLs in 90/10 TWI programs achieve the same levels of proficiency in English as students in 50/50 programs even though the latter have more exposure to English in school (Genesee, 2004; Lindholm-Leary, 2010).

Question: How can we explain the finding which shows that students in DL programs do just as well in English as students in English-only programs even though they have less exposure to English?

The results we have just reported, which have been well documented in both the U.S. and Canada and in programs for both ELLs and English-speaking students, seem to be counterintuitive. How can we explain them? One obvious explanation is that students are exposed to so much English outside school that any reduction in exposure to English in school is relatively minor. In other words, when you take a broad view of DL students' language learning experiences, their exposure to English in total is still extensive even if instruction in English in school is reduced somewhat.

While this might be part of the explanation, it is not the total explanation because the kinds of language skills that students acquire outside school are often not the kinds of language skills they need to succeed in school. Researchers and educators distinguish between language for social communication and language for academic purposes as a means of understanding academic success. More specifically, it is now widely thought that, to succeed in school, it is not sufficient for students to have language skills that are adequate for social communication with their peers and others outside school; they must acquire the forms and functions of language that are linked to mastering academic content. We discuss this distinction in greater detail in Chapters 3 and 5. For our purposes here, it is sufficient to say that academic language includes oral and written language skills that are required to understand academic instruction and written texts, to write about academic subjects, and to participate in discussions of academic subjects in school.

A significant part of the explanation of why DL students can attain the same levels of proficiency in English despite less exposure to English in school is related to how literacy and academic oral language skills develop in children learning two languages. Jim Cummins (1981) was one of the first researchers to point out that the languages of DL learners do not develop entirely independent of one another. To the contrary, he argued, aspects of language that are linked to literacy and academic achievement develop in an interdependent fashion in DL learners. That is, the development of literacy and academic oral language skills in Language X facilitates the development of the corresponding skills in Language Y. Riches and Genesee (2006), similarly, argue that DL learners have a *bilingual reservoir* of skills and knowledge that they can draw on to develop literacy skills and academic oral language. For example, when ELLs in a DL program are learning to read in English, they can draw on their knowledge of letter-sound relationships in their home language to decode in English. A list of the kinds of language-related skills that transfer cross-linguistically is given in Chapter 3. What is important here is that there are a lot of literacy and academic oral language skills that do not have to be taught twice. As a result, students in DL programs are able to attain the same levels of proficiency in English as students in English-only programs because the skills they acquire in the non-English language facilitate their acquisition of literacy and academic oral language skills in English.

But, there is still another question that we need to answer: Why do students in DL programs sometimes *outperform* students in English-only programs? This has been found for both English-speaking students and ELLs in DL programs (Lindholm-Leary & Borsato, 2006). This might be explained by the fact that DL students often develop enhanced metalinguistic awareness and executive control functions (e.g., Bialystok, 2007) which, in turn, can enhance their achievement in academic domains, including literacy. Enhanced metalinguistic awareness is especially important for the development of literacy skills since research has shown that one of the most significant predictors of young children's ability to decode is phonological awareness. Executive functioning is important because it involves the control of attention, including shifting or changing attention, focusing or inhibiting attention, and planning, all of which are important in reading, writing, problem solving, and other complex behaviors.

Question: Do DL students attain the same levels of achievement in academic subjects as students in all-English programs?

An additional concern that is often expressed about DL education is that students will not attain the same levels of achievement in academic subjects such as mathematics and science as students in English-only programs. To fully understand this concern, we need to look at it from the perspective of ELL and English-speaking students separately because the concerns take different forms.

▶ ACADEMIC OUTCOMES OF ELLs

When it comes to ELLs, the concern is that many, although not all, of these students underachieve in school because they do not speak English proficiently upon entry to school. Critics of DL education have argued that the best way for ELLs to close the academic achievement gap with English-speaking students is for ELLs to learn English only, and as quickly as possible, so that they are not hindered in their academic development by low levels of English language proficiency. However, the vast majority of ELLs in the U.S. is and always has been educated in English-only classrooms—approximately 70 percent, depending on which year data are examined. Despite this, national statistics have repeatedly shown that ELLs lag behind their English-speaking peers in most academic subjects, and the gap often increases the higher the grade level (Abedi & Dietel, 2004; Fry, 2007). If instruction in English only were the best solution to this problem, one would not expect to continue to find such significant gaps in the achievement of ELLs. Thus, clearly, educating ELLs in English only is insufficient to close the achievement gap.

In fact, contrary to the English-only argument, most studies that have compared the academic achievement of ELLs in DL versus English-only programs have found that students who receive bilingual instruction in elementary school are as or more successful academically than students in English-only programs. Moreover, most long-term studies report that the longer students stay in a DL program and the more instruction they have in the home language, the more positive are their academic outcomes. Here are some important research findings on the academic achievement of ELLs in DL programs.

- ○ Systematic syntheses of research on the academic achievement of ELLs in late elementary and middle school have found that they score significantly higher than ELLs in general on norm-referenced standardized tests and criterion-referenced state tests in mathematics and that they perform on par with English-speaking students in English-only classrooms (Block, 2007; Lindholm-Leary & Howard, 2008; Gomez, Freeman, & Freeman, 2005; Howard & Sugarman, 2007; Lindholm-Leary & Borsato, 2006; Thomas & Collier, 2002).

- ○ With respect to achievement in mathematics, studies of DL education have found that although ELL students often begin elementary school with low to below-average scores in mathematics on standardized tests, they score average to above average in English mathematics by grades 4 to 6 (Block, 2007; de Jong, 2002; Lindholm & Aclan, 1991). ELLs in these studies also meet district or state proficiency standards (de Jong, 2002; Gomez et al., 2005) and score above district and state averages for ELLs in general (de Jong, 2002; Lindholm-Leary, 2001).

- ○ Lindholm-Leary and her colleagues, as well as other researchers in California, have found that ELLs with high levels of bilingual proficiency also attain high levels of academic achievement (e.g., Lindholm-Leary & Howard, 2008; Lindholm-Leary & Hernandez,

2011; see also Genesee & Lindholm-Leary, 2012, for a review). Thus, contrary to the argument that proficiency in English only promotes academic achievement, it has been found that bilingual proficiency is associated with relatively high levels of achievement.

There are several explanations for these findings.

1. Bilinguals store information, concepts, and abstract knowledge in a common conceptual system that can be accessed through either language (Dijkstra & van Heuven, 2002). This means that even though DL students may have learned something in the non-English language, that information can be accessed through English, and vice versa.

2. DL learners use their two languages jointly to solve problems, think critically, and acquire new knowledge. The multiple ways in which DL learners use the combined resources of their two languages for learning have been referred to in different ways: *cross-linguistic transfer, translanguaging* (Garcia, 2011), bridging (Beeman & Urow, 2012), or as a *bilingual reservoir of skills and knowledge* (Riches & Genesee, 2006). Regardless of terminology, this means that when DL students are trying to solve mathematics or science problems in English, or to think critically about something they have just read, they can draw on skills and knowledge acquired in the non-English language as well as those acquired in English to perform these tasks and to learn new skills and knowledge. This also means that the reduced exposure to English that DL students have in school is offset by time saved using resources from their combined resources in both languages.

3. Because ELLs in DL programs get initial academic instruction in a language they already know, they can keep up academically as soon as they start school, even if their proficiency in English is limited. When they begin to get instruction in English, the academic knowledge and skills they have acquired through their home language can be accessed through English. As a result, they are less likely to fall behind in their academic subjects during the primary grades when their proficiency in English is limited, and it is easier for them to close the achievement gap as they advance through the elementary grades. In contrast, ELLs in English-only programs cannot benefit fully from instruction because they are still learning academic English. As a result, they are unable to

SPECIAL NOTE

About Chinese- and Korean-Speaking ELLs in DL Programs

Research on the English language development and academic achievement of Chinese- and Korean-speaking ELLs in DL programs has found that:

1. They score as well as or significantly higher than similar students on norm-referenced standardized tests and criterion-referenced state tests in English and mathematics.

2. They perform on par with English-speaking students in English-only classrooms (Garcia, 2003; Ha, 2001; Lindholm-Leary, 2011).

keep up academically from the beginning, and they fall further and further behind as academic instruction becomes more demanding in the higher grades. In short, teaching academic subjects in a language that ELLs already know can help them overcome challenges that can jeopardize their learning and achievement.

4. In a related vein, teaching ELLs in the home language allows them to engage in instructional activities and not sit on the sidelines. ELLs are often left on the sidelines when instruction is in English before they are competent in English. Engagement in classroom activities is critical for learning (Goldenberg, 2008).

▶ ACADEMIC OUTCOMES OF ENGLISH-SPEAKING STUDENTS

In the case of English-speaking students, the concern is that they will not be able to achieve grade-appropriate levels of achievement because they are receiving academic instruction in part or in whole for several grades in a language that they have not fully mastered. Contrary to these concerns, evidence from research conducted over more than 40 years in the U.S. and Canada indicates quite clearly that this is not an issue—the academic achievement of English-speaking students in DL programs is not compromised. Here are some important research findings on the academic achievement of English-speaking students in DL programs (see Genesee, 2004, for details).

○ English-speaking students in IMM programs attain the same levels of achievement in mathematics, science, and other school subjects as similar students in English-only programs; this has been found for students in early, delayed, and late immersion.

○ English-speaking students with below average levels of academic ability achieve the same levels of achievement in their school subjects as similar students in English-only programs; in other words, the challenges posed by low academic ability do not jeopardize their achievement more than that experienced by similar students in English-only programs.

Question: Are DL programs suitable for students with special learning challenges?

We have reviewed research so far indicating that DL programs are effective for students in general. But what about students with learning challenges? Children can struggle in school for a variety of reasons—for example, because of primary language learning difficulties, low academic ability, autism, severe cognitive deficits, significant socio-emotional or sensory-motor problems, or disadvantaged socioeconomic backgrounds. All of these factors have been shown to be associated with poor performance in school. We lack research on children in DL programs who face many of these challenges, but we have evidence on others. Once again, we discuss research on ELL and English-speaking students separately because available research on each population differs.

▶ OUTCOMES FOR ELLs

With respect to ELLs (Spanish-speaking students) in DL programs (primarily TWI), there is evidence concerning students from disadvantaged socioeconomic backgrounds and students with special education needs (Lindholm-Leary & Howard, 2008; Lindholm-Leary & Hernandez, 2011). Like research on English-speaking students, the evidence from these studies indicates that DL education is effective and suitable for such students—they are not at greater risk of low achievement in TWI programs than similar students in English-only programs. Here are more detailed findings from research on the performance of ELLs with learning challenges in DL programs.

○ Lindholm-Leary and Howard (2008) report that there were no significant differences between TWI students with special education needs in grades 4 to 8 and California state norms for students with disabilities, despite the fact that the TWI students had had much less instruction in English than students who comprised the California norming sample (see Lindholm-Leary, 2008, for a review).

○ Lindholm-Leary (2008) also reports that grade 4 to 6 ELLs with speech-language impairment scored significantly higher on a number of English language measures than similar ELLs in English-only programs and in so-called structured English immersion programs.

○ Similarly, TWI students from disadvantaged socioeconomic backgrounds scored as well as disadvantaged students who comprised the California state norming sample for students with socioeconomic disadvantage; the TWI students included both ELLs and native English speakers.

► OUTCOMES FOR ENGLISH-
  SPEAKING STUDENTS

With respect to English-speaking students, there is
evidence on students with these characteristics:

1. Primary language difficulties

2. Low academic ability (as assessed by IQ tests)

3. Disadvantaged socioeconomic backgrounds
   (assessed as low levels of parental education
   and/or income or eligibility for free lunch)

4. English-speaking students from minority cultural backgrounds, such as Hawaiian and
   Mohawk children (Genesee, 2004)

Findings from research indicate that DL students with these learner/background characteristics
can do as well in DL programs as students with similar background and learner characteristics in
English-only programs. Much of this research has
been done in Canada, but the results are pertinent to
educators in the U.S. because the research was carried out on students who speak the socially dominant
language—English. Here are more detailed of findings on these students.

○ Working with IMM students in Canada,
  Genesee found that English-speaking students
  with below-average levels of academic ability who were in early
  total French IMM programs attained the same levels of achievement in English and in their academic subjects as students with
  comparably low levels of academic ability in English-only programs. At the same time, the IMM students achieved advanced
  levels of functional proficiency in their L2 (French) that were significantly higher than those achieved by comparable students in
  conventional French-L2 programs.

○ The same pattern of results has been reported by Bruck (1978; 1982)
  in research on English-speaking students with disabilities in their
  home language who were attending early immersion programs.

○ Bruck also found that students from families with low socioeconomic status (Bruck, Tucker, & Jakimik, 1975) attained the same

> ◄ **On the Suitability of Dual
> Language Education for
> Students with Special
> Educational Needs**
>
> *"Until there is strong research evidence
> indicating that learners with certain
> language and/or learning disabilities
> are better served when schooled through
> one language only, there is no reason to
> deny the cognitive and linguistic enrich-
> ments of a dual language education to
> any child. Indeed, by achieving some level
> of bilingualism, a competence that is per-
> ceived as beyond the norm by some, dual
> language learners who struggle in school
> can earn a much-needed boost to
> their self-esteem."*
>
> —Tara Fortune, Immersion
> Projects Coordinator, Center for
> Advanced Studies in Research on
> Language Acquisition,
> University of Minnesota

1. Individual children whose parents select to have their child in a DL program and who might be at risk for academic difficulty in school should be permitted to participate in DL programs. Their progress should be monitored carefully and regularly so that they can be provided with additional learning support and to determine whether they are achieving to the level one would expect given their learning challenges. They should be withdrawn from the program only if there is clear evidence that their progress is being hampered as a result of DL instruction. For more discussion of this issue with respect to students at risk for reading disability, see Chapter 10 in Paradis, Genesee, and Crago (2010).

2. It is particularly important that special needs children for whom the acquisition of both languages is important (because a non-English language is spoken primarily or exclusively at home, for example) participate in DL programs. They should continue in the program unless they exhibit academic difficulties and those

levels of academic achievement and English proficiency in early IMM programs as similarly disadvantaged students in English-only programs. At the same time, the IMM students attained significantly higher levels of functional proficiency in the L2, French in this case.

○ The students with learning challenges or from the disadvantaged backgrounds in these studies did not perform as well in English or in their academic subjects as students who were not challenged or disadvantaged in these ways. What is important, however, is that they were not at greater risk of low achievement in a DL program than similar students in English-only programs.

Overall, available research indicates that students who experience socioeconomic disadvantages, difficulties in their first language, and, in the case of English-speaking students, those with low academic ability, are not put at greater risk in DL programs than similar students in English-only programs and, at the same time, they benefit from enhanced levels of bilingual competence.

RESOURCES

Working with Students with Special Learning Needs

Genesee (2007)

Hamayan, Marler, Sanchez Lopez, & Damico (2013)

Paradis, Genesee, & Crago (2010)

Fortune (with M. R. Menke) (2010)

Summary: Building a Successful Program

Now that we have described the salient features of the most common forms of DL education and have reviewed important research findings concerning critical issues linked to program effectiveness, let's examine what each program model requires for effective implementation. In the case of new programs, it is important to have the necessary prerequisites to get a new program up and running successfully. In the case of existing programs, it is a matter of deciding whether the program alternative that was originally selected and implemented is still the best choice in light of changes in the community and school system. In the checklist at the end of this chapter, we identify key features and activities that need to be in place for success. The key features we identify are the same, for the most part, for all program models; we identify important differences where they exist. We have organized the key features according to students, teachers, administrative support, curriculum and instruction, assessment, and families and communities.

difficulties can be linked directly to DL instruction. To exclude such children from DL programs would be to deny them the opportunity to develop a language that is important in their day-to-day and future lives.

DUAL LANGUAGE VOICE: CONTINUOUS PROFESSIONAL DEVELOPMENT

My first year as a supervisor at The Rafael Hernandez Dual Language School PS/MS 218, I knew professional development was going to be critical in the development of a successful dual language school. After observing teaching practices, debriefing with staff, and engaging in professional dialogues with staff, parents, and community stakeholders, I assessed their professional needs as a school community and realized that a strategic action plan was needed to fulfill, support, and foster a successful dual language program. I began by inviting teachers to a book study: *Designing and Implementing Two-Way Bilingual Programs* by Dr. Margarita Calderon. We met on a weekly basis and discussed the strategies described in the book and the general implications for teaching at our school. Teachers practiced the strategies in their classrooms, and I would go in to support and give constructive feedback to foster bilingualism, biliteracy, and multiculturalism. My experience taught me that having a dual language coach and supervisor that is passionate and knowledgeable about dual language education yields many benefits.

As a dual language supervisor, it was important to provide professional development that would give the teachers the knowledge of research-based pedagogy that supports a rigorous program for students, aligned with bilingual education tenets. Specific content could include but was not limited to the following:

❑ Collaborative planning strategies among all teachers

❑ Analyzing student data in both languages for the purpose of informing instruction and program implementation

(continues)

- Vocabulary strategies for ELLs
- Identification of language proficiency stages
- Scaffolding strategies
- Identifying language and content objectives
- Review of research in the field of bilingual and second language education
- Teacher collaboration and co-teaching
- Curriculum planning across two languages
- Inquiry-based research
- Spanish word study

Professional Development at our school occurred during Lunch and Learns, common planning time, and after school. The most beneficial professional development came through teaching learning communities (TLC) that fostered teamwork and collaborative planning; these were led at first by me and eventually released to teachers. Teachers began to do inquiry-based research within their classrooms and schoolwide. As a result, we have designed our own dual language curriculum, Spanish word study, and writing prompts. Ongoing professional development is a key to dual language program success.

—Vivian Bueno, Assistant Principal
The Rafael Hernandez Dual Language School
50/50 Side-by-Side English and Spanish
District 09 Bronx, NY
(now Principal of PS 73, Bronx, NY)

RESOURCES

Sources for Evaluating DL Programs

Guiding Principles for Dual Language Education, Second Edition (2007)

A useful reference for self-evaluation of DL programs; available at the Center for Applied Linguistics website: www.cal.org/twi/guidingprinciples.htm

Normas para la enseñanza de las artes del lenguaje en español para programas de inmersión doble

Standards for Spanish language development: Mid Atlantic Equity Center (2011); available at http://maec.ceee.gwu.edu/sites/default/files/NormasDL_MAECSu2011.pdf

Evaluator's Toolkit for Dual Language Programs (2007)

The purpose of this Toolkit by Lindholm-Leary and Hargett is to assist staff in DL programs that serve ELLs to understand how to meet assessment and accountability guidelines. This Toolkit assumes no prior knowledge of data collection, data management, or data analysis on the part of the user. It is truly "A Beginner's Toolkit." Available at the Center for Applied Linguistics website: www.cal.org/twi/EvalToolkit/

Checklist of Key DL Program Features

Students

☐ For IMM programs: Is there a sufficient number of English-speaking students for two classes in kindergarten and in the primary grades for ongoing programs (to allow for attrition in higher grades)?

☐ For DBE programs: Is there a sufficient number of ELL students for two classes in kindergarten for new programs and in the primary grades for ongoing programs (to allow for attrition in higher grades)?

☐ For TWI programs: Is there a sufficient number of both ELL and English-speaking students for two classes in starting grades for new programs and in the primary grades for ongoing programs (to allow for attrition in higher grades)?

☐ Also for TWI programs: Half of each class is ELL and half English-speaking.

☐ ELL students all speak the same language or different varieties of the same language. *(continues)*

✓ Checklist of Key DL Program Features *(continued)*

❑ There are firm commitments from parents who understand the program, its requirements, and the importance of continued participation in the program.

Teachers

❑ Teachers have native or native-like competence in English and/or the non-English language.

❑ Teachers have appropriate credentials—a standard teaching credential and a bilingual credential, as applicable.

❑ Teachers are knowledgeable about DL programs—their structure, goals, and critical instructional elements.

❑ Teachers know how to teach content through students' second (and perhaps not yet proficient) language.

❑ Teachers understand the importance of collaboration and are prepared to work collaboratively with other DL teachers.

❑ Teachers who are native English speakers and/or native speakers of the other language are in place or available at every grade level, starting in K.

❑ Teachers have cross-cultural understanding and awareness of funds of knowledge of the cultures of their DL students.

❑ A plan is in place to provide professional development opportunities to DL and other teachers in the school to prepare them to work with DL learners.

Administrative Support

❑ School principal and administrative assistants understand and support DL education and are prepared to advocate on its behalf.

❑ Support staff (including clerical, custodial, and special support personnel) understand (or are prepared to become knowledgeable about) DL education and how to make it work.

❑ Preferably, administrative personnel know both languages or have some competence in the non-English language.

❑ District-level leaders understand and support DL education.

Curriculum and Instruction

❑ High-quality curriculum and instructional materials in English and the non-English language are available, as required by allocation of languages of instruction.

✓ Checklist of Key DL Program Features (continued)

☐ For beginning programs, instructional resources for year 1 (usually K) are available in year 1.

☐ A plan to develop curriculum and instructional materials for years 2, 3, and so on, is in place.

☐ Most importantly, the curriculum includes a comprehensive and coherent set of language and content objectives and, secondarily, general school skills and learning strategies, cross-linguistic, and cross-cultural learning objectives.

Assessment

☐ There is a comprehensive and sound plan for program evaluation.

☐ A person or team has been designated to oversee and manage the evaluation process.

☐ Professional development activities are planned to assist school personnel to interpret and use evaluation information in helpful ways.

☐ Collaboration is planned with local and/or regional university personnel who are knowledgeable in school assessment and are willing to provide support to the school.

Families and Community

☐ There are sufficient numbers of families who support DL education and are committed to having their children participate in the program for the elementary grades.

☐ Families have a full understanding of DL education (language of instruction allocation, content and language goals, etc.).

☐ There is a group of parents, community members, and others who will plan, oversee, and implement advocacy activities on behalf of the program, with assistance from the school.

About DL Education in General

Cloud, Genesee, & Hamayan (2000)

Cloud, Genesee, & Hamayan (2009)

De Jong (2011)

Genesee (1999)

Hamayan & Freeman (2012)

Howard & Christian (2002)

Howard, Olague, & Rogers (2003)

Howard & Sugarman (2007)

Improving Education for English Learners: Research-Based Approaches (2010)

Montone & Loeb (2000)

CHAPTER TWO

The First Steps: Planning a Dual Language Program

IN THIS CHAPTER, we describe the foundational steps that are fundamental to establishing a Dual Language (DL) program, be it IMM, DBE, or TWI. For existing DL programs, the information presented here can help school personnel adjust aspects of the program that made sense in the beginning, when the program first started, but that may not be effective now. With experience, program administrators and teachers can see flaws that can be corrected—they may have started the program without enough preparation, or they may have had a different understanding of various aspects of the program. They may know how to follow the desired model in a way that is more effective for teachers as well as for the learners. Established programs also need to be modified for external reasons: new developments in the community, innovations in pedagogy, a new superintendent, a different student population, the availability of new materials, and recent legislation. Sometimes, a new dissenting voice within the school, district, or community at large may also make it necessary to revisit the initial steps in order to solidify the foundation. Regardless of how satisfying the results of the program are, it is healthy to periodically adjust the program for even greater success.

DUAL LANGUAGE VOICE: IMPORTANCE OF YEARLONG PLANNING PRIOR TO STARTING

The Margarita Muñiz Academy is the first dual language, college preparatory high school in Boston Public Schools. Our school opened in August 2012 on the Boston University campus and the Museum of Fine Arts for our summer program. Our first student and family orientation marked the birth of our community, including staff, board members, local politicians, and district representatives. The orientation was the culmination of months of planning, collaboration, and decision making, and it marked the next phase of our community, living and learning in two languages.

Muñiz Academy was named after the principal of the well-known K–8 Rafael Hernández School in Roxbury, Massachusetts, and was the vision of a group of educators committed to dual language education. As we embarked on this journey a full year before the orientation date, we knew that a year of planning is a luxury, but also a necessity, for starting a new school. Dedicating a year to planning was important enough that the dual language founders did fundraising and then the district added some matching funds.

Our work was grounded in a deep passion for dual language education as well as the shared vision with the school's founders. As instructional leader, my prior experience as a teacher, school principal, staff developer, and leadership coach informed key parts of the plan, but input from others was equally invaluable. Here are things that we worked on during our planning year:

❑ Gaining school committee approval and community support by vetting key points in our plan and sorting out questions regarding our complex instructional model

❑ Planning the logistics, such as length of school day/year, size of school, hiring and student recruitment policies, planning key platforms that would drive instruction (the arts, technology, etc.), and the language allocation plan

❑ Establishing key alliances with families, the local community, district staff, and city officials

❑ Talking with students

Selecting our founding faculty has been a critical part of the work, as has been making the decision to begin one grade at a time. As a team, we will build our practices and "habits" as a community of student and faculty scholars. Because our students consistently said that teachers who guide them through challenging and authentic experiences inspire them, we looked for staff who are content experts and who also could proficiently teach academic subjects in both languages. Most of all, for our start-up year, we looked for educators who were passionate enough to weather the complexities of a new school. With a strong team, excited students, and families, we have built a solid foundation to begin our school.

—Dr. Dania Vázquez, Headmaster,
Margarita Muñiz Academy;
Two-Way Dual Language,
College Prep High School
Boston Public Schools, Massachusetts

For schools and districts that are just beginning to consider starting a DL program, this chapter presents a step-by-step description of what needs to take place before the first day of classes. It could take a whole year of planning before the first class begins, so it is essential that schools take the necessary time to plan the program in advance of this. If this essential planning time is not taken, the program is likely to have a shaky start and unstable foundation.

Set a Solid Foundation

Bilingualism is the value-added learning that DL programs can offer in contrast to other school programs. As we have shown in Chapter 1, students in DL programs can become bilingual at no cost to either the development of English (whether it is the students' home language or their second language) or achievement in their academic subjects. However, as attractive as this is (see the Teacher Tip entitled "Benefits of Being Bilingual"), many people both within the school community as well as in the larger society may not see the benefits of bilingualism, while others may fear that, at least for native speakers of English, learning an additional language might take time away from learning the core curriculum or from developing English, the home language, to its fullest. Fears may also be expressed that DL programs will impede ELLs' acquisition of English.

TEACHER TIP

Benefits of Being Bilingual

❖ Students who acquire advanced levels of proficiency in a second language often experience cognitive advantages compared to monolingual students.

❖ Young bilingual children show more flexibility in thinking, greater sensitivity to language, and a better ear for listening.

❖ Bilinguals generally have a better understanding of their home language.

❖ Knowing a second language offers the chance to communicate with people they would otherwise not have the chance to know.

❖ Bilingualism opens the door to other cultures, and it helps a person understand and appreciate people from other countries.

❖ Proficiency in a second language gives students a head start in language requirements for college.

❖ Job opportunities are increased for careers for which knowing another language is an asset.

Solid support for DL education must be established before embarking on a DL program to avoid unwarranted opposition to the program after planning or instruction has begun. For new programs, as soon as the idea for DL education materializes, it is critical to begin spreading the word and involving key people who will make the program a success. Before planning for instruction, student selection, teacher recruitment, choice of materials, and so forth become too far advanced, it is important to start advocating on behalf of the program.

For established programs, new questions about the value or effectiveness of the program may make it necessary to revisit the foundation that was set early on when the program was first started, or to

Research Notes

One of the characteristics of effective DL programs is a timely and appropriate means of addressing any incongruity between the model, school-community needs, and systems of implementation (Howard, Sugarman, & Christian, 2003).

remind people of the success and advantages of the program. Areas of weakness that need fine-tuning may have been discovered that have created dissatisfaction among key constituents which, in turn, can make the program vulnerable to funding cuts. The first step is to have a clear message about the key advantages of the DL program.

Get the Message Heard

The simplest and strongest message that all constituents—be they school board members, parents, teachers, students, or community members—need to hear is the following:

> By offering a dual language program to our students, we can give them the gift of proficiency in two languages without risk to their academic achievement or the development of full proficiency in English. If we acquire the resources that such a program needs and if we use these resources well, we can guarantee the best learning environment that a school can offer to the students and the community that it serves.

This message applies to monolingual native speakers of English as well as to ELLs who begin school with a language other than English. Fortunately, as indicated in Chapter 1, the research is plentiful and clear in showing the following:

1. Native speakers of English do not lose anything by being in a well-designed DL program; their achievement in English and academic subjects is at least as high as that of students in monolingual English programs. At the same time, students in DL programs gain proficiency in an additional language.

2. Well-designed DL programs can also provide the most effective learning environment for ELLs. Not only can ELLs reach higher levels of English proficiency and academic achievement than

their peers in all-English programs, they can also perform on par with, and in some cases better than, English-speaking students.

Publicize Research Findings About DL Education

The constituents affected by the DL program need to hear about research that supports this type of education. These constituents include the superintendent and other high-level administrators, school board members, teachers and staff in the school that houses the DL program, teachers and staff in other schools, parents of children where the program will be housed, residents in the community that the school serves, business owners, and community organizations. The Teacher Tip below gives suggestions about planning to publicize a new program.

TEACHER TIP

For Constituents Planning to Implement a DL Program

❖ Become familiar with research that shows positive results for DL education. You can use the references and resources presented in Chapter 1.

❖ Learn about criticisms of DL programs that often occur in the popular press (e.g., www.jewishworldreview.com/cols/chavez032300.asp).

❖ Become an expert in answering the question, "Why is DL education beneficial?"

❖ Establish a close connection with a researcher who can provide an "outside expert voice." Conveniently, technology makes it possible for this expert to "be present" virtually at meetings as necessary.

❖ Develop a brief summary of important research findings, written in clear and easy-to-understand terms.

Show Success Through Students' and Parents' Voices

It is also crucial that the voices of students who have gone through a DL program are heard. Students are the focal point of interest for all constituents—and constituents need to see with their own eyes that DL students become fluent in both their languages. In addition, they need to be assured that students in DL programs are achieving to the same high levels in their academic subjects as they would in an all-English program. To do this, testimonials and work samples from students should be collected; or, if a new program is being established, obtain testimonials from DL programs that have been up and running for some time so that the value of the program can be shown. Video

---

RESOURCES

A List of Selected Videos on DL Education

To promote DL programs:

- http://migrantmedia.com/learning.html
- www.dlenm.org/index.php?option=com_content&view=article&id=209
- http://pusd.mirocommunity.org/video/94/mandarin-dual-language-immersi
- http://blog.syracuse.com/video/2008/01/the_dual_language_academy_at_s.html
- www.youtube.com/watch?v=qteup56qSg0
- www.youtube.com/watch?v=B2SB4TTCuHA
- www.youtube.com/watch?v=B2SB4TTCuHA
- http://schools.u-46.org/index.pl?id=102095

To raise issues regarding concerns about DL education:

- http://speakingintonguesfilm.info/

To be used for parent meetings:

- www.tdsb.on.ca/_site/ViewItem.asp?siteid=13&menuid=20006&pageid=17500

clips of DL students talking in both languages are also very effective. Many DL programs have created such video clips; alternatively, you may want to create your own video. Begin from the first week in kindergarten by recording short clips of individual children and return to the same children during the next three or four years. This way, it can be shown how students develop competence in their languages from year to year. A long-term video that follows the growth of two or three students can be extremely effective in convincing others that there is no need to worry when children do not seem to show great progress in the early years. Videos of DL programs on the web can also be useful for promoting the program.

Show Confidence in the Model

The constituents in your community need to see the confidence that you have in DL education and the value-added aspect of the program. Constituents need to hear that:

- ○ You have a solid understanding of research on DL education.
- ○ You have strong data that show how well students in your program are doing (or in other DL programs if you are just starting).
- ○ You base pedagogical decisions on sound research and theory.
- ○ You know the various models of DL education and their advantages and disadvantages.
- ○ Your knowledge of and experience with best practices in DL education guides you in every aspect of the program.
- ○ With the help of parents and community members, you use this knowledge to guide you in choosing the educational model that best suits your community.

Advocate on Behalf of the Program

The first step in advocating on behalf of the program is to become familiar with the opposing opinions that have either emerged or are likely to emerge from major constituents and the unwarranted fears of uninformed critics. You must sound out as many people as you can, including teachers, administrators, school board members, parents, and other community members, to see what their (informed or uninformed) opinions are of the program and what concerns they have. Some of these individuals will have some knowledge of DL education, while others will not—which may not keep them from having strong opinions anyway! This preliminary fact-finding can be done informally by simply having casual conversations or, more formally, by having focus groups and interviews. The purpose is to find out what the sensitive issues or sources of anxiety are and to prepare responses to them. Knowing the research behind an instructional approach or program and being able to anticipate doubts and anxieties are both very important for advocacy.

The connection that the audience feels toward the person relaying the message is crucial as well. Advocacy is most effective when the person relaying the message is someone to whom the audience can relate. If you are addressing a group of parents, solicit help from a parent to share his or her experiences with their child in a DL program, in the parents' preferred language, if possible. A presentation to the school board must include the views of a board member from another DL program. Superintendents need to hear from other superintendents. So, it is useful to create a group of spokespersons who can speak on behalf of the program as parents, community leaders, teachers, administrators, or board members.

Prepare the Groundwork

The foundation described in the preceding sections must be established both within the school and in the broader community where the students live. For new programs, the team that is setting in motion plans for a DL program should hold meetings, disseminate information, and have formal and informal conversations with key people in the school and broader community. In established programs, the team may need to arrange these meetings for individuals who are new to the school district or broader community. Established programs can provide local and regional leadership by paving the way for new programs and by opening their doors to teachers and administrators who are just beginning to develop their program.

Within the School

It is important for school staff to be involved in preparing the groundwork, and to do this they must have information readily accessible to them so that they clearly understand the rationale and elements of the program.

▶ Make It a Participatory Process

It is essential to involve all staff in the school where the DL program is housed in the general decision-making process. Staff should be able to at least make their opinions and preferences known on issues such as whether to make the whole school a DL program or a strand within the school. You can use Table 2.1 to start a discussion on the advantages and disadvantages of each option. More detailed decisions about such matters as the curriculum, scheduling, and instructional frameworks need not involve more than a small team consisting of administrators, teachers, and an outside resource person.

Table 2.1

Some Advantages and Disadvantages of Within-School and Whole-School Programs		
	Advantages	**Disadvantages**
Strand within a school	• Families have a choice of which program to enroll their child in. • Monolingual English teachers can find a role in the school more easily.	• The program may come to be dominated by English because of high stakes testing in English. • DL programs may be isolated or misunderstood by the rest of the school.
Whole school	• The program takes on an importance or higher status within the district. Resources do not need to be divided among programs.	• Students entering at higher grade levels will need extensive support. • Schools may be perceived to be elitist.

▶ Have Information Readily Available

It is useful for established programs to have an information packet readily available for anyone from the district who wants to know what the DL program is like. The following photo shows an example of a program brochure from Mission Valley Elementary in El Paso, Texas. This packet can also be given to other schools that are interested in starting a DL program. For new programs, at the very least, everyone should be kept well informed of the general plans for the program, its goals, and timeline for implementation. Entire school and small group meetings should be held with ample time for questions and discussion. The accompanying checklist provides information that could be included in the packet.

As a Parent, how will I be able to help my child if I don't know the target language?

■ Continue reading to your child in your primary language

■ Maintain close communication with your child's teacher in order for you to be able to help your child at home

If Spanish is the home language, how will my child acquire the English language?

■ In an immersion program the English language is modeled by the teacher as well as the students and reinforced during English Language Development (ELD) through a content area.

How many schools in the Ysleta district offer this program?

We currently have 26 campuses implementing the program

■ Seventeen elementary schools

■ Six middle schools

■ Three high schools

Dual Language
Immersion Program

Dual Language
Immersion Program

PARTICIPATING CAMPUSES

Elementary Schools

Capistrano Elementary	434-8600
Cedar Grove Elementary	434-7600
East Point Elementary	434-4500
Hacienda Heights Elementary	434-2500
Lancaster Elementary	434-3400
LeBarron Park Elementary	434-3500
Marian Manor Elementary	434-3600
Mesa Vista Elementary	434-2700
Parkland Elementary	434-6600
Pasodale Elementary	434-8500
Ramona Elementary	434-7700
Thomas Manor Elementary	434-7800
Tierra Del Sol Elementary	434-8900
Mission Valley Elementary	434-3700

Elementary/K-8

Alicia R. Chacon International	434-9200
Eastwood Knolls	434-4400

Middle Schools

Eastwood Middle	434-4300
Ranchland Hills Middle	434-2300
Rio Bravo Middle	434-8400
Valley View Middle	434-8200

High Schools

Bel Air High	434-2000
Del Valle High	434-3000

Ysleta Independent School District

Mission Valley Elementary
8674 North Loop
El Paso, TX 79907
(915) 434-3700
http://www2.yisd.net/missionvalley

Bilingual Education
Department

Two-Way Dual Language Immersion Program
Questions and Answers

What are the goals of the program?
■ To develop a high level of proficiency in understanding, speaking, reading and writing in both English and Spanish

■ To develop positive attitudes toward those who speak the other language and toward their culture

■ To prepare students to perform at or above grade level in both languages

■ To promote self-esteem and leadership skills

What are the characteristics of the program?
■ An additive bilingual environment that has full support of school administrators, teachers and parents

■ A minimum of a 5-year commitment, ideally 12

■ English speakers enter only at kinder and first grade

■ Both English and Spanish speakers are instructed together

■ Teachers use the language of instruction; separation of the two languages is a key component

■ There are no translations or repeated lessons

■ Quality language arts instruction in both languages

■ All students learn to read and write in Spanish first

■ Language learning is accelerated in the classroom by a combination of 1/3 of students who speak Spanish, 1/3 who speak English and 1/3 who are bilingual

■ Rigorous core academic curriculum that is tied to the TEKS

■ Active parent-school partnership

How much English and Spanish instruction will my child receive at every grade level?
■ Middle Schools
All students take a Spanish language class and at least one additional core content class taught in Spanish.

■ High Schools
Students must complete a minimum of 8 credits in dual langue classes, 4 of which come from any combination of Math, Science, Social Studies and Spanish Literature.

Why is this program beneficial for both English and Spanish speakers?
■ Two-Way dual language is an additive model for both groups

■ Spanish speakers maintain their first language while learning a second language

■ This program presents no risk to the English speakers' dominate language. They are taught academics in Spanish with second language approaches to ensure their success.

Is my child a good candidate for the program?
■ Students who can enjoy an additive language program that enables them to add a second language to their first, whether they are language minority or language majority students are welcome to the program.

Language of Instruction Across the Grades

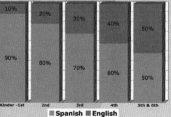

Dual Language
Immersion Program

These show sample pages from a brochure for Mission Valley Elementary School Dual Language Program. Information packets and program brochures communicate program goals and answer families' questions.

Checklist for a School Information Packet

It should include:

☐ A description of the basic features of the program or a brief summary of the proposal that was submitted to the school board/district

☐ Program goals and the rationale for the model that was selected

☐ A summary of research showing the effectiveness of DL education

☐ Testimonials from parents and students from DL programs; for new programs, these can be obtained from schools with programs that are similar to your own

☐ A sample schedule

☐ A language allocation plan

☐ A short discussion of how the program fits in with the rest of the school or district, educationally and fiscally

☐ FAQs: See www.cal.org/twi/faq.htm for a sample list of questions and responses.

▶ VISIT OTHER DL SCHOOLS

Visits to schools with successful DL programs can be arranged. New program staff can see a program in action, and staff from established programs can see how others run their program and get new ideas. Make sure that all constituent groups go on these visits, not just teachers.

- ○ Before you go:
  - ▶ Find out as much as you can about the program.
  - ▶ Clarify the similarities and differences with your program as much as possible.
  - ▶ Determine what you want to see (for new programs this may be difficult)—all aspects of the program will be of interest.
  - ▶ Formulate questions that have come up in your community that might be answered during the visit .
- ○ During the visit:
  - ▶ Have people with the same roles from your school and the school being visited talk to each other—teachers to teachers, parents to parents, and so forth.

- ▶ Observe students and teachers in different settings, not just the academic content classroom—for example, the lunchroom, the physical education class, the playground.
- ○ After the visit:
  - ▶ Debrief as soon after the visit as possible, reviewing the items that most interest you.
  - ▶ Consider setting up some type of partnership with the school you visited so you can collaborate on projects—students can set up a common blog, teachers can get together to do a book study, for example.

In all new DL programs, it is essential that everyone know what role they will play during the planning stage as well as once instruction begins. A highly contentious issue that often emerges during early discussions of new DL programs is the fear that monolingual English-speaking teachers have no place in the program. It is essential that these teachers be assured of a role in the first year of the program as well as in the coming years as the program expands. This is not necessarily difficult since the first year of the program (pre-K or K) will likely require a full-time English-speaking teacher to teach the English part of side-by-side kindergarten classes (see Table 1.4, "Role of Teachers" section). The English-speaking teacher and the other-language teacher will share two groups of students. This would limit the choice of program model to 50/50. As the program expands, teachers who teach in the non-English language can be hired whenever an opportunity arises for instruction in any subject area or for any position (e.g., music, physical education, speech pathologist, librarian).

▶ PLAN FOR STRONG PROFESSIONAL DEVELOPMENT

It is critical that a solid program of professional development be planned specifically for DL teachers as well as, more generally, for all teachers in the school and district. In addition, the topic of DL education should be included in district and/or school professional development plans. Also, whenever a professional development session is offered to the general education staff, the implications of the topic or issue to be addressed in the session should be discussed from the point of view of the DL program. A glossary of commonly used DL terms can be included with materials distributed at these sessions (see, for example, the glossary in Howard, Sugarman, Perdomo, & Adger, 2005). Video clips can also be shown.

The following is a sample of professional development topics for both new and established DL programs:

- ○ What the DL program is all about and who it is for
- ○ Why this program is suitable for the school
- ○ Pedagogical principles of the program
- ○ The basic design of the program
- ○ Who will be teaching in the program
- ○ How the program is funded
- ○ How the program fits into the rest of the district
- ○ A five-year projection of the educational features and outcomes of the program
- ○ Possible collaborations among program and non-program teachers
- ○ Opportunities the program can offer members of the school community
- ○ The importance of the program to different constituents of the school

In the Local Community

It is essential to both elicit information from and provide information to the community that is impacted by the DL program. By doing this early on we ensure open communication between the community and the school, an essential factor for the success of the program.

▶ KNOW WHAT THE COMMUNITY THINKS

It is important to get a clear sense of parents' needs and goals for their children:

- ○ Identify leaders in both the English-speaking as well as the ELL community who can be your link to those groups.
  - ▶ Who are the individuals or families that people look to for advice and support?
  - ▶ What community organizations play key roles in bringing the residents and business owners together?
  - ▶ Which businesses are key information brokers in the neighborhood? Where do people gather and talk? (Don't overlook the beauty salon, the grocery store, or the Laundromat.)

○ Investigate parent and community concerns. Before meeting with community members, make inquiries about possible concerns that the community might have so that you are prepared to respond to their questions and doubts. This can be done informally at the same time that you make contact with individuals who have been identified as leaders. Be sure to get information from native English-speaking as well as ELL groups; each group might have different concerns. Existing programs should revisit the concerns that parents had in the beginning of the program to make sure that parents are comfortable with their concerns.

 DUAL LANGUAGE VOICE: DEVELOPING COMMUNITY SUPPORT FOR THEIR PROGRAM

Going from an English-only mindset to that of Dual Language (DL) enrichment in our demographically changing district required a great deal of planning to ensure successful implementation. We needed the support of numerous stakeholders, a few of those being the staff, parents (both English proficient and Spanish proficient), and our Board of Education. At a faculty meeting for all staff we announced our plan for a yearlong investigation of local DL programs. We were sure to invite teachers, parents, teaching assistants, interventionists, and the principal to be part of our exploratory committee; our committee was comprised of people on board, people on the fence, and people seriously opposed to the DL instructional model. Here are four key things we did:

1. We used *Designing and Implementing Two-Way Bilingual Programs* as an anchor text for our six meetings that year.

2. To hear from all constituents, we asked all school employees (secretaries, custodians, cafeteria workers, and instructional staff) to complete an anonymous survey.

3. We provided public updates during the exploratory process, and I was available to meet with anyone who had additional questions.

4. During year one of implementation we invited a consultant to speak with teachers after school about the latest findings in DL research, as well as to evaluate our program model.

(continues)

Getting the support of our Latino families was a challenge, as parents struggled to understand how instruction in Spanish would help their child acquire English. Networking with parents to advocate on behalf of the program and inviting these same parents to join us on a district-run, Spanish TV program to convey the added benefit of DL instruction for our Latino students was very effective. The parents of our English-dominant students wanted reassurance that students in the DL Academy would be held to district benchmarks in English, wouldn't lose valuable instructional time, and would also acquire a second language. After addressing concerns from both language groups it was time to bring everyone together, so we hosted a bilingual parent information session that was facilitated by a respected local administrator involved with ESL and DL. Even now, six years later, we continue to hold an annual information session for incoming K families and conduct two or three DL update meetings during the year.

One of the most rewarding moments since we began this journey happened just this year: Questions from parents and Board members shifted from whether or not this was a beneficial instructional model for students to our plans for growing the program to a third elementary building and extending it to the secondary level. It's great to know that the message "El que habla dos lenguas vale por dos" is catching on!

—Suzanne M. Lasser
Director, ELL Programs K–12
Dual Language Academy; Two-Way; 50/50
White Plains City School District
White Plains, NY

▶ INFORM THE COMMUNITY

Distribute information packets. Have information packets ready to give to community members and the parents of all entering students. The materials in the packet prepared for school staff (refer to the previous checklist for a school information packet) can be modified, making it more reader friendly and focusing on students—parents' primary interest—rather than on school matters such as curriculum, scheduling, or assessment.

Information packets can be formatted in different ways:

○ Dual language versions, where both languages appear on the same page or under the same topic. This can also be done by having each language on different sides of the information packet. If you turn the packet in one direction, it appears in one language; and if you start from the other side, turning it upside down, it appears in the other language.

○ Single language versions in each language.

○ DVD versions with the option to choose the language of the sound track.

Myth

MYTH: *Language minority parents don't support dual language education. They want English only.*

FACT: Some language minority parents may feel that way, but most families welcome the opportunity to maintain their linguistic and cultural heritage once they are assured that their children will develop the highest level of English proficiency possible (Freeman, Freeman, & Mercuri, 2004; Shannon, 2002).

Have community meetings. Since the concerns may be different for ELL parents than for English-speaking parents, some of the meetings can be held separately for the two groups. These meetings can cover research and pedagogical issues briefly, but they need to focus more extensively on what children will gain, both academically and affectively, from the program. You can reassure ELL parents that others just like them have mentioned the following as the main benefits of the DL program to their children:

○ Children develop full proficiency in English.

○ Children feel proud of their heritage and maintain connections with their culture.

○ Children can speak with relatives who speak the home language only; they feel stronger bonds and connections to all members of their family.

○ Children are able to use their home language throughout their careers wherever they may work in the world.

TEACHER TIP

Sample Agenda Items for Community Meetings

For community members:

❖ Why are DL programs important? What are the benefits of being bilingual to the students, the community, the state, and the nation?

❖ What does the DL philosophy of value-added education encompass?

❖ What are the components of a DL program?

❖ How does DL education work for native speakers of English and for English language learners?

❖ How does DL education differ from other programs offered in the district?

❖ What is the relationship of the program to other programs in the school/district?

❖ What can parents do if they do not speak one of the languages of the program?

❖ What are the expectations in the next three to five years regarding student progress/achievement, especially in language and literacy development?

In addition, for parents of participating students:

❖ What can I expect from my child in the first year and in subsequent years?

❖ What can I do at home to help my child?

❖ What resources will I have in the language that I am not proficient in?

❖ Will my child learn what he or she would have in a mainstream class?

❖ Will my child learn English?

It is useful to show video clips at parent meetings because they give an inside view of the type of education that their children are (or will be) receiving.

Ensure easy accessibility. Community meetings should be accessible to all parents.

- Make sure the meetings are at a convenient time and location.
- Offer transportation to and from the meeting, if possible and if necessary.
- Arrange for child care or on-site activities for children of parents attending the meeting.
- Offer translation services for parents who need it.

Provide other useful services. Here are some examples of other services you could provide.

- Contact the local newspaper or television channel to feature the program.
- Offer services that provide a language and culture resource for the community. These could include language resources for local businesses with international interests or that serve speakers of other languages locally, or perhaps courses in English-as-a-second language and in the language other than English.

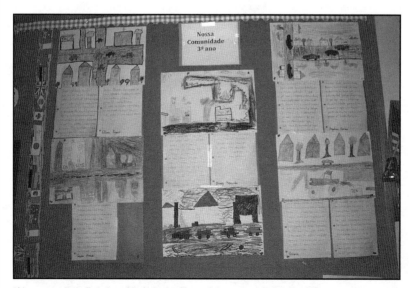

This community bulletin board includes families and the community in school life.

○ Create a parent café or lounge in the school.

○ Include a parent liaison position when requesting funds for the program.

Program Goals

Certain DL program goals are nonnegotiable:

1. high levels of academic achievement,

2. high levels of literacy and academic proficiency in both languages, and

3. positive cross-cultural attitudes.

Other goals will vary to reflect the wishes of the community and to meet state and federal requirements (see the Special Note at left).

Incorporating Cross-Cultural Learning

An incidental outcome of DL programs is increased understanding of another culture. Students in successful DL programs form friendships that cross cultures (Cazabon, Nicoladis, & Lambert, 1998), and they develop cross-cultural skills that their peers in monolingual programs usually do not. Sadly, cross-cultural learning is rarely a primary goal for most schools and is not seen as an important part of learning. However, cross-cultural skills, although not valued in the environment of high-stakes testing that is prevalent currently in education, can play a significant role for these students as they become adults who live in a global society. This then is an added benefit of DL education.

Setting Long-Term Goals

It is essential even during the initial planning stage to set long-term goals. For example, with respect to English language development, native English-speaking students may lag during the early grades when the non-English language is the main language of instruction. However, parity with other native speakers of English is achieved within one year of instruction in English. Also, keep in mind that for ELLs, it usually takes at least three to five years for them to achieve the same levels of proficiency in academic English as their English-speaking peers in all-English programs (Collier & Thomas, 2009). However, during these

SPECIAL NOTE

For School and District Administrators

With the strict testing requirements currently imposed on schools and districts, the length of time it takes for DL students to become proficient enough in English to take the required tests may become a challenge. If students are forced to take statewide tests in English at third grade, some of them will not yet have developed enough proficiency in English to perform their best on the test. However, you can rest assured that, given one or two more years, DL students—be they native English speakers or ELLs—will perform at the same or even higher levels than students in all-English programs. Research has shown this repeatedly and unequivocally. As described later in this chapter, it is important to advocate with political and educational leaders to establish assessment guidelines that are appropriate for this group of students. Collect and publicize your own data along with statewide measures to show other benefits, such as L2 proficiency, better integration of two linguistic communities, and parental satisfaction.

grades, ELLs progress normally in their academic subjects and acquire proficiency in the non-English language. It is important to discuss these long-term developments so that parents, teachers, and other educators understand the full benefits of DL education—such as that DL education requires a long-term commitment. Schools that offer only primary-level education, lasting for only two or three years, should consider how they can extend their students' dual language learning when they leave their school. This is necessary so that students get the full benefits of DL education. This can be done by arranging for another school in the district to continue students' DL education.

Myth

MYTH: *A few years in a DL program will bring advantages for a lifetime, so any amount of time in a DL program is worthwhile.*

FACT: It can take up to six years of extended exposure to academic language to become fully proficient in that language. If we do not give students that amount of time, they may not attain full academic language proficiency and their mastery of academic material taught through the language may become a challenge (Genesee & Lindholm-Leary, 2012).

For established programs, it is recommended that the goals set in the beginning of the program be revisited every couple of years to determine whether they are being met, and if not, to figure out the reason(s) why. At that time, anything that needs to be changed in the program and/or goals must be determined, and the necessary changes must be made. In addition to in-class testing and formal assessment results, the following types of information can be gathered:

○ Interviews with parents, teachers, and students
○ Analyses of student work, using locally or nationally developed rubrics, and language proficiency and academic content area standards

Phasing in the Program

It is a good idea for new programs to start with one cohort and expand naturally by adding a new cohort every year. Start with the lowest grade level that the school offers. Ideally, the program should begin at the pre-K level to establish the strongest foundation possible in the language other than English. This is necessary for English speakers as well as ELLs so that English does not overpower the other language from the onset. If pre-K education is not offered, then the program can start at kindergarten. In the second year, when the kindergarten students move to grade 1, another cohort can begin in kindergarten, and so on. It is best to start with two classrooms at the same level in pre-K or K to avoid having too few students at the higher levels due to attrition later on. The mobility rates that are typical in the district should give some indication as to how to plan for attrition. The following options are possible:

- ○ Make the pre-K, K, and grade 1 classes slightly larger than usual.
- ○ Go from side-by-side classrooms in the earlier grades to self-contained classrooms in the higher grades.

It is also a good idea to begin with just one non-English language in a school or district to avoid exceeding any personnel and other resource capacity limitations. After the program is up and running in one non-English language, another language can be added based on community needs.

Designing the Program

Two decisions must be made when designing a DL program. The first is choosing a program model and the second is determining the languages of instruction for different parts of the curriculum.

Choosing a Program Model

When choosing a program model, it is important to become familiar with the various DL models, including the benefits, challenges, and resources associated with each model. Choose the model that best fits with school and district resources, community goals and wishes, the availability of educational personnel, the demographics of the community populations from which students will be drawn, and the level of competence in the L2 you aim for, as documented in the research for each model. As described in Chapter 1, there is no significant difference in the long term in English language outcomes between models that provide more instruction in English and those that provide less instruction in English; for example, between 50/50 and 90/10 (or 80/20) TWI programs or between total versus partial IMM. In other words, more English does not usually result in better outcomes than less English. However, more instruction in the non-English language, as in 90/10 models, results in higher proficiency in that language in the long term than programs with less time devoted to the non-English language, as in 50/50 programs.

The choice of a model often depends on very practical issues, such as the availability of teachers and resources, and the level of community acceptance. For example, programs that provide more instruction in the non-English language require more resources and possibly more teaching personnel trained to work in that language during the early grades. Thus, if teachers in the language other than English are difficult to find, then perhaps a program model that provides less instruction through the non-English language would be preferable—for example, 70/30 instead of 90/10. Or, if the community balks at their children receiving very little instruction in English, as the 90/10 model would entail, a proportion closer to 50/50 might be preferable.

It is critically important that a model be selected that can be sustained over time so that the proportion of instructional time in each language does not fluctuate. For example, avoid going from 80/20 in kindergarten to 50/50 in grade 1 to 70/30 in grade 2. Such fluctuations and drastic changes in the proportion of time spent in each language make no developmental sense. It is also important that 90/10 or 80/20 programs reach the 50/50 level at around grades 5 or 6 gradually rather than by making a significant jump, say, from 80/20 directly to 50/50 from one year to the next. These are issues that illustrate once again why long-term planning is critical.

When choosing and implementing a program, it is important to remember that the two languages of most DL programs rarely enjoy the same status in the broader community. English typically holds a more powerful position, not just economically and in popular culture, but also in practically all aspects of life. The power of English is also evident in school when, for example, tests in English take on such importance that use of the non-English language is progressively reduced to prepare students for mandated standardized testing in

DUAL LANGUAGE VOICE:
HELPING SCHOOLS CHOOSE A DBE
PROGRAM MODEL

In our region, we hold a two-day Dual Language Institute to showcase local dual language programs and highlight the most current research on effective programs. To help districts make decisions on whether a school should choose a 90/10 versus a 50/50 model, a one-way versus a two-way dual language model, we conducted an analysis of the demographics of both the school and the community, examined enrollment trends, conducted parent surveys, discussed staffing considerations, and facilitated book studies. We also conducted a cost analysis to compare early exit models to dual language programs. Most administrators were stunned to learn how nominal the differences were between the two programs. We witnessed their excitement about implementing a program with proven success in developing high-level bilingual and cognitive skills in ELLs.

School districts transitioning from a TBE to a DBE program have taken distinctly different approaches. For example, in a large suburban district with a large number of Latino ELLs and more than fifteen school campuses implementing a TBE program, it was determined that it would be best to pilot a DBE program in three of the schools. By piloting only a few campuses, the school district was able to effectively manage the implementation of the DBE program in diverse cultural and socioeconomic settings that were representative of that school district. All DBE programs started at the kindergarten level. Each year the school district added another grade level to the existing DBE school campuses, and three additional DBE schools were added per school year. The goal was to completely phase out the TBE program within five years. This gradual "TBE phase-out" approach had tremendous benefits: School administrators were able to evaluate program effectiveness and student achievement on both programs, side-by-side, and to communicate the academic impact that the DBE program was having on ELLs. More importantly, the data motivated campus administrators, teachers, and the community. This is important because *effective communication for effective implementation* has been one of the greatest challenges we have witnessed in those large urban and suburban districts that have decided to do a districtwide transition from a TBE to a DBE program. The lack of communication has resulted in unclear DBE program goals, confusion at the campus level, and the implementation of a variety of DBE program approaches that ultimately have not yielded the desired results. For these reasons, it is imperative that school administrators develop a strategic plan for how the DBE programs goals will be communicated, monitored, and supported.

In the end, the goal should be that every program design meets the unique needs of the school. The more strategically aligned the program is to the needs of the students, teachers, and the community, the more successful it will be. Districts that have adopted a DBE program have seen the academic growth of Spanish-speaking students, along with receptiveness from Latino parents and the community as a whole. Most importantly, the participating students become empowered to compete in the worldwide economy of the future.

—Diana L. Madrigal-Hopes and Alejandra Ortiz
Bilingual/Dual Language Program Development Consultants
Region 10 Education Service Center*
Richardson, Texas

*Region 10 Education Service Center is one of 20 regional service centers in Texas providing services that impact more than 150,000 English learners who speak more than 100 different languages; however, an estimated 89 percent are from Spanish-speaking backgrounds.

English. It is important to foresee this inequality in the status of the two languages and to make plans from the very beginning to raise the status of the non-English language in the school and, if possible, even in the broader community in which the students live. Because English enjoys such high status, it may not be sufficient to raise the other language to be on par with English; rather, it is often necessary to elevate its status so that it takes precedence over English. Otherwise, English will prevail at the expense of use of the other language and students' proficiency in that language.

The Language Allocation Plan

Once a program model has been selected, the next decisions with significant implications for language allocation are: (1) how to allocate

TEACHER TIP

Elevating the Status of the Non-English Language

In the school, by:

- ❖ Making the majority of the visuals and signs on the walls in the hallways and in the classrooms in the non-English language

- ❖ Making the morning announcements in both languages

- ❖ Celebrating achievement in the non-English language

- ❖ Inviting writers from languages other than English as featured authors to the school

- ❖ Having the bilingual teachers in the program use the non-English language exclusively with each other in the hallways and on the playground

In the broader community, by:

- ❖ Planning cultural events, such as cooking classes in the cuisine that is typical of the non-English community

- ❖ Holding song recitals in that language

the language of instruction to each content area and for how much time, important considerations when creating a curriculum that is compatible with the chosen model (see next section), and (2) how to use each language during instruction (discussed after curricular-level planning). Hilliard and Hamayan (2012) provide more detailed discussion of how to make these decisions.

▶ CURRICULAR-LEVEL PLANNING

Language allocation at the curricular level involves two main issues:

1. which subjects to teach in each language (science, social studies, mathematics, art, music, and physical/health education) at each grade level, and

2. whether to use both languages during a short period of time for a specific subject or whether to teach subjects exclusively through one language over an extended period of time.

Unfortunately, there is no research to indicate that it is desirable to teach certain subjects in English or in the non-English language. A great deal of judgment and opinion comes into play when making these decisions. Here are some issues and factors to consider when allocating languages to specific subjects:

1. The availability of qualified teachers to teach specific subjects in each language

2. The availability of appropriate instructional materials to teach specific subjects in the language, or expertise in the school or district to create such materials

3. How the language allocation of a content area fits into the scheduling

DUAL LANGUAGE VOICE: IMPORTANCE OF PLANNING, MONITORING, AND REVISING

The decision to start a dual language immersion program is just the first of many you will make. Among the first and most important, you will be deciding how much time to allocate to each language—the home language of your students and their new language. If less than 100 percent of the school day is in the target language, then you will need to decide which subjects will be taught in English and which in the target language. The choice of subjects to be taught in the target language is often based on the current or desired language outcomes of the program. For example, a Spanish program selected those subjects at a particular grade level that present language-rich opportunities for students to enhance their ability to read and write. A Chinese program made their choice of subjects at a particular grade level based on current level of Chinese literacy, while another program selected social studies to teach in French because it would require students to engage in discussions using utterances longer than a word or two.

Teachers are among the most important resources for your program. Dual immersion teachers are most effective when (1) they are trained and experienced teachers of the grade level(s) they will teach, and (2) demonstrate native or near-native proficiency

(continues)

in the target language so that they can communicate success-fully with parents, administrators, and their partner teachers (if your program teams teachers). In addition to being highly effec-tive in the classroom, dual language teachers must be collabora-tive, flexible, and willing to take on the unique time and work challenges characteristic of these programs.

Like all teachers, dual language teachers will be more effective if they have regular and frequent opportunities for professional development. In addition to keeping up with new standards and related instructional practices, dual language teachers have to take the extra step to determine how new standards and/or practices across the curriculum will be implemented in the dual language setting. Many schools find it useful to plan for profes-sional development that allows the dual language team to deter-mine how best to align the dual language classroom with initiatives in their school or district.

Instructional resources are also critical for your program. Careful consideration of criteria for literacy materials is a major first step. These criteria should go beyond what you might consider for any classroom and take into account the following: the appropriate-ness of the progression skills and strategies for second language readers, the level of language knowledge (particularly vocabu-lary) required for successful reading experiences, the cultural content in relation to its effects on the interactions between readers and texts, and how well the materials can be imple-mented in the time allocated for literacy development.

—Myriam Met
Former district supervisor, Montgomery County Public Schools (MD)
Immersion Educational Consultant to Dual Language Programs

The second language allocation issue to address when planning the curriculum of a DL program is how much continuous instructional time should be devoted to teaching a particular subject in a specific language. For example, if the decision is made to teach social studies in Spanish, will Spanish be used for the entire grade to teach social studies, or will you switch to English during the school year to teach social studies? If you choose to switch during the school year, when will the switch happen—at the end of a semester, at the end of a unit, or at the end of a grading period? Some DL programs choose an alternate-day model of language allocation such that the language of instruction is switched from day to day. This means that the same subject is taught in English one day and in the non-English language the next day.

Research Notes

Research indicates that L2 acquisition is better when exposure is intensive (Collins, Halter, Lightbown, & Spada, 1999). Frequent switches and short exposure to the L2 during the day and from day to day can make it difficult for students to consolidate their L2 skills.

This arrangement can be quite challenging for teachers and students alike because they have to switch languages when discussing the same subject from day to day. This is not a particularly authentic form of bilingualism because it rarely occurs that languages are switched arbitrarily like this, because of the day of the week. There is also the risk in the alternate-day approach that students will "turn off" when instruction is in the L2 because they know that their home language will be used the next day.

Alternate-day programs provide low-intensity exposure. Moreover, an alternate-day approach requires materials and lesson plans in both languages for all subjects at all times, and teachers must be prepared to teach the same subject in two languages. If different teachers are teaching in each language, then they need to collaborate on a day-to-day basis to make sure that instruction is coordinated and coherent.

We prefer that each language be used to teach specific subjects for longer stretches of time than one day. The language allocation plan that we recommend is using one language to teach the same subject for the entire school year. We also recommend that students have exposure to each language on a daily basis, if possible. Table 2.2 lists our reasons for preferring this plan.

If it is not possible to use the same language of instruction for a specific content area for the whole year, then the language can be switched after a semester, quarter, or marking period—all of these are natural breaks in a school's schedule and will not disrupt instruction. The shortest period of time that we recommend for switching the language of instruction would be at the end of a unit. If you choose this option, one unit can be taught in English, followed by another unit in the non-English language. Table 2.3 illustrates how languages can be allocated for teaching subjects using different allocation plans.

Whatever language allocation decisions you make must respect the program model (e.g., 50/50 or 90/10) that you have chosen. In

Table 2.2

Advantages of Daily Use of Each Language
1. Students have exposure to and practice using their L2 every day, and this promotes retention and fluency.
2. Students know exactly when they are expected to use each language (mathematics in Spanish and science in English, for example), making it easier for everyone to promote use of the L2; otherwise, it can be difficult to keep students using their L2.
3. Students can consolidate their ability to communicate in the L2 when their exposure to and practice in the language focuses on one subject; switching languages between subjects too often may leave students with insufficient vocabulary and subject-specific ways of speaking to communicate fluently.
4. Finally, the allocation of instructional resources, including materials, is efficient because each subject is taught in one language at a time. If the same subject is taught using two languages, as in an alternate-day approach, then materials need to be prepared in both languages, and teachers need to be prepared to teach the same subjects in both languages.

Table 2.3

Alternate- and Single-Language Instruction Models of Language Allocation			
Year 1	**Single-Language Instruction by Subject**	Science in Spanish	Mathematics in English
	Alternate-Language Instruction by Marking Period (or semester)	First marking period (or semester): Science in Spanish	Second marking period (or semester): Science in English
	Alternate-Language Instruction by Unit	Metamorphasis (ladybug and butterfly) in Spanish	Growth cycle/stages in mammals (humans and cats) in English
Year 2	**Single-Language Instruction by Subject**	Mathematics in Spanish	Science in English
	Alternate-Language Instruction by Marking Period (or semester)	First marking period (or semester): Mathematics in Spanish	Second marking period (or semester): Mathematics in English
	Alternate-Language Instruction by Unit	Vertebrates in Spanish	Invertebrates in English

Tips for Planning the Schedule

❖ First, account for subjects that must be taught through English because there is no one who could teach them through the other language of your program.

❖ Account also for school-controlled time periods, such as recess and lunch, if those too will take place in English.

❖ Plan to add an equal number of minutes into the schedule in the language other than English to make up for uncontrollable instructional time lost to English.

❖ When assigning languages to subjects, determine which subjects will be taught in each language. Also, determine whether the allocation will last for a marking period, a semester, or for the entire school year. Then plan what will be done in the following year, making sure each subject is taught through both languages over the period of two to three years.

❖ If using both languages to teach specific subjects within the same year, decide whether you will do an alternate day, week, or other arrangement (e.g., every two weeks), while still maintaining your language allocation model. Note that switching languages frequently may not be practical from the standpoint of resources—twice as many materials may be required. From the learners' perspective, more continuity may also be desirable.

❖ If you have a collaborating teacher or side-by-side program model, arrange time beforehand so partner teachers can plan lessons and share information as the unit progresses.

❖ If implementing a DL program at the middle school level, consider the language abilities of all personnel in the school, and try to ensure that the program has flexibility and is not bound by the language proficiency of specific teaching staff.

❖ Before expanding a program to the middle school level, ensure that there are sufficient bilingual personnel to properly staff the program and maintain the programs' plan for language use, never dropping below 50/50; and be sure to account for all special subjects (i.e., technology labs).

Due to the complexity of allocating languages in DL programs, principals or other building administrators responsible for the program will want to give priority to the DL program when making schedules for special subject teachers (art, music, physical/health education). Many problems can be avoided by consulting program staff prior to making these decisions. Also, when hiring special subject teachers, or when assigning special subject teachers to schools, hiring bilingual personnel will alleviate scheduling headaches in the future. In middle schools this will be particularly important, because the more bilingual staff among the faculty, the less programming will have to be determined by personnel factors alone.

other words, the time allotted to teaching in each language—regardless of the subjects taught in each language and how the two languages are coordinated—must add up to the total required by the program model you have chosen. We also recommend that you do not teach specific subjects exclusively through one language over the course of the entire program or for more than one or two years in a row. Doing so would mean that students would not be given the opportunity to learn the language skills associated with all the subjects in the curriculum in both languages. To avoid this, science, for example, should be taught in English as well as in the non-English language during the K to grade 6 span of elementary-level DL programs. Thus, planning ahead is critical for deciding for how to use each language to teach the curriculum.

It is important that established programs revisit their language allocation plans from time to time. This is particularly true if they are not seeing the gains that were expected in language learning. In this regard, the drift toward English as the language of use in the program is a powerful force in English-speaking countries, and it takes continuous effort and attention to counteract this powerful social force. In addition, some programs may find that they did not account for special subjects such as art, music, and physical/health education when planning the original schedule and, therefore, they need to rethink the schedule to take better account of all the instructional minutes in a day or week. There may also be personnel changes that require scheduling changes, or perhaps there are curricular reasons for doing so (e.g., adoption of a new curriculum). Finally, community demographics might change resulting in fewer or more ELLs in the program than initially and, as a result, the original model no longer applies. Vigilance is called for to detect these changes and correct the imbalance they create. While the schedule should be reexamined periodically, avoid changing it too frequently because this can compromise program outcomes and result in teacher frustration.

Administrators should make sure that teachers who must coordinate with one another are given the time to do so in their schedules. This should be considered regular planning time, and it cannot be disrupted by class coverage and other duties; it is essential time needed by DL teachers and coordinators to insure the success of the program. Each pair of teachers needs at least 30 to 45 sacrosanct minutes built into each week's schedule dedicated to this purpose. If necessary, accountability measures can be built in so that teachers account for how they are using this time. For example, they can keep meeting logs—simple recording systems of what was discussed and the decisions that were made. These may become important program records that help justify shared planning time in the future, especially during tight budget years.

▶ LANGUAGE USE DURING INSTRUCTION

Language allocation also involves decisions about how the two languages will be used during classroom instruction. These are important decisions because the way the two languages are used in the classroom has a significant impact on student attainment of linguistic goals. Thus, it is critical that teachers consider how they and their students will use language during instruction—whether both languages should be used when teaching the same subjects during the same instructional period. On the one hand, it has traditionally been argued that the use of each language should be strictly separated when teaching specific subjects. In fact, there are compelling reasons for following this rule. The more students are encouraged to use the non-English language, the more likely their proficiency in that language will be enhanced. Conversely, the more English is used, the greater the risk it will dominate classroom use, with the result that the non-English language will be disfavored by students and, consequently, their development in that language can suffer. On the other hand, and more recently, there is growing recognition that there are some benefits to students using both languages as a resource for learning (e.g., Cummins et al., 2005; Cummins, 2007; Lyster, Collins, & Ballinger, 2009). The way to align these two seemingly conflicting points of view is to let the *languages of learning* (used by the student) rely on and feed one another, but keep the *languages of instruction* (used by the teacher) separate (Hamayan, 2010).

By using the same language of instruction for designated periods of time, teachers provide students with valuable exposure to each language, exposure they need to acquire the language. This is especially important when it comes to learning the non-English language, which, as we have pointed out before, often enjoys less status than

English and, thus, is often the less favored language in and outside the classroom. Thus, we recommend that teachers stick to using a single language during designated instructional times.

In programs where the language allocation plan has the language of instruction switching within a single day, depending on the content area being taught, teachers should determine how that switch is signaled. The language that students are expected to use should be a routine and as clear as possible to students; see the Teacher Tip entitled "How to Indicate a Switch in Language Instruction When the Same Teacher Uses Both Languages During the Day." This is especially important when a thematic structure is used and the day flows smoothly without clear separation of different subject areas. Students could become confused as to which language they are expected to use, especially in stand-alone classes where one teacher uses both languages for different subjects, unless a switch in the language of instruction is clearly indicated to students.

TEACHER TIP

How to Indicate a Switch in Language of Instruction When the Same Teacher Uses Both Languages During the Day

❖ Wear a different color scarf or cap for each language.

❖ Change the direction of the classroom by having a teacher's desk at each end of the room.

❖ Turn the lights off for a minute before switching languages.

❖ Use different classrooms for each language.

❖ Switch languages in different parts of the day.

❖ Have students get up and do a predetermined movement— for example, walk around their table, clap their hands to a rhythm—before switching.

❖ Have a song for switching languages (the music teacher can help with this).

At the same time, there are advantages to allowing students to use one or both languages for learning during the same instructional period of time: (1) Students can become engaged relatively early on in the program or school year even during an L2 class if they are allowed to use their L1 with one another or their teacher; (2) students can make connections among related topics that have been taught using different languages; and (3) students can better make connections between their two languages in either their oral or written forms. Here are some examples of how teachers can take advantage of dual language learning without switching the language of instruction and when instruction is in the students' less-proficient language:

1. Students work in groups to produce a report. They discuss how they are going to complete the task and determine the content of the report using their more proficient language. Then they prepare the report in the language of instruction. If it is an oral report, they deliver it in the language of instruction.

2. After finishing a lesson on folktales, for example, students investigate whether there is a similar folktale in their other language; they examine the text and find differences in various aspects of the story as well as the language. For example, they might do a word count or observe that there is less dialogue in one language.

3. After a lesson on metamorphosis, for example, the teacher, staying in the language of instruction, points out cognates in the other language or asks students to identify cognates in the other language. Students produce a poster listing the cognates, or even a rule for transforming a word into its cognate—for example, all words ending in -*cion* in Spanish have -*tion* as an ending in English.

If students use both languages for learning, it is critical that teachers be strategic in how they do this—they need to keep control and prevent students from gravitating to using their more proficient language at all times simply because it is easier. One strategy is for teachers to set aside time for *bridging* between the two languages so that, at the end of each

> "Students and teachers alike have been enthusiastic about our biliteracy projects. The bilingual read-aloud activities crossed borders between French and English classes in ways that enabled all students, regardless of their dominant language, to understand the stories. Students seemed especially appreciative of the scaffolding teachers provided to help them discover productive connections between languages."
>
> —Roy Lyster, Professor, McGill University

lesson or unit, time is available to point out relationships between the two languages based on the content of the lesson (see Beeman & Urow, 2012 for more details). Teachers may also want to set some ground rules as to when it is appropriate for students to switch to their other language—for example, when they are working in groups, or individually on a project or short-term activity. This is especially important when the language of instruction is in the non-English language.

Coordinating with Other Programs in the School or District

A major decision regarding the design of DL programs is how they fit in with the rest of the school. If the DL program is the only program in a school, it is important to ensure that it is included in all districtwide events and professional development opportunities. If the DL program is a strand within a school, it should have access to whatever the school has to offer and should be seen as a vital part of the school. For communities with a large number of ELLs, a DL program can be offered to these students in addition to other options. The DL program need not replace a traditional transitional bilingual or sheltered English program that is already in place. Offering a range of options makes it possible for ELLs who arrive in the middle of the school year or after grade 1 to attend a program that provides at least some support so they can better master academic content taught in a language they are not proficient in.

However, even when DL programs are well integrated with other programs in the school, they call for special policies, especially with respect to assessment, because of what research tells us about how long it takes DL students to develop proficiency in two languages. More specifically, because it can take DL students at least three to five years, and often six, to acquire full proficiency in English for academic purposes, it is important to delay testing in English until you can be reasonably assured that students have been given adequate time to attain this level of proficiency. In other words, avoid premature standardized testing in English to give DL students the time they need to attain expectations based on English-only instruction. Given the current focus on standardized testing in English of younger and younger children, changing attitudes about when it is appropriate to test

English achievement will require extensive advocacy with legislators and high-level state and district administrators.

Ways to Prepare for Teaching

Teachers who have not taught in a DL program in the past will need to spend time before school starts preparing for the special bilingual environment that a DL program offers. This is especially true for teachers who will be working in TWI programs where about half of the students are learning through a second nonproficient language, at least during the early grades, at all times. To prepare for instruction, new DL teachers can be paired with an experienced teacher to do the following:

- ○ Explore publishers.
- ○ Examine instructional and assessment materials.
- ○ Decide on L2 teaching techniques.
- ○ Devise assessment strategies that can be used during content instruction.
- ○ Plan how to set up their room to maximize learning.
- ○ Think about how to work with parents who are not proficient in English.

Before classes start, the curriculum and instruction plans should be developed, materials should be chosen, and the school and classrooms should be prepared to receive students.

Curriculum and Instruction

The broad grade-level curricular frameworks that are used in the district can apply to the DL program so that the general aims and core grade-level expectations are the same. However, DL programs need flexibility in the curriculum, and the order in which it is taught, so that the content and the way it is taught are well adapted to the DL setting. In Chapters 4 and 5, we discuss what is, in our opinion, the most effective way to deliver the curriculum in two languages and in two cultural contexts—through integrated thematic units.

▶ CURRICULAR ARTICULATION ACROSS THE GRADE LEVELS

It is critically important that DL program personnel meet on a regular basis to explore overlap in the curriculum across grade levels. While some redundancy and spiraling of content, language, and cross-cultural learning is desirable, avoiding repetition of topics, materials, and activities across grades is advised. For this reason, it is recommended that quarterly meetings be planned each year, and even summer curriculum articulation projects when extended time is provided, for contiguous grade-level teachers to meet and learn how their units may overlap in undesirable ways. Teachers may have to decide in which grade level they will offer particular topics, or in which grade levels particular curriculum materials will be used. It is possible that certain activities (say, field trips or museum docent visits) happen more than once in identical ways across the grades. This can only be known if teachers meet. In addition, teachers can collect feedback from parents and from the children themselves to learn where they are experiencing overlap. If you find children saying "we did this," "we read this," "we studied this last year with Ms./Mr. X," then you need to investigate the possibility of potential unwanted overlap.

Time is precious in DL programs, and no matter how much you like to teach a particular unit or use particular material, everything you do must serve the purpose of helping students learn what they need to learn. This means creating enough redundancy to build on prior learning, but to not repeat so much that other subjects are left out. In short, grade-level articulation is critical to program success.

It is likely that lessons will be taught differently in DL classrooms than in other classrooms in the school or district, especially during the primary grades, because students are learning new concepts and skills through a language they have not yet mastered. Sheltered instructional strategies are useful under these circumstances (Echevarria, Vogt, & Short, 2008). Generally speaking, teachers should use a lesson-planning framework that takes into account their students' language needs when learning new academic concepts and skills, even in special subjects such as music and art. While this is especially important during the primary grades, when DL students are just beginning to learn the new language, it is equally true at all grade levels when new, demanding content is being taught. It is essential that DL teachers establish not only content objectives but also language objectives that correspond to the content regardless of what they are teaching because students always need to learn new language skills to cope with new academic objectives. Since cross-cultural learning is an important aspect of DL programs, objectives should also be set for learning the cultural contexts of the concepts being studied. For example, when studying a unit on recycling, sustainable housing that is typical in different parts of the world can be investigated. Cross-cultural objectives are discussed in the sample lesson presented in Chapters 4 and 5.

▶ ASSESSMENT

An assessment plan should be in place at the beginning of each school year so that all teachers can begin to collect information that is important for monitoring program success regularly and consistently. It is best to include assessment activities as part of the everyday functioning of the classroom and to use strategies for gathering information that serve instructional purposes at the same time. For example, use dialogue journals or students' written work on assigned projects to assess the extent to which students have attained the language, content, and cross-cultural objectives set for them. As you will see in Chapters 4 and 5, it is not difficult to integrate assessment with instruction.

Another way to monitor program success is by examining longitudinal data from various sources in the school or district across grade levels to identify patterns of low performance. Are students writing on level in one content area but not others? Are they strong in science concepts expected at only particular grade levels? Are they developing L2 skills as expected but in only one language? If so, you will want to investigate weaknesses in the program and make specific revisions to the curriculum. Data should be used for their intended purpose—to provide needed feedback to help strengthen the program, and never to punish teachers or question the legitimacy of programs. Reading or mathematics instruction is not abandoned when students do not succeed; rather, the information is used to improve teaching practices and curriculum.

The assessment requirements imposed by mandatory standardized testing in English, which begin as early as grade 3 in some schools, are a major challenge for DL programs. As we know from the extensive research reviewed in Chapter 1, this is too early for most students, even in the best DL programs, to reach parity with students in all-English programs. Standardized tests cannot appropriately assess what DL students know in English or in content areas if tested in English until at least grade 4 when they have gained enough proficiency in English (see previous Special Note, "For School and District Administrators"). Strong advocacy is needed, preferably in the early stages of program development, to avoid these problems or, at least, minimize their deleterious effects on the program. Teachers in DL programs need to gather information, both quantitative and qualitative, in a uniform way to show what their students know and can do in English and in their academic subjects as they move through the grades so that they can make a strong case for their program in the face of such testing demands. A plan should be devised to disseminate information on student achievement as extensively as possible, using, for example, local newspapers and television stations, virtual social networks, political

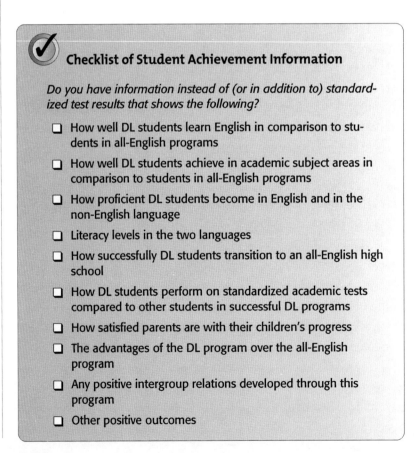

Checklist of Student Achievement Information

Do you have information instead of (or in addition to) standardized test results that shows the following?

- ☐ How well DL students learn English in comparison to students in all-English programs
- ☐ How well DL students achieve in academic subject areas in comparison to students in all-English programs
- ☐ How proficient DL students become in English and in the non-English language
- ☐ Literacy levels in the two languages
- ☐ How successfully DL students transition to an all-English high school
- ☐ How DL students perform on standardized academic tests compared to other students in successful DL programs
- ☐ How satisfied parents are with their children's progress
- ☐ The advantages of the DL program over the all-English program
- ☐ Any positive intergroup relations developed through this program
- ☐ Other positive outcomes

newsletters and briefs, and academic venues such as presentations at conferences in journal articles. The following checklist can help you assess whether the information you gather addresses the questions that various constituents have about the DL program.

▶ SUPPORT FOR TEACHERS

A strong professional development plan should be in place for each grade level and for the whole year. Of course, after classes start that plan can change depending on actual needs of staff. The following is a sample of professional development topics for DL teachers:

○ How language and culture mediate learning

○ How language proficiency and literacy develop in two languages

○ Instructional strategies that promote language development

○ Strategies that promote the learning of subject matter in a second language

○ How to assess student progress

○ How to encourage cross-language transfer by bridging the two languages

○ How best to group/pair students for different kinds of activities

○ How to support all learners with differentiated language practice

---

RESOURCES

Some Excellent Conferences for Administrators Teams of Teachers

- Dual U (www.thecenterweb.org/irc/pages/f_events-dualu.html)
- La Cosecha (www.dlenm.org)
- Two-way CABE (www.twowaycabe.org)

Not only do you learn a great deal in a little time, but you also get unique opportunities to network with others in programs or contexts similar to yours.

Teachers also need different types of support in the classroom, including a resource teacher who can coach them and assistants who can help translate materials that go home (such as newsletters and instructions for completing homework).

Recruiting

The final major aspect of DL programs concerns recruitment of teachers as well as students. Selection criteria and quality standards must be in place for the recruitment of teachers to ensure the best instruction possible. As well, plans must be developed to determine how students are to be accepted into the program.

Teaching Staff

There should be a clear and detailed plan for hiring, preparing, and assigning teachers to subject areas and/or grade levels. The language allocation plan should clearly describe the type of teachers who are needed at each level and what language they need to be able to teach in. Do not forget special subjects, such as music and physical education, in your planning because these subjects also contribute to the proportion of instructional time dedicated to each language. Teachers at or above grade 3 should have proficiency in academic language skills in the language(s) that they will be using for instruction; it is not enough to have proficiency in only social language if you are teaching and discussing abstract academic concepts.

In addition to what you would expect from any teacher (see Crandall, Stein, & Nelson, 2012, for skills needed by teachers who work with L2 learners), the following are important characteristics and skills to look for when selecting staff for a DL program (Freeman, Freeman, & Mercuri, 2004):

- Understanding and commitment to the goals of the program
- Proficiency in the language of instruction
- Ability to work in cross-cultural settings
- Willingness to collaborate or team-teach
- Willingness to find or develop resources
- Willingness to accept coaching in the classroom

The number of teachers needed in DL programs need not be different from general education programs. There is no reason whatsoever to make classes in DL programs smaller than the norm; they function the same way as any other classroom in terms of the number of students they have. If DL class sizes in the primary grades are small, this could result in too few students in higher grades if students withdraw from the program. Small class sizes also make DL programs subject to criticisms of elitism.

Experienced DL teachers should be prepared to act as resources for novice DL teachers. They can do this by serving as coaches or mentors, modeling in classrooms; as well, they can work closely with one or two novice teachers, providing them with feedback on their teaching as they become used to working in a DL environment. Experienced DL teachers can also serve as resource teachers to assist in locating and developing materials, especially in the non-English language, and they can provide professional development to other DL teachers as well as other staff in the district.

Students

Decisions have to be made as to how students will be recruited and selected for the program. The following questions can help guide these decisions:

- ○ Will students be recruited from the neighborhood or from a larger geographical area?

- ○ Will students be admitted on a first-come, first-served basis, or will there be a lottery?

- ○ How will students with special needs be supported?

- ○ Will students who enter school in the middle of the year, or enter in the upper grades, be accepted into the program? If so, what support services will be provided to those whose skills in both languages of the program are not up to par with their peers?

- ○ For TWI programs: How will the proportion of students from the two language groups be controlled? Recall, as we described in Chapter 1, that ideally 50 percent should be English speaking and 50 percent ELL students. Try to avoid creating an imbalance by including too high a proportion of English-speaking students.

SPECIAL NOTE

For DL Programs That Accept Late-Entry Students

Students entering a DL program after kindergarten or grade 1 whose skills in both languages of the program are not up to par with their peers will need extensive support services. Families of children who are not proficient in the non-English language are urged to consider assistance options such as summer language camps or tutoring during the summer before the child attends an IMM or TWI program.

Summary: Planning or Adjusting a Dual Language Program

In Chapter 6, the checklist entitled "Planning a New DL Program and Reviewing an Existing DL Program" summarizes the process that new programs need to go through as they prepare for their first year of instruction. Established programs can use this checklist to determine whether modifications need to be made now that their program has been up and running for some time.

CHAPTER THREE

▶ Planning for Instruction

CAREFUL PLANNING FOR INSTRUCTION is critical for a successful DL program. This cannot be overstressed. Planning must be done carefully because it involves multiple components:

- ❍ planning language, content, cross-linguistic, cross-cultural, and general learning objectives
- ❍ planning resources that are needed to implement the curriculum, and
- ❍ planning for collaboration among teachers who are responsible for teaching each language and teaching through each language.

In this chapter, we discuss all of these aspects of planning. We describe what goes into unit and lesson planning, starting with the identification of objectives. Then we describe resource planning and setting up your classroom. Part of instructional planning also includes tailoring instruction to respond to the individual needs and characteristics of your students. This means you need to get to know who your students are. We talk about research that has been done identifying reading and language learning difficulties in DL students so you can plan for their special needs. Finally, we end the chapter by looking at planning for collaboration.

Unit and Lesson Planning

The main goal of unit and lesson planning is to identify objectives for teaching and student learning. In the case of planning units and lessons in DL programs, this involves "double planning" because you need to plan for both language and content learning to occur in tandem. In the case of TWI programs, you also need to plan for two groups of students: those who are learning through their home language and those who are learning through their L2. Of course, whether a student is learning through the home language or the L2 depends on the language of instruction. Whatever program model you work in, you should have the same set of objectives for all students regardless of whether they are learning in their first or second language. Unit and lesson planning are important because you have to plan for multiple kinds of learning; in addition to the two primary sets of objectives related to language and content, there are secondary objectives related to cross-linguistic transfer, cross-cultural learning, and general learning (see Table 3.1). We discuss how to plan for each type of objective in the next sections.

Table 3.1

Instructional Objectives in DL Programs
Objectives   • *Content objectives* that are based on school, district, and state standards that apply to all students in the school or district   • *Language objectives* that include both academic and transactional (social) oral language skills, and literacy
Secondary Objectives   • *Cross-linguistic transfer objectives* that teach students how to make links between their two languages   • *Cross-cultural learning objectives* that promote an understanding of other cultures and the ability to function effectively in them   • *General learning objectives* that are linked to study skills, learning strategies, and time management

Content Objectives

Content objectives are central to instructional planning in all DL models because learning content is the context in which language learning, and especially L2 learning, takes place. Thus, identifying and sequencing content objectives are the foundations for language learning. Educators and parents would not support DL education if it resulted in diminished academic achievement. Therefore, it is important to take care when writing content objectives—be sure to plan them carefully to ensure that they are appropriate and that students master them. More specifically, it is important that your content objectives are cognitively challenging, grade/age appropriate, and aligned with district and state standards. In other words, do not "water down" your content objectives when you are planning instruction for students in DL programs. If you are working in a TWI program, the content objectives should be the same for both students who are learning through their home language and those who are learning through their second language.

To ensure high academic standards in all DL program models (TWI, IMM, or DBE), we recommend that you first identify the content objectives that are appropriate for native speakers at your grade level. These should be the objectives for teaching both students in DL programs and students in the regular program. It may be necessary to sequence content objectives, especially during the primary grades of a DL program, so that those requiring relatively basic or simple language are the focus of attention early on when students have limited L2 proficiency and those that require more linguistic sophistication are taught later in the unit or year. As well, students learning through their L2 will require special instructional support, such as scaffolding, so they can fully comprehend content being taught through their L2 or by letting them draw on knowledge from the L1. We discuss strategies for teaching students through their L2 in more detail in Chapter 5.

Once you have chosen your content objectives based on the school curriculum, you then need to link them to state and national *content* standards. State and national learning standards should not drive instruction; rather, they should be cross-referenced to your unit objectives after you plan your units. This is usually very easy to do. Be sure to take account of all of your units to ensure that you have covered all critical grade-level state/national standards. The particular standards you choose should be the same for both languages of instruction to reinforce students' acquisition of targeted knowledge and skills.

Language Objectives

Of course, along with content objectives, identifying and planning language objectives is also a cornerstone of DL programs. As a DL teacher, you will want to have clear language objectives for every unit and lesson. When identifying language objectives, it is useful to distinguish between *content-obligatory* and *content-compatible* language, a distinction that was first introduced by Snow, Met, and Genesee (1989).

Content-obligatory language is language that is essential for communicating about specific topics in each academic domain, such as science or mathematics. In general, content-obligatory language includes:

1. specific and often technical vocabulary that is integral to the content you are teaching,

2. sentence or grammatical patterns that are commonly used to talk about specific subjects, and

3. discourse patterns and text genres that are typical of how to talk or write about topics in different academic subjects—such as expository text, which is characteristic of reading and writing about scientific topics; narrative text, which is common when writing about social studies topics; and sequential or procedural texts.

Content-compatible language is language that is not essential for talking or learning about specific academic subjects but can be used during content lessons to expand students' vocabulary, grammar, and discourse skills. Planning for content-compatible language skills is a useful way to include language that might get overlooked otherwise or that needs reinforcement because it is difficult for students.

There is more discussion of content-obligatory and content-compatible language objectives in the Language Objectives section and in the Unit Planning tool discussed in Chapter 4, including Figure 4.13.

Your unit and lesson plans should include clear statements about your content-obligatory language objectives because students must acquire these language skills if they are to master the targeted content objectives. Identifying content-obligatory language objectives requires that you do a careful analysis of the content you intend to teach so that you can identify the vocabulary, grammar/sentence patterns, and discourse/text genres that are called for by your unit and lessons. Collectively, these language skills are also referred to as *academic language or language for academic purposes*. It is important to keep in mind that all students need to develop academic language whether they are learning through their L1 or their L2. However, students who are learning through their L1 will be able to do so in more advanced ways than those who are still acquiring the language. It is critical when teaching through students' L2 that teachers promote their students' L2 skills as much as possible during the lower grades so that they can comprehend complex academic content taught through the L2 in the higher grade. If you do not develop students' L2 skills early on, they will not have the sophisticated language and literacy skills they need to handle academic instruction taught through the L2 in the higher grades.

Myth

MYTH: *Young children are such good second language learners that simply exposing them to the new language is sufficient for them to acquire full native-like competence in the language.*

FACT: This might be true when it comes to learning a second language for day-to-day social communication. However, when it comes to learning academic language, there is growing research evidence that school-age second language learners benefit from systematic and explicit instruction of difficult-to-acquire aspects of language. In other words, when teachers explicitly and systematically focus L2 students' attention on aspects of the L2 that they have not yet mastered and create opportunities for self-correction, students show improvements in acquisition (see Lyster, 2007, for more detailed discussion of this topic).

A number of educators and researchers have proposed definitions of academic language (e.g., Bailey & Butler, 2002; Scarcella, 2003). We like the succinct definition provided by Chamot and O'Malley (1994) who define academic language as:

> the language that is used by teachers and students for the purposes of acquiring new knowledge and skills . . . imparting new information, describing abstract ideas, and developing students' conceptual understanding. (p. 40)

To expand on Chamot and O'Malley's definition, academic language refers to the specialized vocabulary, grammar, discourse/textual, and functional skills associated with academic instruction and mastery of academic material and tasks. Figure 3.1 includes an example of academic language during a lesson on using graphs to represent change in the manufacturing industry in California.

Note this example is an oral exchange between students and their teacher. This illustrates an important feature of academic language—it can be oral or written language. Also note these characteristics:

- technical vocabulary (such as *manufactured, line graph, trace, related rise*),

- sentence patterns that require complex grammatical constructions (such as "What might happen if there were not products to manufacture?"),

- use of explicit reference to what is being talked about (e.g., "... the graph would then indicate a decline. *The line* would go down ..."), and

- specific background knowledge. Without the necessary background knowledge that was part of this lesson, the language used in this interchange would be even more challenging.

T: *Many things are manufactured in California, from airplanes to computer chips. Suppose you wanted to find out how many people worked in manufacturing jobs in California for the last twenty-five years. A line graph could help you. Look at the line graph on page 51 and trace the line to see changes over time. Why would the line be expected to move up over time?*

S: More jobs.

T: *That's right. Because manufacturing had increased over time, the line indicates the related rise in the number of jobs. What happened around 1990?*

S: It stays the same.

T: *Yes, the job market stabilized so there was only a slight increase—hardly discernible—in the line. What might happen if there were not products to manufacture?*

S: People lose their jobs.

S: Some would move away.

T: *That's right, and the graph would then indicate a decline. The line would go down in that case.*

Figure 3.1 Example of Academic Language

The performance of academic tasks also requires that students be competent performing sophisticated "language functions," such as the ability to:

- argue persuasively for or against a point of view
- analyze, compare, and contrast
- evaluate alternative points of view and factual information
- justify one's point of view or to debate different points of view
- synthesize and integrate information
- follow or give complex directions
- hypothesize about the causal relationship between events
- justify a predication, as in a science experiment on osmosis
- present a logical argument
- question an explanation

Academic language differs from one subject to another; for example, the language of mathematics is different from the language used to discuss and write about science and history. The language of different academic subjects can differ in multiple ways. To start, each subject requires knowledge of specific technical vocabulary; sometimes this means that students must learn alternative meanings of common words, such as the mathematical use of the word *table* or *times* versus the day-to-day meanings of these words. Academic language also differs from subject to subject with respect to the specific grammatical forms and discourse patterns that are typically used when talking or writing about these subjects. For example, whereas science might call for grammatical skills that allow students to formulate hypotheses using subjunctive verb forms and to express relationships in probabilistic terms (e.g., "if the boats were heavier, then they would probably sink"), or to express causal relationships (e.g., "humidity is a function of both temperature and proximity to large bodies of water"), mathematics might call on these grammatical forms and discourse functions much less often. There is undoubtedly some overlap in the academic language associated with different domains and, therefore, it is usually a matter of what grammatical forms or discourse patterns are relatively common in each academic domain.

It is also recommended that you include content-compatible language objectives along with content-obligatory language when planning a unit. This is a way of expanding students' language skills to include skills that are infrequent and/or overlooked during academic instruction but that are important for transactional language—that is, language for personal and social purposes. Many words, expressions, and ways of talking or expressing oneself are useful in day-to-day social communication but are not salient or are infrequent during instruction. Therefore, it is useful when planning your language objectives to also identify content-compatible language skills to include in your unit and lesson plans at the same time. For example, in a unit on butterflies, content-obligatory language would include the stages in the development of butterflies—*egg, larva, pupa, butterfly*—or words like *species, male, female, lay, hatch, molt, spin thread, transform*, and *camouflage*. This could be a useful context to provide opportunities for students to learn how to ask questions; students seldom have the opportunity to ask questions in class, but this is a useful language function in day-to-day social communication. You could do this by asking students to read different books on butterflies and then ask one another questions about what they read—some examples are "What did you learn from the book?" and "What was the most interesting thing you learned in the book?" Moreover, content-compatible language skills that are taught during early phases of a unit or early in the school year can include language skills that are obligatory later. Planning ahead in this way gives both you and your students a head start on learning academic language skills that become obligatory later on.

Cross-Linguistic Objectives

Even though we urge teachers to use one language when teaching a unit, we recommend that you:

- ○ create opportunities to draw your students' attention to cross-linguistic similarities and differences between their languages to enhance their metalinguistic awareness, and

- ○ encourage students to draw on the resources of both languages when reading, solving problems, or learning new skills.

One obvious domain for cross-linguistic comparisons is vocabulary and, in particular, how some words in two languages sound and mean the same, yet some sound the same but have different meanings; or how the same letter in English and Spanish (*j*, for example) has a very different sound in each language. Grammar is another domain of language for making cross-linguistic comparisons—for example, how words are organized in different ways in Spanish and English, with adjectives coming before nouns in English but usually after nouns in Spanish; or that you do not need a subject in Spanish but you always need one in English. You could also demonstrate how nouns become verbs or adjectives become adverbs in the two languages. Raising students' awareness of cross-linguistic similarities and differences is also a way of encouraging students to draw on their bilingual resources.

Research Notes

In a study of Spanish-speaking ELLs, researchers found the following with regard to students who were successful in learning to read in English:

1. They used the same strategies to read in Spanish and in English.

2. The strategies they used differed from those of successful English-L1 readers; and, in particular, they used skills related to their L1—such as translation, knowledge of cognate vocabulary, and transfer of comprehension strategies—to understand text in English.

3. In contrast, less successful ELL readers viewed the use of the L1 as a hindrance in learning to read in English.

—Jimenéz, Garcia, & Pearson (1996)

Encouraging students to see cross-linguistic connections can be especially useful when it comes to reading and writing, particularly when students are in the early stages of learning to read in their L2—so, for example, if students get stuck reading a new word or finding its meaning, or making sense of a sentence, ask them how

Make cross-linguistic connections to build reading and writing skills in both languages.

they would figure it out in their L1. In this way, you can draw on literacy-related skills they have acquired in their L1 to advance their L2 reading and writing development and to demonstrate that the skills in one language can be a resource when they are working in the other language.

MYTH: *People often think that bilingual code-mixing (the use of words or grammatical patterns from two languages in the same sentence or utterance) is a sign that a child is confused, is not acquiring language properly, and may even have a language impairment.*

FACT: There has been extensive scientific research on bilingual code-mixing in children acquiring different language combinations. There is absolutely no evidence from this research that code-mixing indicates language delay or problems. To the contrary, this research shows that children mix their two languages systematically so that they avoid breaking the grammatical rules of either language; three-year-old bilingual children have this ability. Children code-mix for a number of reasons: They do not know a word in the language they are currently using but know it in their other language ("lexical gap filling"), there is no appropriate word in the language they are currently using but there is in their other language, or it is an expression of their bilingual identity (see Genesee, 2003, for more detailed discussion of this topic).

The Importance of Cross-Linguistic Bridging

Time should be set aside in every lesson or unit to do what Beeman and Urow (2012) call *bridging*. Bridging is a time when connections are made about content and language through the active use of two languages. Teachers can select language from a lesson that was just taught, for example in English, to transfer into the non-English language. The bridge, therefore, provides students with English words for what they have learned in Spanish, and vice versa, so that they can talk about a certain topic in either language. Bridging can be useful even when a specific content area is taught in one language the entire year. In fact, it might be even more critical to dedicate time to bridging activities in that situation than if the language of instruction were switched for a given content area within the year. We talk about this further in Chapters 4 and 5.

Cross-Cultural Objectives

Given the importance of cross-cultural learning goals in DL programs, be sure to explore the cross-cultural dimensions of your content objectives as you plan each unit. In social studies, for example, cultural objectives could involve a comparison of the perspectives, norms, and values of different groups with respect to specific events you are teaching, such as the Mexican-American War, or differences among groups with respect to key concepts in your unit, such as *community* or *family*. In science or mathematics units, a cross-cultural focus could involve learning about important scientists and mathematicians from around the world. Or, it could involve a deeper exploration with your students of how different groups' beliefs and values affect how they construct knowledge, and what they believe is part of science and mathematics and what is part of folk wisdom—this is sometimes referred to as *ethnoscience* or *ethnomathematics* (see D'Ambrosio, 1985, 2000; Moreira, 2008).

It is important to engage students' families when addressing cultural objectives to ensure that you take advantage of the rich experiences they can share with you and your students and that what you are teaching is compatible with their heritage and background.

General Learning Objectives

Finally, it is important to include general learning objectives in unit and lesson plans. These include:

- ○ making diagrams and charts to represent information
- ○ using print, audio-video material, and online resources to research topics being taught in specific subjects
- ○ previewing a text by reading the table of contents and skimming the index

> "Using the non-English partner language is crucial for all students in dual language programs. In our work with secondary TWI programs, we found that cultural identity and being able to talk with and connecting to family in the home country was a very important reason for Latino students to become bilingual. When we talked with adolescent TWI students in Massachusetts, students unanimously asked for more opportunities to use Spanish for real purposes in the community, especially at the secondary level. Schools can explore issues that matter in the community through community-based project learning, through critical (auto)biographies, interviews, and so forth."
>
> —Esther deJong
> Associate Professor
> College of Education
> University of Florida

○ creating your own picture dictionary or writing your own glossary

○ making notes while reading/viewing (visual and verbal)

○ recording information in science journals or learning logs

○ developing interviewing skills for interviewing experts or family members about a topic.

General learning objectives can also be identified using grade-level specific curriculum guides or core textbooks. You may also want to link these to state or national standards if such cross-referencing is possible given the content of your state standards.

Planning for Instruction

Instruction in DL programs is necessarily different from instruction in all-English classrooms, especially during the primary grades, because students are learning new concepts and skills through a language they have not yet mastered. Therefore, you should use a lesson planning framework that takes into account students' language needs when learning new academic concepts and skills, even in special subjects such as music and art; we discuss this in more detail in Chapter 5. While this is especially important during the primary grades, when DL students are just beginning to learn the new language, it is equally true at all grade levels when new, demanding content is being taught. Sheltered instructional strategies are useful under these circumstances (Echevarria & Short, 2010). You will also want to use some of the common strategies frequently used by teachers in general education classrooms so that the DL program is an integral part of the rest of the school. For example, if science or mathematics journals are used in classrooms elsewhere in your school, you will also want to use these in your DL classroom, but, of course, they should be adapted for DL learners.

Also, avoid the separate stand-alone program trap—having a separate stand-alone program for mathematics, another for science, and still another for social studies, with no points of contact between them and no theme that ties them together. To maximize language learning opportunities in DL classrooms, it is useful to base instruction on themes that link teaching and learning across content areas. By using key thematic concepts and language to teach across content domains, you are able to promote students' understanding of the content while also promoting their development in two languages.

This is important not only in the primary grades, but at all grade levels. We recommend that middle school DL teachers also plan for thematic instruction so that different content areas are interconnected as students go from class to class. This can be accomplished in the middle school grades by placing students in learning teams. Each team of teachers must plan together and establish ways to connect learning across content domains using the chosen theme. For example, middle grade teachers could use social studies or science as curriculum anchors for thematic instruction and then link mathematics, language arts, and other special subjects (such as art, music, or technology) to the anchor subjects. Examples of this would be to teach about ancient civilizations, say, Mesopotamia, in an Arabic-English program or the Maya in a Spanish-English program, and discuss the innovations made in farming, writing systems, and social organization. Using these broad themes, you can then teach about plant cell structure in science that is related to crops grown in Mesopotamia or Mexico; or work on liquid and solid measurement concepts in mathematics, again tied to the theme, and use theme-appropriate texts, genres, and authors in language arts.

High school teachers may be able to build connections by creating dedicated academies or "houses" with specific missions: STEM (science, technology, engineering, and mathematics), the hospitality industry, the arts, or international careers. In these cases, themes will emerge from the mission itself. Magnet schools or charter schools established around particular missions have similar possibilities. The main point here is that by providing connected learning experiences to students you can avoid the fragmentation that makes learning difficult for them in complex and rigorous programs.

If a subject is so specific or disparate from other subjects that it does not work well as a curriculum anchor, you can choose broader, more abstract concepts as themes, such as exploration, survival, discovery, change, innovation, and so forth. The important point here is that, whenever possible, it is useful from an instructional point of view and certainly beneficial from a learning point of view to make thematic and conceptual connections among subjects during instruction in DL programs. Building connections among the subject areas and between languages enhances student achievement by reinforcing both content and language learning without taking extra time; this is useful in DL programs where time is at a premium.

Obtaining Resources

Although DL teachers work toward the same objectives and standards as teachers in general education classrooms in the school and district, sometimes they cannot use the same materials or textbooks, or even teach mandated units in the same order, because the best curricular anchor for DL classrooms is to use "themes" as the connector. DL teachers must be given flexibility to work toward the same goals and standards, but in ways that work best within the DL program framework and by using materials that are authentically written in each language rather than translations (except where absolutely necessary). See the checklist on the next page for suggestions on how to judge the quality of non-English books.

Textbooks and additional materials need to be obtained in both languages for all of the following:

- classrooms and school libraries, with non-English materials displayed as prominently as those in English,

- the community library, not only to ensure that materials are accessible to everyone but also to raise the status of the non-English language, and

- lending libraries, for parents, so that all families can access materials in both languages. Non-English speaking families may not feel comfortable going into the neighborhood library to borrow books in English, and English-speaking parents may not know what non-English books to borrow because of their lack of proficiency in the language.

In addition to published books and series, books developed by students, recorded books, and video books can be included.

Checklist for Checking the Quality of Books in Languages Other than English *(adapted from Cloud, Genesee, & Hamayan, 2009)*

Regardless of the language it is written in, a book should have appeal and be interesting, refreshing, and imaginative. It should present new insights and knowledge. In addition, check books in languages other than English to determine whether:

- ❏ the language contains no errors
- ❏ the language is not too formal
- ❏ the language is not artificial
- ❏ the cultural context is authentic to the story
- ❏ the quality of the type is adequate
- ❏ the print quality is adequate—the colors, images, and words are sharp and well defined
- ❏ the binding can withstand classroom use.

In addition, in translated books, check to determine whether:

- ❏ the translation represents the original well
- ❏ words or phrases in the illustrations are in the appropriate language
- ❏ photographs and illustrations are culturally appropriate for the story so that there is a good fit between pictures and text.

In addition, in bilingual books, check to determine whether:

- ❏ the two languages are printed in the same size and quality font
- ❏ at least in some of the books, the non-English language comes first
- ❏ the writing in the illustrations is in both languages
- ❏ the names of the characters are appropriate to both languages
- ❏ the directionality of the book is appropriate to both languages, even if the other language goes from right to left
- ❏ one culture does not take precedence over the other, and the non-English language is not nested in the English-dominant culture.

SPECIAL NOTE

For DL Programs with Low-Incidence Languages

Obtaining books in languages other than English and Spanish can be quite challenging. High-quality trade books can be difficult to find, and materials that connect to academic content even more so. It may be necessary to have a full-time curriculum development specialist whose job is to develop materials for classroom use, obtain grants for material purchase or development, and work with language-specific centers or departments at universities. Explore whether you can collaborate with another DL program of the same non-English language to share such a person.

For languages other than English and Spanish, it can be a challenge to find good materials, especially because it is important to favor books in the non-English language in order to establish equality with English. Most publishing houses that produce books in languages such as Korean and Chinese print storybooks, rather than academic, content-based materials built around U.S. curriculum—for example, Martin Luther King and the Civil Rights Movement. Materials in these low-incidence languages can be found, but they tend to be translations and they tend to be fiction; there are few in science, social studies, and mathematics that align with U.S. school curricula.

Established programs may want to plan a "materials redistribution" event every couple of years where teachers move materials they are not using from their classroom to a book room for other teachers to consider; after some time has passed, leftover books can be discarded or donated to other schools. Teachers in established programs also need to go through their curriculum materials every so often to decide whether to:

- ○ continue to use them or not,
- ○ transform them into the other language,
- ○ keep them at the current grade level or move them.

Setting Up the Physical Space

The school where the DL program is housed as well as classrooms in the school should reflect the unique bilingual and bicultural features of the DL program. The bilingual/bicultural character of the program should be reflected on school and classroom walls for all to see. New programs that do not yet have posters and work produced by students can use store-bought materials and gradually replace them with student work. The sounds heard throughout the school should also reflect the unique bilingual and bicultural character of the school: in the announcements broadcast over the PA system, in the languages heard in the hallways or on the playground, in the music coming from the music room, and in the main office of the school. As mentioned earlier, because of the predominance of English in the community at large, it is advisable to favor use of the non-English language.

Inside the classroom, furniture must be arranged in a way that will encourage interaction among students. In TWI programs, the purpose of having language minority and language majority students in the same class is so they can support each other's learning and be native-speaking models of the language being learned. To take advantage of the linguistic diversity of the students, plan the layout of the classroom to create opportunities for students to interact and learn from one another as they talk about school work. Make the classroom space work for you.

Sometimes large areas of the classroom are wasted by warehousing oversized teacher desks or furniture that serves no purpose in the day-to-day life of the classroom—remove these barriers and maximize available space for learning. The best use of classroom space is flexible-use space rather than permanently dedicated learning areas, although it may be necessary to dedicate some space to specific functions (e.g., a classroom library). Ensure that it is easy to gather all students together for whole-class lessons, sometimes on the rug/floor and sometimes at tables. Tables are better than individual desks because you can arrange them flexibly for small group and teamwork much more easily than separate desks. Determine which areas will be used to store materials, and put material away that you are not using. Use the wall space to reflect the current unit, and don't keep charts up for the entire year unless you can justify this instructionally.

Create classrooms that promote interactive learning and literacy development.

Bring in equipment as needed, and organize materials on carts as much as possible so that they can be integrated easily with your teaching during a lesson. Display students' work prominently and use it as models that other students can consult as they work. Be sure students know how to use classroom space productively, to share resources, to use learning tools posted in the classroom, and to support one another when native speakers and L2 learners are working together.

Getting to Know Your Students

Plans for instruction should also take into account individual differences among students because students learn better if instruction is tailored to their individual needs, interests, and styles. Understanding individual differences is particularly important in DL programs because students in these programs can have widely different backgrounds. This is particularly true of students in TWI programs because half speak English as a native language and half speak another language at home. As we noted in Chapter 1, there can also be considerable diversity among ELLs—they can differ with respect to the dialect they speak, their immigration history, their cultural backgrounds, and so on. All of these differences can affect learning. Therefore, to maximize the achievement of all the students in your DL classroom, it is important to collect as much background information about them as you can. Table 3.2 identifies important background information about DL students that you will want to collect so you can plan instruction effectively. This information is useful for planning units and lessons, selecting materials, and evaluating performance.

Identifying Reading and Language Learning Difficulties in DL Students

Difficulty learning language and learning to read are two of the most prevalent causes of academic difficulty in school. Moreover, it is also often thought that raising or educating children bilingually if they have language or reading impairment or are at risk for language or reading impairment is not a good idea because their difficulties will be made worse if they learn two languages. There is no evidence that this is true

Table 3.2

Background Characteristics of Learners That Are Important to Collect: Check Off the information You Have Collected for Each Student
❏ Language(s) spoken at home by parents and other children; dialect of home language—for Spanish-speaking ELLs, for example, do they speak Puerto Rican, Mexican, Colombian, or other varieties of Spanish?
❏ Family history: places where they have lived; mobility patterns; parental education and literacy levels
❏ Level of oral proficiency in English and other languages
❏ Type and extent of previous schooling (e.g., day care, preschool, educational experiences before joining your class); language(s) of previous schooling (i.e., English or another language); level of performance in previous schools, particularly with respect to literacy
❏ Extent of student's literacy skills in English and the non-English language
❏ Language skills, including literacy, of students' parents in English and in the non-English language
❏ Oral language and literacy practices in the home: access to print in any form and language; uses of literacy in the home; extent to which English and non-English language are used in spoken and written form in the home
❏ Extent to which literacy instruction is provided in English or in the non-English language in institutions in the community: church, community centers, private programs, or through tutoring
❏ Student's early language developmental milestones (age of onset of first words and simple sentences, evidence of delayed or unusual communication skills relative to other children of the same age) to assist in the identification of at-risk learners
❏ History of language or reading impairment/difficulty in immediate family members to assist in the identification of children at risk for reading and language learning difficulty

(Paradis, Genesee, & Crago, 2011). Nevertheless, it is important for educators to be able to identify students who are at risk for academic difficulty owing to language or reading difficulties so that they can provide them the extra support they need. In the next two sections, we provide some suggestions on how to identify such learners.

▶ READING DIFFICULTIES

Many of the same predictors of reading difficulty/impairment in students who learn to read in their first language are the same predictors for students learning to read in a second language (from August &

Research Notes

The Value of Family Literacy

In the *Early Childhood Longitudinal Study*, children's home literacy activities were examined using an index that counted parents' reports of how often they read to their children, sang to them, told them stories, as well as the number of children's books and audiotapes or CDs in the home. The children who ranked higher on this home literacy index also scored higher on reading and literacy skills when they entered kindergarten. This positive relationship between home literacy environment and children's reading knowledge and skills was evident regardless of the family's economic status.

National Center for Education Statistics, 2003, p. 74.

Shanahan, 2006; Erdos, Genesee, Savage & Haigh, 2011; Genesee, Savage, Erdos & Haigh, in press). The following are good predictors of ability to decode words in either an L1 or an L2:

○ phonological awareness (e.g., blending)

○ knowledge of letter-sound relationships

DUAL LANGUAGE VOICE: DUAL LANGUAGE WORKS FOR SPECIAL NEEDS STUDENTS

In 2012, Key School–Escuela Key celebrated twenty-five years of immersion in Arlington Public Schools. I have been the principal for seventeen of those twenty-five years. Ten of those years were spent on my doctorate researching the question of the achievement of children with special needs in immersion schools. We now know that the language used to teach basic academic concepts to children with special needs is irrelevant.

Special needs students must have strong teachers who can work collaboratively with classroom teachers with children who are integrated in the mainstream. The academic environment must be challenging, but the language of instruction matters naught. Students with special needs must start early in DL programs to learn in their first (L1) and second languages (L2). Teachers must believe in the dual language program and stay in the target language despite the challenges. The students must be held responsible and accountable for their learning regardless of their disabling condition. The bar for all children must be set high and remain high.

One of the challenges to success is when Special Education teachers practice "short-range kindness." They slip into English to ensure the students understand the academic concepts, and in the early years this practice can undermine the goal of bilingualism.

I have done research on the achievement of students with special needs in dual language programs (see Myers, 2009). The
results are that children with special needs do as well or better
in dual language programs than their peers in English-only programs. When our students complete a dual language program
they have more than their comparison peers—they have two languages, they are bilingual.

The bottom line is: Pick a language (any language), be true to
the language, support it, respect it, honor it, celebrate it, and
teach *in* it . . . and the special needs students will learn as well
or better than they would if they were in a regular English-only
school. Dual language works—trust it.

—Dr. Marjorie L. Myers, Principal
Key School–Escuela Key
Arlington Public Schools, Arlington, Virginia

The following are significant predictors of ability to comprehend written text:

- word reading ability
- oral comprehension skills

Research also indicates that these predictor skills of word decoding and of reading comprehension transfer across languages. This is
very important because it means that early identification of L2 learners
who might be at risk for reading difficulties and impairment can be carried out in students' L1, before they have learned the L2. Identification
as early as kindergarten enables teachers to provide additional support
early on to students who are likely to struggle when learning to read.
Research shows that the earlier support is provided to struggling readers, the more effective it is in relieving or minimizing long-term difficulties (see Chapter 10 in Paradis, Genesee, & Crago, 2011, for more details
on identification and intervention for dual language students who
might be at risk for reading difficulties or impairment).

▶ LANGUAGE LEARNING DIFFICULTIES

Identification of students with or at risk for language impairment is
more difficult because there is no single or simple set of indices that
can be used unequivocally to identify language impairment or risk for
language impairment. Rather, the process of identification must consist

of examining a set of factors that point to the possibility that a child has an underlying language learning impairment and, at the same time, examining factors that might explain a child's language difficulties but that are not linked to an underlying impairment. The following factors are often associated with language impairment in both L1 and L2 learners:

- ○ delayed L1 milestones
- ○ family history of language impairment
- ○ difficulties in both languages
- ○ both receptive and expressive language problems
- ○ both parents and school personnel identify the child as having language skills that are not typical for the child's age
- ○ the child's language skills lag those of peers with similar backgrounds
- ○ limited response to additional language support

Because there is no single factor or maker that can be used to identify children with language learning difficulties/impairment, multiple indicators of difficulty must be used. Moreover, exclusionary factors should also be considered (see Chapter 9 in Paradis, Genesee, & Crago, 2011, for details on identification and intervention for dual language students who might be experiencing language learning difficulties). For example, before identifying a child as having a language learning impairment or being at risk for language impairment, it is critical that you rule out the following possibilities: visual or auditory problems, neurocognitive problems, and lack of opportunity to learn the target language. If any or all of these factors apply to a particular child, this would suggest that the child's language learning difficulties are not due to an underlying impairment, but to other deficits or experiences.

It is useful and important to investigate your students' language abilities, including literacy, prior to their joining your class so that you can plan instruction that meets their individual needs and, in particular, so that you can identify students who might need additional support in acquiring literacy skills. Some students may have had enriched literacy-related experiences at home (see Table 3.3) and, thus, they are ready for formal literacy instruction in school. Other students may not have had these experiences, so they may need additional support establishing the foundational skills that underpin literacy.

DUAL LANGUAGE VOICE: CURRICULAR CONNECTIONS WITH COMMUNITY

The International Charter School (ICS) is a dual language, K–5 public school located in Pawtucket, Rhode Island, with two dual language strands: Portuguese-English and Spanish-English. Approximately 50 percent of ICS students are dominant in a language other than English, 60 percent live in poverty, and 50 percent are Latino. Thirty-five countries of birth are represented at ICS. ICS truly represents the diversity of Rhode Island.

Until 2008, ICS had used a prepackaged social studies curriculum, taught only in English. The school wanted to remain true to the DL model and teach social studies in both languages of instruction, and it was disappointed with a curriculum that was fragmented and not student centered. To be able to teach social studies in a culturally and linguistically appropriate manner, ICS embarked on developing its own social studies curriculum.

Funded by the Rhode Island Foundation, ICS's faculty and administrators developed a social studies curriculum that facilitates students' meeting national and local social studies standards as they explore and document the school's unique community of students and families. The units integrated National Council for Social Studies (NCSS) standards; RI Grade Span Expectations (GSEs) in social studies; the Grade Level Expectations (GLEs) in writing, reading, and oral communication; and language objectives for each of the languages of instruction (Spanish, English, and Portuguese). The units were developed incorporating the models of both Understanding by Design (UBD) (Wiggins & McTighe, 2005) and Two-Way Sheltered Instruction Observation Protocol (TW-SIOP) available at www.cal.org/twi/twiop.htm.

At every grade level the cultural diversity of ICS comprises much of the content of the curriculum. For example, in a unit called "Documenting Cultural Communities," third-grade ICS students explore the cultural communities of themselves and their classmates. They use photography to document their communities, resulting in student-created images and text of their families, their hobbies, and their religious and cultural celebrations. Their classmates then read these texts and view the images to learn

(continues)

about one another. Families are very involved as they are frequently the subject of the photos, and they always attend the exhibitions of student work.

While we faced the challenge of not being able to obtain adequate materials for our school initially, the social studies curriculum not only provided professional development for our faculty, but also allowed us to create resources that meet our program goals.

—Julie Nora, Ph.D.
Director, International Charter School
Pawtucket, Rhode Island
Two Way; 50/50
www.internationalcharterschool.org

Myth

MYTH: *People think that parents of minority language children (children who speak a language other than English at home) should use English in the home to prepare them for schooling in English.*

FACT: It is not recommended that minority language parents who do not speak English well use English to raise their children. There are several reasons for this. First, if parents do not speak English well, they will not be able to provide good models of English to their children and, thus, their children's acquisition of English will be of little benefit in school. Second, when minority language parents try to raise their children in a language they have not mastered, they are unable to communicate effectively with them and, thus, they are unable to fulfill the critical socializing role that all parents must play in their children's development. Third, research shows that minority language parents are able to support their children's transition to schooling in English if they use the home language, especially in ways that are related to academic language and literacy development, because these kinds of skills transfer from the home language to English (see Riches & Genesee, 2006, for more detailed discussion of this topic).

As we discussed in Chapter 1, there are considerable cross-linguistic and cross-modal interactions between the home language and learning to read and write in a second language, specifically with respect to print, metalinguistic, and phonological awareness; knowledge of the alphabetic principal; and initial reading skills such as decoding, vocabulary (cognates), and comprehension strategies (Genesee & Geva, 2006). Research reviews by Riches and Genesee (2006) and August and Shanahan (2006) have taught us that ELLs draw on skills and knowledge acquired in their home language to break into literacy in English. Research by Genesee and other researchers in Canada have taught us that mainstream English-speaking students do the same when learning to read and write in L2 IMM programs. For example, students who have been told stories in their home language understand story structure, and students who know how to write their names using letters for sounds in the home language have an understanding of sound-grapheme correspondence and that print communicates something meaningful. Thus, when you assess your students' language abilities, consider abilities that they have in the L1 and the L2 because both of these will provide valuable information for planning instruction. Students who already have foundational literacy skills do not need to be taught them again, although reinforcing them is probably useful. Students who have not had the opportunity to acquire the

TEACHER TIP

Language Skills and Knowledge That Transfer Cross-Linguistically

❖ print awareness

❖ letter-sound

❖ phonological awareness

❖ vocabulary

❖ decoding skills

❖ knowledge of narrative structure and narrative skills: ability to understand and tell stories foundations of literacy in the home will benefit from additional support that focuses on the acquisition of these skills.

Acquiring knowledge about your ELL students' experiences with reading and writing, and other literacy-related experiences in English or the non-English language, can better inform you of their readiness for learning to read and write in school and, thus, how to plan appropriate literacy instruction for them. This is particularly important if you belong to the mainstream language group (English) because you may not be familiar with the ways in which literacy is practiced in your ELL students' homes and, more widely, in the community. Simply asking ELLs whether they were read to at home and whether they have books and magazines can grossly underestimate their actual literacy-related language experiences outside school. Therefore, it is important to be prepared to discover that they have had experiences with reading and writing that fall outside your expectations based on your experiences with middle-class mainstream homes. Table 3.3 identifies some valuable literacy-related experiences that ELL students may have had before coming to school, experiences that you might not readily think of as literacy but that support literacy-related language development in school.

Table 3.3

Valuable Early Literacy-Related Practices
• Storytelling
• Sharing traditional nursery rhymes and/or finger plays
• Sharing traditional sayings in the non-English language (*dichos* in Spanish) used for teaching purposes (i.e., *Dime con quien andas, y te dire quien eres*; "Tell me who your friends are and I'll tell you who you are")
• Singing
• Reciting poetry, or listening to recited poetry that expresses important cultural values (love of country and of mother, importance of teachers)
• Reading religious books, reciting prayers, singing hymns
• Writing letters (or email) to relatives, reading letters from relatives
• Writing lists for shopping or other family purposes

Summary: Planning for Collaboration

As you can tell from the previous discussions, planning instruction in a DL program is complex because you must plan to teach through two languages, and in the case of TWI you must plan to teach to students learning through their home language as well as students learning through their L2. What's more, you must accomplish all this in the same time frame as teachers in conventional monolingual programs. Thus, collaboration with other teachers who are working in the same program is critical for the success of teaching in a DL program. Collaboration can enhance:

○ peer support and a spirit of collegiality

○ a sense of shared mission and purpose

○ understanding of shared goals and objectives

○ strategies for working together to achieve shared objectives, including language, content, general strategies, and cross-cultural learning objectives

○ planning broad themes to frame and connect instruction in all subjects (as explained earlier)

○ planning how and when to switch languages within and across subjects during the school year, and the timing of units in each subject so that semester breaks occur at logical points across all

Collaboration is critical for program success.

subjects being taught, particularly if languages are to be switched across subjects at the semester break

❍ best use of available curricular resources

❍ planning for program assessment, including scheduling assessment and identifying individual teacher responsibilities

❍ planning homework and community-based projects to ensure that families are not overburdened with too many things to accomplish at home across all the subjects being taught

❍ planning field trips and other special events.

It is also important to actively coordinate:

❍ outreach to, and meaningful involvement of, families

❍ the additional support you provide struggling students who are not progressing as much as you want, or who need additional support to acquire targeted language or other objectives

❍ best use of personnel, such as volunteers, paraprofessionals, or push-in support personnel (special educators, speech and language teachers, reading specialists, volunteers, and so forth).

Ensure that time is included in your weekly schedule so that these critical aspects of coordination take place. It is also important to coordinate instruction from year to year and grade to grade to ensure that students continue to learn to the maximum. In other words, even if you are not crossing languages during the same year within subjects, it is important to include planning time for coordination among teachers across grade levels.

CHAPTER FOUR

▶ # Teaching Academic Content

IN THIS CHAPTER, we model how to plan science instruction, and to a lesser degree social studies, in Spanish and mathematics in English. We discuss how to promote academic language and literacy development during content instruction and how to tie content instruction to language arts (LA) instruction using children's literature. Chapter 5 goes into greater depth about the development of language and literacy in two languages during LA times of the day. We discuss academic content learning first because, although the hallmark of DL programs is the development of proficiency in two languages, learning academic content is fundamental to any educational program. In addition, language and literacy in two languages are developed in DL programs across the entire school day, not just during language arts. As recommended in Chapter 3, we plan content instruction using an overarching theme because this ensures that connections can be made across the curriculum and, also, because themes provide extensive opportunities for language use and language learning. The planning process is organized around the five major types of learning objectives we discussed in Chapter 3: (1) content, (2) language, (3) cross-linguistic, (4) cross-cultural, and (5) general learning skills and strategies. As we model this process, we show how to:

- ○ tie content instruction to standards (both content and language)
- ○ plan activities that promote acquisition of all objectives in a unit
- ○ select materials that support learners of various proficiency and literacy levels

- ○ evaluate student learning, and
- ○ extend language, literacy, and content learning through meaningful outreach to home and community.

Overview of Our Model Science Unit

The unit we model in the rest of the chapter focuses on stages of growth in insects. Typically, this topic is taught in grades K–4, most commonly in grades 1 or 2. We recommend that each unit be linked to several content areas and that the content areas be tied together using a broad theme. In our unit, the concept of "change" is used to tie the content areas together. When devising a unit, one content area typically takes on primary importance, serving as the anchor for the unit. For this sample lesson, we chose science as our anchor, focusing on stages of growth in insects (metamorphosis). Once an anchor is chosen, other content areas in the curriculum that are most compatible with the overarching theme of the unit can be identified and then integrated into the unit as it unfolds. For our sample unit, we have included mathematics and tied it directly to the topic of "change" by focusing on time (days, hours) and linear measurement (inches, centimeters). We felt that geography (social studies) could be included as a secondary content area because it allows us to study locations in North America, reinforcing the cardinal points, as we discuss butterfly migration. We extended the unit in other ways to include the arts and language arts. To demonstrate how instruction might work in two languages, we plan the science and social studies components in Spanish and mathematics in English, allowing us to demonstrate how to plan bridging activities between two languages (Urow & Beeman, 2011), thus ensuring that what is learned through each language is easily accessible through the other and that students can discuss all concepts learned in both languages with facility.

Finally, our model unit teaches metamorphosis in both ladybugs and butterflies in order to illustrate that it is a general phenomenon in insects. This also permits us to draw on a richer array of supportive trade books and activities. For teachers in the upper grades (5–8), this same unit can be made more appropriate to life science concepts by extending it to consider the interdependency of plants and animals in temperate habitats, insect adaptations, migration, or preservation.

Before we begin, it is important to consider the context in which you are teaching. More specifically, TWI programs offer students the invaluable opportunity of using their L2 with peers who are native or proficient speakers of that language. We need to take advantage of this tremendous opportunity when we set up group work in the classroom. In contrast, students in IMM programs have limited exposure to the non-English language in school and, thus, teachers need to systematically enhance their opportunities to use the language outside of school. As for DBE programs, the hallmark of this model is use of the non-English language to teach academic content and literacy to ELLs for whom this is the primary, or an important, language. DBE programs seek to strengthen students' home language (L1) skills as a means for promoting academic achievement and decontextualized language abilities that will then transfer to English. In fact, DBE programs often include heritage language students with varied levels of proficiency in the L1 and in English, an important consideration when planning content instruction through the L1 and through English to ensure that access to content is optimized for all learners. The same is true if the focus of instruction is on language instruction. Otherwise, the overall planning process is largely the same. As we describe the planning process in the sections that follow, we focus on common planning activities that apply to teachers in all program models and provide additional suggestions when one of the programs requires special attention.

Inside the Planning Process

Dual language classrooms have a degree of complexity that is not present in monolingual classrooms, precisely because we have multiple learning targets. To address all learning objectives (i.e., content, language, cross-linguistic, cross-cultural, and acquiring general learning skills and strategies), the planning process must be systematic.

A Thematic Unit Planning Tool

To facilitate this process, a planning tool that accounts for multiple learning targets is needed. We find the template in Appendix A to be helpful and model its use throughout this and the next chapter. In the sections that follow, we use "cutaways" of this template to better describe each aspect of the planning process. First, we show how to use the template to teach science in Spanish, with links to social studies, in this case geography. Then, we provide the complete template for the mathematics component of the unit on time and linear measurement, which will be taught in English. In cases where two teachers are working together, the teacher teaching in Spanish would teach science (with some social studies), while the teacher teaching in English would teach the mathematics component of the unit. They would both link to LA and the arts in their respective instructional languages. In cases where one teacher is teaching both subjects, the subjects would be allocated to languages based on the plan suggested above, with science and social studies in Spanish and mathematics in English.

Figure 4.1 shows the first part of our unit template completed to show our theme, its guiding questions, and the standards that will be addressed.

It is advisable to revisit the standards that you identified in the template once all the objectives have been set to make sure that you have connected the unit to all the standards that fit in with the theme of your unit, without exceeding the number that can be reasonably attained in one unit. Toward the end of the year, you may want to check state standards to make sure that you have addressed all critical grade-level standards.

▶ CONTENT OBJECTIVES

As stated in Chapter 3, content objectives include knowledge, skills, and dispositions. In the case of our unit on metamorphosis, we would want children to gain knowledge of the transformative growth cycle experienced by both ladybugs and butterflies in comparison to the way other animals in the animal kingdom grow, particularly humans, since this is a growth process children are familiar with already. They should know the specific stages of growth that insects experience as they grow from egg to larvae to pupa to adult. We would also want children to develop the skills scientists use to observe, measure, compare, and graph the changes they see occurring in the ladybug or butterfly they study. Target dispositions could include objectivity when observing scientific processes or phenomena, exactness and care when conducting experiments (for example, when hatching ladybug larvae), and in recording and collecting data (for example, in their scientist's note-

Unit Theme/Topic: Stages of Growth in Insects (Grades K–3; Most Commonly Grades 1–2); taught in Spanish

Guiding Questions:

1. How do insects grow and change over the course of their lifetime?
2. What types of measurement are useful to monitor this process?
3. What is migration, and what are the migratory patterns insects follow as they go through their growth stages?

Time Frame for the Unit: 2–3 weeks

Content Standards (National or State):	Language Standards (Spanish—the language of instruction for science in this sample unit):
The National Research Council et al. (January 2013). *Next Generation Science Standards (Second Public Draft Version).* Washington, DC: Achieve, Inc. Available at www.nextgen science.org/next-generation-science-standards.	
	Normas WIDA del español (WIDA Spanish Language Arts Standards) (WIDA Consortium, 2005), www.wida.us/ standards/slaspanish.pdf
	Primaria Inicial:
	Normas Seleccionadas: 3 A, B *(primary importance)*; 1 A, C *(secondary importance)*
LS1.B. [LS1: Disciplinary Core Idea: Life Sciences Standard 1: From molecules to organisms: Structures and processes] B. Growth and Development of Organisms: Plants and animals have predictable characteristics at different stages of development. Plants and animals grow and change. (National Research Council, *A Framework for K–12 Science Education: Practices, Crosscutting Concepts and Core Ideas*, 2012).	3: Escuchar y hablar eficazmente en español en situaciones diversas.
	A. Escuchar eficazmente en situaciones formales e informales;
	B. Comunicar oralmente información, opiniones e ideas usando el lenguaje apropiado según la situación, el propósito y la audiencia.
LS1.B. Growth and Development of Organisms. Reproduction is essential to the continued existence of every kind of organism. Plants and animals have unique and diverse life cycles that include being born (sprouting in plants), growing, developing into adults, reproducing, and eventually dying. (National Research Council, *A Framework for K–12 Science Education: Practices, Crosscutting Concepts and Core Ideas*, 2012).	1: Lectura y literatura;
	A: Aplicar estrategias de lectura para mejorar la comprensión de textos impresos en español;
	C: Leer, interpretar y analizar críticamente materiales literarios y no literarios de países y comunidades hispanohablantes.

Figure 4.1 Thematic Unit Planning Tool: Theme and Standards

book or in diagrams they produce to visually reflect the changes they observe).

All of the skills included in the Teacher Tip on key science and engineering practices can be practiced in our unit as students observe the differences among the stages of growth in insects.

> **TEACHER TIP**
>
> ## Key Science and Engineering Practices
>
> The National Research Council (2012) identified eight practices that mirror the practices of professional scientists and engineers. They urge that teachers strengthen students' skills in these areas at the same time as they develop their understanding of the nature of science and engineering. The key science and engineering practices from the Framework include:
>
> 1. Asking questions and defining problems
> 2. Developing and using models
> 3. Planning and carrying out investigations
> 4. Analyzing and interpreting data
> 5. Using mathematics, information and computer technology, and computational thinking
> 6. Constructing explanations and designing solutions
> 7. Engaging in argument from evidence
> 8. Obtaining, evaluating, and communicating information.

To understand the migratory patterns of butterflies in North America, a secondary content objective, students could learn specific social studies content, in this case geography, by learning about the places in North America where butterflies live as they migrate and be able to describe the locations in relation to one another using the cardinal points.

▶ LANGUAGE OBJECTIVES

As was noted in Chapter 3, when planning academic language objectives you need to pay attention to both the content-obligatory and content-compatible language skills you want students to learn as they work through the unit. In the sample unit template, we have included content-obligatory as well as content-compatible language skills that span the range from vocabulary to grammatical structures (linguistic targets) to language functions (communicative goals). Objectives that comprise the language arts (LA) curriculum as well as learning objectives that identify what students need to learn in order to master LA skills are discussed in Chapter 5.

Active learning promotes language use and development while advancing content learning.

With respect to identifying vocabulary for inclusion in the unit, there are some obvious content-obligatory words that teachers must teach as part of this unit, such as *metamorphosis, stage, egg, larva, pupa, adult, hatch,* and *lay.* In addition to relying on your own judgment, websites such as Wordle (www.wordle.net/) or TagCrowd™ (http://tagcrowd.com/) can be used to identify high-frequency words that occur in text. By inputting content area text for your unit into Wordle or TagCrowd™, you can get a visual summary of the words that are used frequently in the text. One advantange of TagCrowd™ is that you can input fifteen different languages, including Spanish. Figure 4.2 shows the word map that emerged when we input text from the book *Cómo crece una mariquita* (Marsico, 2008).

You can see that some of these high-frequency words are specific to our unit, words such as *marquita, larvas, huevos, insectos,* and *pupa,* and, thus, fall into the category of content obligatory. Other high-frequency words that emerged would be useful in different communicative contexts in and out of school and, thus, would be content

Research Notes

There is evidence that ELLs need to learn a great deal of vocabulary, but focusing on only this aspect of language will not likely result in increased student achievement. Students need to know more than the terms for the things they see and the ideas they have. Students need to use these words in grammatically correct sentences and understand the function of the language. Knowing individual words will not ensure that students are persuasive when need be, informative as appropriate, and entertaining when the occasion arises.

—Fisher and Frey, 2010, p. 330

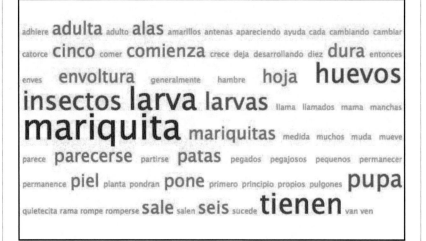

Figure 4.2 Word Map Identifying High-Frequency Vocabulary Using TagCrowd™

compatible—words such as the verbs *parecerse, poner,* and *tener* (all –er verbs), counting words (*cinco, seis, diez, trece, catorce*), the affix -des in *desarollar* (-des + arrollar), and the transition words *después, entonces.* By repeating this process across the main texts in the unit you are planning, you can identify what words to target for instruction, especially for those students who are learning through their L2.

There are published lists that identify words that teachers may want to target because of the frequency with which students will find them in the texts they read; see the following Resource suggestions for Academic Word Lists. Some researchers have found that a high percentage of technical words that appear in science and other academic texts are cognates of Spanish, thus providing another argument for teaching them in DL programs (Bushong, 2010; Lubliner & Hiebert, 2011).

RESOURCES

Academic Word Lists

❖ Academic Word List (Coxhead, 2000) identifies 570 academic words found in content area texts

❖ General Service List (West, 1953)

❖ Word Zone List (Hiebert, 2005)

Teachers must also identify grammatical structures and patterns to teach. From the sample science texts that follow, notice that science texts often include particular grammatical patterns and structures that are not common in everyday language use, such as passive forms of verbs, nominalizations (that is, verbs that are used as nouns, such as distillation, condensation, and transformation), and modals such as may, might, and could.

Four Stages of Butterfly Metamorphosis

*The butterfly and moth develop through a process called metamorphosis (**passive voice**). This is a Greek word that means transformation (**nominalization**) or change in shape.*

There are four stages in the metamorphosis of butterflies and moths: egg, larva, pupa, and adult.

*Egg: Eggs are laid (**passive**) on plants by the adult female butterfly (**noun group**). These plants will then become the food for the hatching caterpillars. Eggs can be (**modal**) laid in spring, summer, or fall. This depends on the species of butterfly. Females lay a lot of eggs at once so that at least some of them survive. (The Academy of Natural Sciences of Drexel University, 2013)*

Science texts often use complex and lengthy sentences with many embedded clauses, as shown in the following text. Students may need assistance comprehending such complex sentences when reading science texts or when producing complex sentences as they write summaries about what they have learned.

Caterpillars grow in stages because of the way their bodies are made. Their skin is tough and does not expand as they grow, so the caterpillar has to burst out of its old skin and form a new, larger skin in order to grow. (Porter, Discovering Butterflies and Moths, 1986, p. 14)

Teachers should also identify the communicative functions (or what are sometimes referred to as "tasks" or "behaviors") they want to teach as part of their unit. A useful source for identifying language functions is the *Common Core Standards for English Language Arts* (National Governors Association Center for Best Practices and the Council of Chief State School Officers, 2010) for *Listening and Speaking*.

Here are core language functions/tasks that they identify:

1. Ask and answer questions.
2. Participate in conversations.
3. Express thoughts, feelings, and ideas clearly.
4. Report on a topic or text.
5. Tell a story.
6. Summarize points made by a speaker.
7. Recount or describe key ideas or details from a read-aloud.

It is possible to perform some of these functions at lower proficiency levels, while others require more advanced proficiency that L2 speakers may still be in the process of developing. As language specialists, it is important for you to always consider the levels of listening and speaking proficiency demanded of the tasks you expect students to perform and to find ways to allow learners to show that they can perform these tasks, either by using scaffolds in their L2 or by assessing their abilities in their home language. For example, you might need to provide scaffolding to "tell a story" by having lower-proficiency students order pictures that tell the story; or, if you think that a student is not proficient enough to "express thoughts, feelings, and ideas" in response to something read in class, the student might name or identify the feeling instead. To ensure that all students attain the language objectives you have identified, use differentiated communicative functions to reflect the different levels of language proficiency of your students, as suggested in Table 4.1.

With respect to planning for the development of literacy-related skills, current literacy standards require that teachers focus on reading

Table 4.1

Communicative Functions	
For beginners	Name Identify
For intermediate-level students	Describe
For intermediate/advanced and native speakers	Explain Summarize

Table 4.2

A Sample of Reading and Writing Skills Required in the Common Core State Standards for English Language Arts
• Read with purpose • Find the main idea and details • Use context clues to determine the meaning of unknown words • Use illustrations as support for the written text • Use text features to locate key facts (captions, bold print, subheadings, indexes, etc.) • Identify the support provided for key ideas • Write different types of texts (informational, explanatory, opinions) • Write clear and well-organized text • Support points with evidence

and writing skills associated with each academic discipline; see Table 4.2 for a sample of reading and writings skills standards from the National Governors Association Center for Best Practices and the Council of Chief State School Officers (2010). We recommend that you use district curriculum guides to identify the disciplinary reading and writing skills for your grade level or identify these from grade-level language arts standards that focus on informational reading and writing skills.

The following part of our thematic unit planning template (see Figure 4.3) shows examples of the primary objectives (content and language) just discussed, as well as secondary objectives (cross-linguistic, cross-cultural, and general learning skills) that fit with our sample unit.

▶ CROSS-LINGUISTIC OBJECTIVES

In our unit, as Figure 4.3 shows, we can highlight cross-linguistic knowledge about the following:

- ○ Sounds and letters: Pronunciation and letter-sound similarities and differences in Spanish and English; for example, contrasting *adult* and *adulto*, the letter *u* is always pronounced in the same way in Spanish whereas it varies in English (as in *up* versus *wonderful*).

- ○ Word meanings: Cognates and root words; for example, *trans* in *transform* and *transformar*.

- ○ Grammatical forms: Morphological features; for example, plurals are formed similarly in English and Spanish while possessives are formed differently.

Content Objectives:	Spanish Language Objectives:
• To show understanding of metamorphosis by describing the transformative life cycle in insects and listing the stages of growth in chronological order (from egg to larva to pupa to adult)	**Content Obligatory:**
	• To learn the names of common insects that undergo metamorphosis
	• To learn the names of the stages in the life cycle
• To observe differences among the stages of growth in insects	• To learn the names of the body parts of insects studied (differentiate vocabulary taught by proficiency level)
• For social studies/geography: to locate places in North America where butterflies live at various times of the year as they go through their life cycle and to describe the locations in relation to one another using the cardinal points	• To describe the stages of growth in butterflies and ladybugs (language function) and how to use transition words for sequential or chronological text structure (*después, entonces, finalmente*, etc.–differentiate by proficiency level)
	• To learn the names of the cardinal points and to describe locations in relation to one another using the cardinal points
	Content Compatible:
	• To practice simple present tense with *-er* verbs
	• To learn how reflexive verbs function (*parecerse*)

Cross-Linguistic Objectives (Bridging):

• To identify the following words as cognates: *metamorfosis/metamorphosis, insecto/insect, adulto/a/adult*, and to name the stages of growth in insects in both languages
• To learn the prefixes *-des/-dis* and how they function to indicate "the opposite" in both languages (*desaparecer, descansar, desconocer; disagree, dislike; dissimilar*)

Cross-Cultural Objectives:

1. To explore cross-cultural beliefs and meanings associated with ladybugs and butterflies: *ladybug*–luck and love, protection; *butterfly*–transformation, social butterfly

General Learning Skills and Strategies Objectives:

1. Summarize a sequentially/chronologically organized nonfiction text
2. Advance visual literacy skills (read maps, charts, graphs, and diagrams)
3. Use the Internet to research information (through online virtual natural history or science museums).

Figure 4.3 Thematic Unit Planning Tool: Objectives

▶ CROSS-CULTURAL OBJECTIVES

In our unit on butterflies and ladybugs, we have identified the common symbolic meanings that insects have for members of the two cultural groups represented by students in the class (i.e., ladybug signifying *good luck*; butterfly signifying *change*) for both Spanish- and English-speaking people. We have also identified popular sayings that these groups have about people's personalities that are associated with the insects being studied, such as "she's a social butterfly." For the mathematics part of the unit, which we describe later in this chapter, we might reference different systems of measurement that are used around the world, or point out how people from different cultures think about time as an elastic or fixed resource.

Since our unit focuses on science and extends into mathematics, we could include discussions of how scientists and mathematicians from around the world have contributed to our understanding of certain phenomenon—a surface contribution perspective; or we could have deeper discussions of group-specific beliefs, knowledge, and ways of understanding scientific phenomena, drawing from the *ethnoscience* or *ethnomathematics* literature (D'Ambrósio, 1985, 2000; Moreira, 2008).

▶ GENERAL LEARNING SKILLS AND STRATEGIES OBJECTIVES

It is important to include general skills and strategies objectives in your instructional units so students can become independent learners. These objectives could include things such as taking notes or using reference collections. Strategies might include ways to plan and organize oneself in order to complete a project. Typically, general learning skills and strategies apply across disciplines and, in fact, can be taught across units, with sufficient repetition to ensure mastery.

Selecting Materials

While the materials you select for a unit should obviously match the objectives of that unit and be at an appropriate age/grade level, it is also important to select a variety of materials that respond to the diverse needs of your students. Include books that require different levels of literacy so that all students can read or listen to "just the right" text. To differentiate instruction systematically, it is necessary to determine the level of the materials you have chosen; this means not just the interest level, but also the general language and literacy levels. Chapter 5 provides more details on how to determine the readability level of written materials.

In addition to printed materials, you will want to have lots of visuals, including multimedia, to support learning. Nonfiction trade books often come with helpful charts and diagrams; books that provide activities and websites make learning interactive and engaging. Be sure to include storybooks that relate directly to the theme of the unit; wordless storybooks can be useful because family members who are not literate in that language can interact with their children about what they are learning. Books that are well illustrated and have limited text as well as books with patterned language are also useful for students who are in the initial stages of literacy. Even books and other print material that may seem beyond the level of your students may provide useful visuals (such as diagrams and charts) that can be linked to your unit. Such materials are useful because they can often be adapted easily to other languages. Graphs and other visuals can be magnified using a document camera or scanned and then displayed on a Smartboard™. In short, consider all potential uses of the materials at your disposal.

In our planning tool, you will see references to the use of technology (see Appendix B); for example, there are many Internet resources, from videos to poetry and songs to natural history museums around the world, with special collections related to students' interests. As well, there are teacher websites that can provide useful resources.

Technology can also be used to communicate with families to show them what you are doing at school and to invite their participation. Blogs and class websites are ideal for this purpose. When using these resources, you can embed videos, recordings of songs and books, digital photographs, and other sources for learning. These can be enjoyed by parents and their children together, or you might be able to make it possible for parents to upload their own resources for other families to access.

The next step in the planning process is to fill out the section of the Unit Planning template dedicated to materials; see Figure 4.4.

DUAL LANGUAGE VOICE:
EMBEDDING WEB 2.0 TOOLS INTO DUAL
LANGUAGE ISTRUCTION

As dual language teachers in a Portuguese-English setting we wanted to look for a way to make parents more aware of daily activities and language used in our classrooms. Finding ways to build a strong bridge for home-to-school communication has always been a struggle, as well as finding resources in Portuguese to meet our students' needs.

Creating a classroom blog has become an easy and quick way of gathering Web 2.0 tools in one easily accessible page for use in class and at home. Our classroom blogs came about after many attempts to involve parents and keep them aware of our every-day activities.

In order to capture special classroom moments, we have used different Web 2.0 tools. One of our favorite tools has become Audioboo® for voice recording (http://audioboo.fm/). It's a simple-to-use application that allows you to record any conversation or reading and upload a picture as well. Audioboo® has also become a great assessment tool. We have been able to evaluate our student's oral language progress throughout the year.

Another great tool has been PhotoPeach, www.photopeach.com, which allows you to upload pictures and create interactive digi-tal slide shows. With this tool, we motivate students to read and reread in both languages. Students have become eager to talk to their parents about reading, and they beg their parents to use the computer so they can listen to themselves through audio recordings—which took the teacher seconds to upload.

—Cynthia Simé
Second and Third Grade English Dual Language Teacher
http://mscynthias.blogspot.com/

—Francisca Silvia Lima
Second and Third Grade Portuguese Dual Language Teacher
http://srasilvia.blogspot.com/
International Charter School; Two Way; 50/50
Pawtucket, Rhode Island

When seeking resources in languages other than English, consider not only publishing houses and distributors of books in other languages but also the following:

• Other dual language programs with whom you could share teacher-developed materials

• Student-produced materials

• Websites from schools and classrooms around the world; teacher blogs and wikis

• YouTube or Teacher Tube videos in languages other than English that align with your content area topics

• Government- or agency-sponsored websites such as museums; mathematics, science, and history/geography associations; professional association websites

---

Materials:

Hall, M. 2007. *Mariquitas Mariquitas/Ladybugs* (Pebble Plus Bilingual, Spanish Edition). Mankato, MN: Capstone Press

Marsico, K. 2008. *Cómo crece una mariquita.* New York: Children's Press, an imprint of Scholastic, Inc.

Rau, D. M. [Spanish translation and text composition by Victory Productions]. 2007. *¡Vuela mariposa, vuela! Parte de la serie ¡Vamos criaturita, vamos!* Tarrytown, NY: Marshall Cavendish Benchmark.

Rice, D. H. 2012. *La vida de una mariposa* (part of *Time for Kids Nonfiction Readers*). Huntington Beach, CA: Teacher Created Materials.

See Appendix B for a more complete list of materials related to our unit.

Figure 4.4 Thematic Unit Planning Tool: Materials

Teaching Strategies and Activities for Active Learning

We are now at the stage of planning what will actually happen in the classroom. We find that a framework for teaching that consists of three phases—Preview, Focused Learning, and Extension (Gordon, 2000)—is very useful for this purpose. No matter the phase of a lesson, it is important to favor active learning strategies, or as Himmele and Himmele (2009, 2011) call them, "total participation techniques," as these promote the greatest cognitive and linguistic learning for students (Kagan, 1995). Also, consider what grouping arrangements are most suitable for certain activities or groups of learners; some suggestions for how to group students are given in the Teacher Tip about grouping arrangements.

In order to make decisions about teaching strategies for each phase, you should determine the background knowledge that students need so that you can make the most of your lesson. For this we turn to the section of our Unit Planning tool called "Background Knowledge Needed"; see Figure 4.5.

Background Knowledge Needed:

Awareness of butterflies and ladybugs as well as other insects in the environment

Awareness of growth of living organisms

Awareness of the continent of North America and of political maps (maps showing the boundaries of countries and states)

Figure 4.5 Thematic Unit Planning Tool: Background Knowledge Needed

TEACHER TIP

Grouping Arrangements

It is important to vary grouping arrangements to maximize learning. While it is likely that, early in the unit, instruction will feature whole-group learning, the focused learning and extension phases should feature small-group and partner-grouping arrangements so that students can work with one another or in small groups. This promotes talk among students which, in turn, promotes learning—not only language learning, but also content, general skills, cross-linguistic, and cross-cultural learning.

1. Use *simultaneous* participation structures. Some examples of this are: All students respond on whiteboards at the same time; all students read with a partner and each is either in the role of reader or listener; all students participate to complete an assigned task, with each having a well-specified role and contribution to make in their group or team through cooperative-learning task structures as opposed to *sequential* participation structures (e.g., where the teacher calls on only one student at a time and all other students wait silently for their turn). While students are working in groups, carefully monitor how much practice each student is getting to ensure concept and language learning for all students. De-centering the classroom brings many benefits to language learning, in comparison to only allowing certain students to participate when called on by the teacher while all other students remain silent and often disengaged (Himmele & Himmele, 2009, 2011; Wrubel, 2002).

2. It is beneficial for students to work together in their more comfortable language, as long as the product is presented in the language of instruction. So, it is okay to let students figure out in their more-proficient language how to say or write something in the other language, provided it leads to stronger performance in the less-proficient language.

3. As appropriate, favor individual learning so that you can clearly see the progress that each student is making.

▶ THE PREVIEW PHASE

The preview phase provides an opportunity to accomplish two things: (1) Find out what your students know, and (2) prepare them for learning new concepts or the big ideas in a lesson. To find out what your students know, investigate students' prior knowledge on the topic, skills they already have that are related to the unit, and questions they would like to explore. For the science part of the unit, for example, it is useful to know whether students have basic awareness of insects, such as butterflies and ladybugs, of the continent of North America, and of wall maps. For the mathematics part of the unit, you will want to find out what students know about clocks, size, length, and making comparisons in size or length. A variety of techniques can be used to collect this information: class surveys, checklists, peer interviews, think-pair-share, teacher-led discussions, students' entries in journals, KWL charts, short pre-tests, anticipation guides, and quick draws or writes.

Once you have found out what your students already know, you need to prepare them for the unit. The best way to do this is to engage them in some type of activity that establishes the linguistic foundation they need in order to learn the concepts included in the lesson. It is essential that you think through the oral language students will need to understand and talk about new concepts. You might write needed words and phrases on word cards and sentence strips, or you might display key terms and phrases on the classroom walls. The Preview phase also serves to stimulate interest in the topic so that students are motivated to engage in learning. Figure 4.6 shows some examples of preparatory activities. These activities can be done separately or together, depending on how much preparation you think students need. Since the purpose of this phase is to set a common foundation among students, most of these preview activities are done using a whole class format.

It is important to vary the activities you use to preview concepts so that each lesson starts in its own interesting way and puts all students on an equal footing as they begin a new unit. Appendix C lists other possible activities to conduct in the Preview phase.

Figure 4.6 is an example of how to fill out the Unit Planning tool for the Preview phase.

▶ FOCUSED LEARNING PHASE

Once you have prepared students to tackle the linguistic demands for learning new concepts and have established a common knowledge base for those concepts, it is time to carry out the focused learning phase—teaching the new concepts more directly and in more depth. Many of

Major Teaching Activities Preview Phase *Sample Preview Activities*	Grouping Arrangements
1. Demonstrate growth in human beings by showing photos of you as a newborn, toddler, teenager, etc.	1. Whole class
2. Focus on key vocabulary that you have selected, demonstrating each word and writing them on the Word Wall; for beginning- level students, engage them in a game where they have to run and stand by a word or take it off the wall. Don't forget to also capture key phrases or "scripts," sentence stems that help students express ideas around a particular topic (i.e., "I noticed that …"; "I wondered why …").	2. Whole class
3. Ask students to bring anything from home that shows how they grew, for example, photos, baby clothes, and height measurements. Ask students to imagine and to estimate how their growth will continue.	3. Individual and whole class
4. Do a whole-class or small-group writing task describing the activities so far using the key vocabulary.	4. Whole class or small groups
5. Explore the insects students know using insect picture cards. Have the students do a picture sort into various categories—those they have seen before, those they can name, those about which they know some facts, etc.	5. Partners

Figure 4.6 Thematic Unit Planning Tool: Preview Phase

the strategies that are used in this phase are the same as those used in the Preview phase. The difference is that here your attention is primarily focused on concept attainment, with language taking a back seat.

Before looking at some strategies that are useful for this phase, we need to go back to our objectives briefly. Because instruction in DL programs is complex and involves multiple types of learning objectives, you want to make sure that your students are aware of what they will be learning and the things they should be able to do by the end of the unit. Therefore, in this phase you want to make sure that your students are aware of what they need to accomplish. Find interesting ways of helping students know what they will learn and be able to do at the end of the unit; consider strategies that go beyond simply posting unit objectives on the board or having students recite them at the start of each lesson.

Here are some ideas to determine whether students are aware of your instructional objectives. These activities can be done after teaching a portion of the unit or a lesson.

1. Before teaching, provide students with a list of the big ideas you will teach and the language features you want them to know. Then, after teaching, ask them to put the big ideas into two piles—those they can explain/use/do without help and those they still need help with.

2. Ask teams of students to become detectives so that they can figure out why you did a certain activity or what a specific activity was intended to teach. Place their answers under the appropriate headings: "language," "content," "cross-cultural," and so on. This can be done before, during, or after the lesson.

3. Have students write down "exit slips"—one new thing they learned about language, content, cross-cultural understandings, and so on—and put them on the board. Then, have them review their slips the next day and identify those that best capture what you hoped they would learn.

4. At the conclusion of the unit, give students "either/or" choices to circle the language, content, cross-cultural, or other objectives they feel best represent what they have learned.

New concepts in a unit or lesson can be introduced using a variety of strategies while maintaining the rigor of instruction for the grade-level and curriculum requirements. In general, we recommend using an inquiry approach, letting students discover aspects of the concept under study. Many of these strategies can be done using cooperative learning groups. This allows for face-to-face communication and engages students in enjoyable activities where they can use the vocabulary, phrases, and structures that they just learned in the Preview phase. Ensure that you create opportunities for extended production, not just one-word answers. Make certain that you are creating plentiful opportunities for all students to use the target language. Opportunities for extended expression and participation patterns are governed by the grouping structure and tasks assigned to students. So if students are not getting enough practice, consider how to change the grouping and task structures to ensure more participation. Remember this maxim: "Language use is language learning." Give support as needed, and also give feedback to make sure that each student's language repertoire grows. The cycle of language input, practice, and

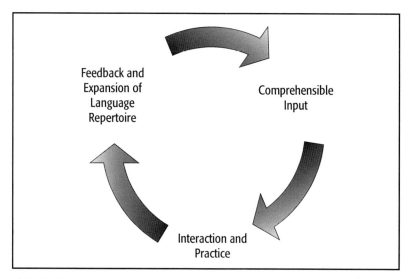

Figure 4.7 Cycle of Language Practice

feedback to extend and stretch student language capabilities is shown in Figure 4.7.

The following strategies are particularly useful during the Focused Learning phase because they ensure conceptual clarity despite linguistic modifications.

1. The use of realia, hands-on exploration of objects, and manipulatives.

2. Multimedia presentations (BrainPOP® (www.brainpop.com) and BrainPOP Español® (esp.brainpop.com), Teacher Tube, and other teaching video sites.

3. Models and demonstrations to enhance verbal input.

4. Readings in small cooperative groups, each with appropriately leveled texts for proficiency levels in class or partner reads.

5. Jigsaw reading followed by reciprocal teaching among partners.

6. The use of visuals—graphic organizers, and other visual means of organizing information such as concept maps, graphs, or outlines—which ensure that the input is comprehensible to all students.

7. Research projects or experiments conducted in the classroom.

8. Partner "think-pair-share" activities. In TWI programs, create dyads or triads, and prepare students to be good language-

learning partners; ensure that they know how to elicit language and give practice to their non-native-speaking partners.

9. Accountable talk, where students must give reasons or show support for statements they make.

10. Discussion starter cards for small group discussions. Groups report in.

When involved in whole-class discussions, ask for responses from students through appropriately worded questions and prompts taking into account the current proficiency levels of students. Give

---

TEACHER TIP

Ways to Reinforce Student Learning

❖ Help students learn to take notes in ways that match their language proficiency and the demands of the topic. For example, for lower-level proficiency students, jotting down words on graphic organizers may be the most efficient way for taking notes. When jotting down notes for this unit, use a sequence chart or a timeline to show stages of growth, or use a T-chart to show what is similar and what is different in the ladybug and butterfly growth stages. Many graphic organizers are available online. One of them is www.eduplace.com/graphicorganizer.

❖ Keep learning logs and journals.

❖ Create student-constructed texts, done alone or jointly with a partner or small group, at different times during the introduction of the concepts.

❖ Play games, use simulations, and have dramatizations.

❖ Use WebQuests or online explorations.

❖ Select additional readings (text sets) to match learner language proficiency and literacy levels.

❖ Use songs and performance poetry, both of which are particularly useful for integrating new language patterns into students' long-term memories.

equal turns to all students to promote language and content learning by all. Monitor your turn allocation to ensure that you are giving all students equal practice opportunities. Do not ask questions such as "Who knows . . . ?" or "Can anyone tell me . . . ?" because this invites unequal distribution of turns as well as calling out answers, both of which diminish opportunities for others to speak.

Always be sure to give clear directions for all projects and tasks, including behavior expected during group or partner work before starting an activity. Provide sufficient practice opportunities for all learners to use the target language and demonstrate understanding of key concepts. Use simultaneous participation structures, such as those recommended by Himmele and Himmele (2009, 2011) in their *Total Participation Techniques* (see the Teacher Tip, page 194, in Chapter 5). During activities, circulate to provide targeted support to individual learners.

Appendix D lists some websites with highly purposeful, yet fun activities you might include if you were to teach the stages of growth in ladybugs and butterflies. Our Unit Planning tool includes only a few strategies, as is typical of a lesson of limited time; it would look like what is shown in Figure 4.8 for the Focused Learning phase of our lesson.

▶ EXTENSION PHASE

The next phase of teaching and learning is the Extension phase. Learning can be extended by allowing students to pursue their own

Focused Learning Phase	
Sample Teaching Activities	**Grouping Arrangements**
1. Introduce the topic using a BrainPop Español® video (Metamorfosis).	1. Whole class
2. Science experiment (hatching ladybug larvae) with science notebook for recording (takes 2 to 3 weeks; www.nature-gifts.com/ladybug-gifts.html).	2. Cooperative learning groups
3. Guided reading groups or literature circles (with appropriate-leveled books on the topic).	3. Small groups
4. Diagram of the ladybug life cycle; vocabulary notebook.	4. Individual
5. Performance poem: see www.mamalisa.com/	5. In partners
6. Place push pins in countries where ladybugs flourish, or use yarn to track the migration pattern of Monarch butterflies when they migrate to and from Mexico.	6. Teams of students

Figure 4.8 Thematic Unit Planning Tool: Focused Learning Phase

interests and choices using skills and knowledge they have learned from the unit; for example, you could ask students to generate research topics or to conduct individual investigations. These might involve investigations using interviews, research on the Web and other media, or visits to facilities in the community.

Ideally, this phase would also allow students to apply what they have just learned to their daily lives or to their community or neighborhood, and it would allow you to bring to school the funds of knowledge from your students' families and communities (Moll et al., 1992). For example, there may be families who know how to attract ladybugs into a garden to combat unwanted infestations; other families may have witnessed butterfly migrations or seen a butterfly sanctuary (e.g., Monarch butterflies in Mexico—see www.learner.org/jnorth/ tm/monarch/LifeSanctuaryRegion.html). Family members may know fables, folk tales, and *dichos* (sayings) that you can draw on to extend your students' learning about the topic of the unit.

Students could complete interesting activities together with their families. They could do data collection projects, such as the Lost Ladybug Project (www.lostladybug.org/); or perhaps they could complete art projects at home (see www.youtube.com/watch?v=qfN73_W7_4E for ideas). Extension into the community can also involve project-based learning; some examples are growing a butterfly garden in the neighborhood or bringing community resources to the classroom (such as a docent from a museum or a ranger from a nature preserve). You can also take students on virtual field trips by accessing museums' and other organizations' websites—for example, www.andeanbutterflies.org/index _sp.html or www.miucr.ucr.ac.cr/descarga2.html.

During this phase, you can also incorporate other content areas. You have already seen in our Unit Planner how geography was incorporated into the science unit, and later you will see how grade-appropriate mathematics concepts and skills can be taught or reinforced through the unit. You can also extend into the following:

1. Language Arts
    a. Have an author study with Eric Carle (starting with www.eric -carle.com/home.html and www.eric-carle.com/SPbooks.html and including *La mariquita malhumorada* and *The Very Hungry Caterpillar*).

b. Read *La Mariquita Juanita* by Angélica Sátiro (www.angelica satiro.net).

   c. Write bilingual poetry using metaphors and other types of figurative language based on models of renown authors (i.e., "Las Mariposas/Butterflies" poem by Francisco X. Alarcon in *Animal Poems of the Iguazu/Animalario del Iguazu*).

   d. Sing children's songs.

   e. Do a writing project (use shape/accordion books for recounts or simple narratives constructed by students to accompany their diagrams).

2. Art

   a. Make use of drawings and pictures to illustrate stages of growth.

   b. Do craft projects such as those modeled in our activities.

3. Dance and Movement

   a. Perform scenes from books that students have read.

   b. Do performance poetry.

   c. Do rhythmic play while counting.

The Extension phase is also a time for making cross-linguistic bridges, where the focus shifts back to the language of instruction, but in both of the students' languages (Beeman & Urow, 2012). The following are possible strategies to make that transfer possible.

   ○ Identify cognates from the language that have been used during the lesson and list them side-by-side on the blackboard or classroom wall.

   ○ Turn any poster or word wall that has been created into a side-by-side poster that shows items in the two languages next to each other, showing similarities or differences in the ways concepts are expressed across languages.

   ○ Give explanations using charts and graphics; produce videos of the explanations given by students to place on the class website.

   ○ If there is a bilingual version of a book that the students have read, or will read, do a comparison. What is compared can vary according to the students' age and language proficiency. Even very young children can do a simple word count, and this can be a statistic that can keep building to determine whether there is a pattern.

DUAL LANGUAGE VOICE: BRIDGING BETWEEN LANGUAGES IN THE DUAL LANGUAGE CLASSROOM

One of the prominent features of our classroom is "bridging," the last stage in a unit, when students transfer what they have learned in one language to the other language. It is not about teaching the same concepts twice, but about encouraging students to analyze what is similar in their two languages.

In our 50/50 dual language kindergarten, English is taught in one room and Spanish in another, with the students changing rooms in the middle of the day. We guide our students to pay attention to the similarities in grammar and vocabulary in Spanish and English. We allow time at the end of the unit to bridge into the other language. The bridging is planned at the beginning of the unit, and the two teachers coordinate what vocabulary and grammatical patterns are going to be transferred and how. Even though the lesson is preplanned, there is always a chance that students may take a different turn. As a teacher you can choose to go with it or stick to the preplanned lesson, making sure the focus is on the vocabulary.

For example, if a unit was taught in Spanish, students could "teach" the English teacher the vocabulary learned in the other language. The English teacher encourages them to use the Spanish vocabulary, but the students come up with the English vocabulary and make connections through the use of TPR and visuals. They are responsible for their learning, bridging from Spanish to English or vice versa.

As the photo shows, a tree unit taught in Spanish was bridged to the English classroom. The tree was labeled in Spanish and the students dictated two sentences about what they learned about trees. The students brought the poster they created in Spanish to the English classroom. They taught the Spanish vocabulary to the English-speaking teacher and then proceeded to label the tree in English. After the bridging activity is complete, the students engage in an extension activity involving the new vocabulary, and they practice what they have learned in the new language.

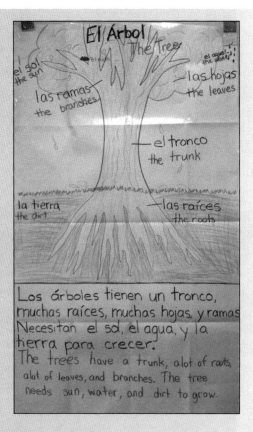

El Árbol / The Tree

el sol / the sun

las ramas / the branches

el agua / the water

las hojas / the leaves

el tronco / the trunk

la tierra / the dirt

las raíces / the roots

Los árboles tienen un tronco, muchas raíces, muchas hojas, y ramas. Necesitan el sol, el agua, y la tierra para crecer.
The trees have a trunk, a lot of roots, a lot of leaves, and branches. The tree needs sun, water, and dirt to grow.

We can only say good things about how the bridge supports students in our classroom. We know that it makes a dual program's instruction more complete, and we encourage teachers to implement this great tool.

—Kimberly Hansen
Dual Language Kindergarten Teacher
and
—Marcos Gómez
Dual Language Kindergarten Teacher

—Verda Dierzen Early Learning Center
Woodstock District 200
Woodstock, Illinois; Two-Way; 50/50

Figure 4.9 shows what our Unit Planner would look like for the Extension phase.

We have shown many ways to use technology during each phase of instruction of a unit. We have used many Internet resources, including YouTube videos, poetry, and songs that are available from specific websites, as well as websites for natural history museums around the world that have special collections related to the topic of instruction. We also pointed out many teaching resources that can be gathered from teacher sites across the web.

Technology is also a great resource for communicating with families to show them what you are doing at school and to invite their participation. Blogs and class websites are ideal for this purpose (see previous Dual Language Voice entitled "Embedding Web 2.0 Tools into Dual Language Instruction"). When using these resources, you can embed videos, recordings of songs and books, digital photographs, and other sources for learning. Parents and their children can enjoy these together, or you might make it possible for parents to upload their own resources for other families to access.

Extension Phase	
Sample Teaching Activities	**Grouping Arrangements**
1. Extension into the community: Grow a butterfly garden in the neighborhood.	1. Whole class or small group with community members
2. Extension to Social Studies: Use maps in Spanish to show migration patterns of butterflies in North America. Practice using cardinal points to describe directionality and relationship of one location to another.	2. Small groups or in partners
3. Extension to Art: Make paper butterflies (Como hacer una mariquita de papel/YouTube video) to decorate the school hallway.	3. Whole class and individual
4. Extension to Music: Song (with actions; e.g., www.doslourdes.net/partitura_mariposa.htm), la mariposa.	4. Small groups
5. Extension to other language: Make "subtitles" of the song la mariposa in English to be held up as the song is being performed in Spanish.	5. Small groups
6. Closing activity: La oruga muy hambrienta (You Tube version: www.youtube.com/watch?v=DC2qSWEjD28); or dramatic performance of story.	6. Whole class

Figure 4.9 Thematic Unit Planning Tool: Extension Phase

Planning Assessment

There are two major types of assessment that teachers use to evaluate student performance: formative and summative. Formative assessment is an evaluation that occurs during instruction. In formative assessment, the teacher monitors the effectiveness of instruction in order to adjust instruction for learners as needed. Summative assessment is done periodically at the end of a unit, marking period, or year to determine whether students are making expected progress. Typical summative assessments include state assessments, district interim assessments, end of unit tests, and so forth. Since summative assessments are often set by district and state policies, we concentrate here on formative assessment—assessment that can guide instruction and make it more effective.

▶ FORMATIVE ASSESSMENT DURING INSTRUCTION

Formative assessment can be done by making assessment activities part of the unit from the beginning. As you plan learning activities, consider which learning activities could also be used to assess achievement of the learning objectives you have set for the unit. In this way, assessment can be integrated with the instruction rather than becoming a separate stand-alone process. For example, you might watch how they are performing during a science experiment (see Appendix E) to examine not only their ability to engage in key scientific practices, but also how well they function as members of a group. Alternatively, as students are making a poster about metamorphosis, observe whether and how quickly they are acquiring language and content objectives. You could also pay attention to how much cross-linguistic transfer is happening, or you might notice how well students are using general learning skills to complete the activity.

Another way to ensure that formative assessment takes place on an ongoing basis is to plan self- and peer-monitoring protocols that students can use during learning activities to assess their own and other students' progress. Peer and self-assessments not only make learners aware of their own progress, they also help them become independent learners.

Many techniques can be used to monitor student learning. The Teacher Tip about formative assessment gives some examples.

◯

TEACHER TIP

◯ Formative Assessment

Sources of Information

1. Exit slips in which students provide answers to key questions like: What do you want more help with? What are you still unsure of? Did you get enough chances to speak/read/write today?

2. Learning logs, student notebooks, and journals (including mathematics and science journals).

3. Work samples, including notes that students are making to help them learn or figure out the answer to a problem.

◯

4. Class checklists to monitor acquisition of language and content objectives. For example, assess students' acquisition of specific content objectives by interviewing the students using prepared scripts. As they explain their understandings of the content taught, listen for particular vocabulary and grammatical structures to see how well they have learned them. Notice the types of communicative functions that students use with ease and those that they are still having difficulty using easily so you can set these as future language objectives.

5. Oral performance during or following instruction.

6. Teacher-student conferences and interviews.

7. Quizzes and tests: Ask students to complete diagrams of the four-stage life cycle of insects, or complete a Venn diagram or T-chart comparing the growth cycle of both insects studied in the unit.

8. Periodic audio and video recordings that give a sample of learners and the classroom overall, from a different angle. Record from different places in the room over time to capture such things as who is on track and who isn't, who is complaining about not being able to do the work, who takes the most turns and whose voice you never hear, and who is still making mistakes conceptually or linguistically that deserve attention.

Ways of Recording Assessments

1. Referring to anecdotal notes that you accumulate for each student.

2. Using a grid to check off which objectives—content, language, literacy, and learning skills—have been attained and by which students.

3. Graphing the correct usage of specific vocabulary or grammatical structures (language objectives) over time.

▶ SUMMATIVE ASSESSMENT AT THE END OF A UNIT

The final activity to plan in a unit is an assessment of learning upon completion of the unit—that is, summative assessment. Our Unit Planning tool for assessment might look something like the one shown in Figure 4.10. To do this, you must decide two important things: (1) how to assess students, and (2) the level of performance you expect. Be sure to evaluate all of the objectives for the unit, not just the content objectives. There are many ways to assess student learning, both formal and informal. Formal assessments might include publisher-, district-, or locally developed unit tests designed to parallel statewide assessments. You can also use any of the informal means described in the previous section. It is advisable to use a uniform scoring protocol, such as a rubric or rating scale, so that you can understand individual students' progress relative to the whole class.

To allow students to demonstrate their attainment of content objectives according to their proficiency levels, you could construct a Performance Indicator Chart, using a template such as the one in Figure 4.11, based on the WIDA system of assessment (WIDA, 2007; 2012). Performance indicators are statements of how learners will express their learning depending on their level of proficiency in the language of instruction. Each strand of indicators is presented in a developmental sequence across language proficiency levels. As the student's level of language proficiency increases, the language function or communicative expectation becomes more complex with respect to both the amount and complexity of language needed to do the task. Document and monitor student growth, and support students so they can advance toward behaviors associated with the next level of proficiency.

Planning Assessments
During the Unit: Formative Assessment
Observe conceptual understanding and language needs during Read-alouds or experiments.
Examine work products, such as diagrams, vocabulary notebooks, and graphic organizers students have completed, to evaluate conceptual learning and language output.
Look at your planner to be sure you are evaluating all objectives for the unit.

At the End of the Unit: Summative Assessment
Have students order and define/describe the stages of growth.
Make an oral presentation to parents or other audiences; use a rubric to rate their performance.

Performance Indicators for Evaluating Student Performance
Use the indicators listed in Figure 4.11. *Note to reader: You should check for updates to WIDA English Language Development Standards, and use the ones that are most recently approved.*

Figure 4.10 Thematic Unit Planning Tool: Planning Assessments

ELD Standard 4: The Language of Science   **Topic: Life Cycles in Insects**

Connection: National Research Council Framework for K–12 Science Education, 2012 (Foundation of the Next Generation Science Standards; www.nextgenscience.org): LS1.B. [LS1: Disciplinary Core Idea: Life Sciences Standard 1: From molecules to organisms: Structures and processes] B. Growth and Development of Organisms. Reproduction is essential to the continued existence of every kind of organism. Plants and animals have unique and diverse life cycles that include being born (sprouting in plants), growing, developing into adults, reproducing, and eventually dying.

Context for Language Use: Students work with partners to show understanding of metamorphosis by describing the transformative life cycle in insects and listing the stages of growth in chronological order (from egg to larva, to pupa to adult) through drawings, diagrams, and text in their science journals.

Cognitive Function: Students of all levels of English language proficiency REMEMBER the stages of growth in insects.

	ENTERING	EMERGING	DEVELOPING	EXPANDING	BRIDGING
LISTENING	Match picture cards and word cards with a partner that depicts the stages of insect life cycles according to oral directions given.	Select and order picture and word cards with a partner based on teacher and partner prompts about the life cycles of insects.	After listening to text read by the teacher or a peer, identify the target vocabulary from a word bank about the life cycles of insects.	Compare the stages of life of two different insects in a side-by-side chart using illustrations after listening to the teacher's description.	Reproduce stories about the stages of life in different insects after listening to stories read aloud by the teacher.
SPEAKING	Answer factual questions asked by the teacher about particular life cycle stages of insects, using single words.	Interact in small groups to restate facts about particular life cycles of insects.	Use extended phrases to describe the processes involved in given life cycles of insects.	Discuss, in small and whole group, the major changes insects go through in their life cycles.	Explain the physical changes that occur throughout the life cycle of a specific insect.

Figure 4.11 Thematic Unit Planning Tool: Performance Indicator Chart for Five Levels of Proficiency

	ENTERING	EMERGING	DEVELOPING	EXPANDING	BRIDGING
READING	After viewing a picture book with captions, work with a partner to order picture and word cards that show the stages in the life cycles of insects.	After reading an assigned section of text, work with a partner to select word cards pertaining to the life cycle stage read about.	After reading a proficiency-appropriate text with a partner, identify and name physical characteristics of each of the stages of life for a specific insect.	After reading a grade-level text with a partner, explain the steps and physical changes involved in the life cycle of a specific insect.	After reading several books on an assigned insect, draw conclusions about similarities in the facts presented and make inferences about details not directly addressed about the insects' major life cycles.
WRITING	Using word boxes, write the single words that represent the steps in the life cycles of specific insects next to a picture that illustrates a given stage.	Working with a partner, list the stages of the life cycle of a specific, chosen insect using a bulleted list and short descriptive phrases.	Using level-appropriate texts as references, write complete sentences to describe the processes and physical changes that occur in the life cycle of a specific insect.	Use a graphic organizer as a source to compose detailed paragraphs to describe the life cycle of a specific insect.	Create a brochure using original text and visuals that explain the life cycle of a specific, chosen insect.

Topic-related language: Students at all levels of English-language proficiency interact with grade-level words and expressions such as *life cycle, stage, egg, larva, pupa, adult, hatch, lay, metamorphosis* (with the unit taught in Spanish but using the key academic language in English during the bridging phase).

Figure 4.11 (*continued*)

Outreach to the Community

The last part of the unit to plan focuses on learning in the community outside of school. Many learning experiences are possible if you venture into the local community and take advantage of the rich resources it offers. You might visit local museums, nature centers, or botanical gardens to learn from master gardeners about the benefits of ladybugs or how butterflies are a benefit to the ecosystem. Since many students' families bring a rich cultural heritage, you can integrate this into some of your cross-cultural objectives during this part of the lesson. It is important to not only take what the community has to offer, but to also give back to the community. For example, a butterfly garden can be created in a corner of the neighborhood that would add aesthetic value to the block.

You can also create themed book bags around children's literature that would go home with learners. They would be the basis for family literacy activities, or they could simply reinforce at home what the students are learning at school. These book bags can include fiction or expository trade books in either language or in both. They can include photographs that would inspire storytelling or projects to complete together with family members. You might also partner with various community-based agencies, such as the local Boys and Girls Club, scouts, or public library, for projects. de Jong (2011) warns educators to avoid engaging parents in ways that demand knowledge or skills they do not have; rather, ensure that you engage them in ways that demonstrate the competencies they do have. Links to home and community should be bidirectional—that is, you want to ensure that resources from the home and community flow *into* the classroom just as you send materials *out of* the classroom home with children, all to extend what is going on at school.

The Outreach part of our Unit Planning tool might look like what you see in Figure 4.12.

Planning Meaningful Involvement of Families and Outreach to the Community

- Invite a parent with rich knowledge to share to talk about butterfly gardens, or show a video of his/her butterfly garden.
- Create teams of children and parents to begin working on a butterfly garden.
- Prepare book bags for students to take home to enjoy with their families. Be sure to include bilingual books.

Figure 4.12 Thematic Unit Planning Tool: Outreach

Planning the Mathematics Component in English

The rest of this chapter presents lessons on the same science topic, but this time the lessons focus on mathematics and will be taught in English. Major objectives are counting forward and backward, addition and subtraction of numbers to 20, and measurement of time and length. According to the National Council of Teachers of Mathematics (NCTM), these are first-grade skills, but if you were to teach the unit in kindergarten, you could focus on greater than or less than, shorter, longer, longest, and basic counting skills (1 through 10). (See www .nctm.org/standards/content.aspx?id=26847.) If you were to do the unit in second grade, you could concentrate on seeing addition and subtraction as inverse operations, and skip counting or word problems with ladybugs and butterflies. For the upper grades (third and fourth), you could present numbers of ladybugs remaining on each page of the book *Ten Little Ladybugs* as fractional parts of the whole and/or concentrate on word problems with ladybugs. We provide sample lessons using the same Unit Planner that we described in the first part of this chapter, but this time include only mathematical concepts; see Figure 4.13. The unit has been designed for grades 1 and 2, and is filled out as though it were part of a real math unit; that is, only a few rather than the whole set of possible strategies, ideas, or suggestions have been included. We have provided suggestions for materials in Appendix F.

Unit Theme/Topic: Stages of Growth in Insects (Grades K–3; Most Commonly Grades 1 and 2); Taught in English

Guiding Questions:

1. How do insects grow and change over the course of their lifetime?
2. What types of measurement are useful in keeping track of this process?
3. What is migration, and what are the migration patterns insects follow as they go through their growth stages?

Time Frame for the Unit: 2–3 weeks

(continues)

Figure 4.13 Thematic Unit Planning Tool: Planning Mathematics Instruction

Content Standards (Common Core Standards for Mathematics, K–2; National Governors Association Center for Best Practices and the Council of Chief State School Officers [2010])	ELA Standards (Common Core State Standards; K–2; National Governors Association Center for Best Practices and the Council of Chief State School Officers (2010) make specific choices based on grade level; those listed are for grades 1 and 2.
Counting and Cardinality: 1. Know the number names and the count sequence; count to tell the number of objects (i.e. insects); compare numbers. (K) Operations and Algebraic Thinking: 1. Understand and apply properties of operations and the relationship between addition and subtraction. (1st) 2. Add and subtract within 20. (1st) Measurement and Data: 1. Describe and compare measureable attributes. (K) 2. Measure lengths indirectly and by iterating using length units. (1st) 3. Tell and write time. 4. Measure and estimate lengths in standard units. (2nd) 5. Relate addition and subtraction to length. (2nd)	SPEAKING AND LISTENING: SL 1c, 2, 5 LANGUAGE: L 4b, c, (Other language standards may apply depending upon the point of year in which you are teaching this unit.) READING: Informational Text (1 and 2) RI 1, 2, 5, 7, 10 FOUNDATIONAL SKILLS: RF 3a WRITING: W 2, 5 Second Language Standards (in English): Standard 3: The Language of Mathematics; Listening, Speaking, Reading, Writing See Sample Performance Indicators below.
Content Objectives: 1. Compare size and length. 2. Tell time in days and weeks. 3. Measure to the nearest inch; centimeter. 4. Count forward and backward using cardinal numbers. 5. Add and subtract to solve basic word problems.	Language Objectives: Content Obligatory: • Know the cardinal numbers from 1 to 20. • Know these terms: *long, short, wide, tall, short, small, large, length, width, height, inch, centimeter, day, week, measure*; and prepositional phrases: *measure between, measure from, height of*. • Know the forms of the word *measure*: *measure* (as verb and noun), *measuring* (as an adjective in *measuring tool*), and *measurement*. • To learn how to form plurals in English; when to add *–s* and when to add *–es*. • Know how to pronounce *th* in the final position (*length, width*). • Use the verb *to be* to express length using the phrase "the _____ is _____ inches long/wide."

Figure 4.13 (continued)

Content Compatible:*

- Use comparatives and superlative adjectives (-er, -est).
- Text structure: Definition. More advanced proficiency students along with native speakers can go further with learning about text structure by focusing on writing definitions of concepts and words with compound and complex sentence structures.

Language Functions:

- Tell the length and width of particular items.
- Express length of time that the ladybug and butterfly are in each of their stages across days/weeks.
- Describe, explain, and report results of mathematical calculations made.

*Note that students whose home language is English (in TWI or IMM programs) may already have the content-compatible language.

Cross-Linguistic Objectives (Bridging)

1. Compare the terms for standard measurement units across languages.
2. Show similarities and differences in how the plural form works in Spanish and English.
3. Compare how English makes comparatives and superlatives with how Spanish does so (*longer, longest* vs. *más largo*).

Cross-Cultural Objectives

1. Know that in different cultures, different systems of measurement are common.
2. Know that time is thought of and valued in different ways across cultures.

General Learning Skills and Strategies:

1. Scan for the relevant facts in insect word problems in order to determine what operation to perform (addition or subtraction) and how to represent the problem.
2. Work with a partner to solve problems.

Materials:

See Appendix F for a lengthy list of materials from which you could choose a few titles to use in this unit.

Background Knowledge Needed:

Some knowledge of how to read a clock, awareness of size, and some life experience in making size comparisons

Figure 4.13 *(continued)*

Major Teaching Activities:	
Preview Phase:	
1. Introduce the mathematics topic for the theme using *The Best Bug Parade* listed in Appendix F (introducing words children need to describe size and length and *-er* and *-est* for comparing sizes) or *Inch by Inch* listed in Appendix F, which shows measurement in relation to body parts of animals. (See URLs for related teacher guides/suggested activities for these books in Appendix F.)	1. Whole Class
Focused-Learning Phase:	
2. To deepen children's knowledge, go further with a more explicit book about measurement (see listed books in Appendix F). Then use your books to show how mathematics text is constructed (e.g., writing definitional text: "It's a measuring stick called a ruler." "An inch is a unit of measurement.") or how to process word problem questions that begin with *How* and *Which* ("How many inches is the wingspan of your butterfly?" "How long is a ruler in inches?" "Which is taller, wider, longer?"). Help learners notice important words they should underline and so forth to comprehend and answer what the question is asking them. Use sentence frames and color coding so they can see the patterns and key words.	2. In Literature Circles
3. Measure different insect parts in inches or centimeters (*wing span, legs, bodies*, or *caterpillars, chrysalis, egg, pupa*) and record the findings. Make sure learners are practicing the vocabulary until it is internalized.	3. In Partners
4. Make timelines in equal intervals by weeks (from 1 to 33); split each week into seven days. Have children decorate their time-lines with butterfly stickers or drawings.	4. Individually
5. Have students make a timeline that shows weeks (from 1 to 33) and is divided into days. Read the book *Life Cycle of a Butterfly* listed in Appendix F, actively marking their own timeline as the book progresses. Make sure they list the stage of growth the butterfly is in each week	5. Whole Class

Figure 4.13 *(continued)*

(*caterpillar, pupa*, etc.). Connect to the science experiments they may be conducting in terms of how they are recording time in their science notebooks.	
6. Practice counting forward and backward with their timeline and then with *Ten Little Ladybugs* listed in Appendix F. Follow up with the Ladybug board game, or with the Ladybug mat and recording sheet.	6. Together as a whole class with individual support
7. For individual practice, use the mathematics activity sheets (Ladybug spots) listed under materials in Appendix F so that students reinforce counting and adding to 20.	7. Individual
8. Make Grouchy Ladybug clocks. Then read *The Grouchy Ladybug*, focusing on reading the hands on the clock and setting their own clock to match.	8. Individual
9. Measure objects in the room in inches or centimeters using a tape measure and record their answer using the right abbreviation (in., cm.).	9. In partners or teams
10. Perform the finger action poem (listed under Extensions to Language Arts below). They can perform the actions (climbing, sitting, landing, or flying) with whole-body movements, while showing the number of ladybugs that remain on their hand.	10. Whole Class
11. As an optional activity (if conditions permit), participate in the Big Butterfly Count project, or go further with the measurement topic for upper elementary-grade students, showing them how to measure and record the distances traveled during butterfly migration.	11. Whole Class

Extensions to Language Arts

Books:

Carle, E. 1996. *The Grouchy Ladybug*. New York: Harper Collins (telling time mostly by the hour). [Reading level 3.3; Lexile 560; GRL: J]

Carle, E. 1994. *The Very Hungry Caterpillar*. New York: Philomel (relates to the days of the week and cardinal numbers). Follow up activities with a pocket chart of placing right number of fruits into a pocket chart. [Reading level 2.2; Lexile 460, GRL: J]

Finger Action Poem:

"Five Little Ladybugs" [Source: uca.edu/steminstitute/files/2011/07/ladybugs.pdf]

Bridging to Other Subjects (Art, Music, Dance, and Movement)

Manual Arts: Making and decorating Ladybug clocks; illustrating timelines.

Dance and Movement: Counting forward and backward as children march, dance.

Figure 4.13 *(continued)*

Planning Assessments

Formative Assessment: Observe how the students are responding during the Read-aloud, the timeline activity, and the mathematics games and projects. Be sure to observe for all objectives set.

Summative Assessment: At the end of the unit, students measure additional items or mark their clocks, count forward and backward, and perform simple addition and subtraction problems up to 20 while the teacher marks a checklist to see the skills they have learned.

Cross-Linguistic Objectives: Have students make their individual "contrast booklets" where they show differences in comparatives and superlatives using words that were not included in the lesson.

Cross-Cultural Objectives: Have a whole-class discussion on how time is used at home, at school, and in the doctor's office in terms of whether time is elastic (stretching as needed to fit the conditions) or exact (no extensions possible, exact time must be honored). Notice what is viewed as being "on time" across cultural settings. Point out culturally dependent phrases such as *spending time, wasting time, take your time*, etc. Observe how students contribute to the discussion.

General Learning Skills Objectives: Scan for relevant information: Give students two or three word problems, and have them circle the key words that indicate the mathematical operation needed.

Performance Indicators for Evaluating Student Performance
ELD Standard 3: The Language of Mathematics Topic: Measuring and Comparing Lengths

Connection: *Common Core Standards for Mathematics: Measurement and Data.* Measure and estimate lengths in standard units. Relate addition and subtraction to length. (2nd grade)

Context for Language Use: Students work with partners to measure specific insects or parts of insects, and make comparisons using standard measurement tools.

Cognitive Function: Students of all levels of English language APPLY their understanding of addition and subtraction and of standard units of length to the comparative measurement of insects.

Listening:

Entering: Match insects with their lengths based on oral discourse with a partner and following a model.

Emerging: Order insects according to their length based on oral discourse with a partner and following a model.

Developing: Categorize insects from smallest to largest according to their lengths based on oral discourse with a partner and following a model.

Expanding: With a partner, follow step-by-step oral instructions given by the teacher to compare the lengths of insects.

Bridging: Follow multi-step oral instructions given by the teacher to compare the lengths of insects.

Figure 4.13 *(continued)*

Speaking:

Entering: After conferring with a native-language peer, point to pictures that show insect body parts of particular lengths when directed by the teacher.

Emerging: Working collaboratively with a partner, state the particular body parts that are particular lengths when questioned by the teacher.

Developing: After practicing with a partner, explain how to use a measurement tool to measure insect body parts.

Expanding: Orally compare and contrast the sizes of three or more insect body parts while placing them in order from shortest to longest, and justify the placement.

Bridging: Hypothesize as to which stage of insect development would be the smallest, and defend the hypothesis.

Reading:

Entering: After reading simplified and illustrated word problems with a partner, identify key words related to numbers and measurement.

Emerging: After reading simplified word problems, identify key words related to numbers and measurement, and demonstrate the meaning through physical demonstrations with measuring tools.

Developing: With a partner, identify key words related to numbers and measurement in simple word problems about insects.

Expanding: With a partner, box key words related to numbers and measurement in grade-level word problems about insects.

Bridging: Underline words and phrases that represent important details that guide the operations required in grade-level measurement word problems about insects.

Writing:

Entering: Work with a partner to label insect body parts with their respective lengths in inches, using a word box for support.

Emerging: Work with a partner to list insect body parts in order of size in a single-column chart.

Developing: Work with a partner to order and then write captions describing the relative lengths of different insect body parts next to their illustrations.

Expanding: Following a model, create a simple descriptive paragraph that explains the relative sizes of different insect body parts.

Bridging: Produce a language experience story that tells what went on during a mathematics investigation in which various insect body parts were measured.

Note to reader: These performance indicators are based on 2012 WIDA English Language Development Standards. You should check for updates to WIDA ELD standards and use the ones that are most recently approved.

Topic-Related Language: Students at all levels of English-language proficiency interact with grade-level words and expressions, such as *long (-er; -est), short (-er; -est), length, inch, centimeter; measure; measuring tool* (with the unit taught in English but using the key academic language in Spanish during the bridging phase).

Planning Meaningful Involvement of Families and Outreach to the Community:
See Appendix G for a list of possible activities from which to choose.

Figure 4.13 *(continued)*

Summary: Teaching Academic Content

In this chapter we modeled how to plan for and deliver a science-based, content-area unit, taking into account the multiple issues that DL teachers must consider when planning instruction. We modeled and discussed in detail how to use our template to plan a lesson for the science learning that will take place in the unit (taught in Spanish) and provided a completed planning template for the mathematics learning portion of the unit (taught in English). We showed how to connect the two languages and to promote cross-cultural understanding and culturally responsive ways of behaving. Throughout, we discussed how to build bridges among the major content areas and other subjects taught in grades K to 8. We urged teachers to view the family and community as partners in the learning process, and to recognize how the "funds of knowledge" and expertise they bring can enrich instruction both inside and outside the classroom. We also demonstrated ways of using technology across primary learning settings.

A checklist is provided in Chapter 6 that will help make sure you have thought about everything you need to consider when planning content lessons or units.

CHAPTER FIVE

▶ # Language Teaching in Dual Language Programs

In this chapter we focus on the development of proficiency in two languages. Throughout this chapter, we refer to two kinds of objectives: (1) objectives that comprise the language arts (LA) curriculum, and (2) objectives that include the language skills that students need in order to learn during LA instruction—that is, the content-obligatory language skills associated with LA itself. We begin by defining what we mean by the development of proficiency in two languages. We list significant principles that should guide teaching for language development, and then we discuss commonly asked questions at the program level regarding language instruction. Next, we explain what goes into planning instruction to advance language proficiency, and we describe strategies for developing language through the three-pronged framework—Preview, Focused Learning, and Extension—introduced in Chapter 4. We illustrate the key ideas of this chapter with an upper-grade LA unit on genres using the topic of hurricanes. This unit allows us to focus on disciplinary literacy as emphasized in the *Common Core Standards for English Language Arts and for Literacy in History/Social Studies, Science, and Technical Subjects* (2010), but it also incorporates literature.

Developing Proficiency in Two Languages

MYTH: *If you can hold a conversation fluently, you are proficient in that language.*

FACT: Being proficient in a language in school entails much more than being able to hold a conversation in that language. Students need to be able to understand how to use academic language to discuss and learn about different subjects in the curriculum, and they need to be able to communicate in different settings and with different audiences (e.g., Chamot & O'Malley, 1994; Schleppegrell & O'Hallaron, 2011).

Language proficiency entails a wide range of different kinds of skills that encompass the different contexts and ways in which the two languages are used as well as the various functions they serve in the student's life at school and in the wider community. It is useful to think of these different kinds of language proficiency as a set of continua rather than as dichotomies (see Figure 5.1). Viewing language proficiency as a set of continua better reflects the complexity of language and the interconnections that exist within and between languages when they are used for authentic purposes. In other words, language proficiency is not one thing, but many.

Teachers and students use language in the classroom in diverse and complex ways rather than in the simplified and often stilted ways in which it is often used in students' textbooks—as, for example, when text is linguistically or phonetically controlled for the sole purpose of teaching particular sound-symbol correspondences. While we want to give readers "stage-appropriate" texts, we also need to ensure that these are authentic. It is important that, in all parts of the LA block, students are exposed to authentic, rich models of language as used in grade-appropriate children's/adolescents' literature.

Oral ⇔ Written:	Oral and written language are interdependent in many ways. We write what we want to say (especially in a technology-rich environment); we read aloud what we have written; and we listen to stories being read.
Social ⇔ Academic:	The distinction between social and academic language is neither definite nor clear. We often move subtly from one to the other. Both are indispensable to succeed in a school setting.
Formal ⇔ Informal:	We use formal and informal language based on the setting, purpose, and audience of communication, often moving from one to the other even within the same setting.
Home language ⇔ Second language:	In many situations we move between our two languages and, as we develop proficiency in our two languages, we use what we know in one to help us learn and use the other.
Home culture ⇔ Second culture:	We learn and use our two languages interchangeably in the context of our two cultures, often moving from one cultural context to the other. Sometimes we behave according to blended norms from both cultures.

Figure 5.1 The Continua of Language

How does this complex, dual set of skills and knowledge develop? It is the result of a long-term process that starts at the beginning of participation in a DL program and continues throughout the program. Dual language proficiency continues to evolve and expand in the six to seven years that a child is in an elementary school DL program, and, preferably, throughout high school as well. One implication of this long-term view is that the attainment of language objectives must be in the forefront during the entire program. Curriculum mapping (Jacobs, 1997; Kallick et al., 2004) can guide this process by setting the language, content, cross-linguistic, cross-cultural, and general learning objectives for each grade level's curriculum as well as by tying these objectives to all relevant sets of standards (common core, or other state standards in use). This makes expectations clear to all educators working in the program and to families with children enrolled in the program.

DUAL LANGUAGE VOICE:
ELEVATING SPANISH STATUS

Numerous steps needed to be taken in our school to elevate the minority language status and to strengthen its acquisition for students. These are the primary decisions we made in our effort to maintain a higher level of Spanish language proficiency:

- ❑ Monitoring the growth of oral language in Spanish is a key aspect of our dual immersion school. Five years ago, we began monitoring students' oral Spanish growth through OLAI-SOLOM—a combination of OLAI (Oral Language Acquisition Inventory) and SOLOM (Student Oral Language Observation Matrix).

- ❑ Teachers designed a Spanish continuum that helps us to teach Spanish in an aligned way in grades K–5. We are convinced that this is necessary to explicitly teach vocabulary, grammar structures, and spelling, which enables us to achieve higher levels of Spanish proficiency.

- ❑ We are striving to improve the consistency of our PLC (Professional Learning Community) for Spanish teachers.

- ❑ Another important feature of our plan is implementation of content language allocation. During 2011–2012, we taught math in grades K–2 in English and math in grades 3–5 in Spanish. Social studies/science were taught in grades K–2 in Spanish and in grades 3–5 in English. During 2012–2013, we decided to teach math in English in grades K–5, and social studies/science in Spanish in grades K–5. This language allocation will allow us to elevate and enhance both academic and social Spanish language acquisition.

- ❑ Bridging is an important aspect of our content language allocation practices, which allows for transfer between the two languages. This practice includes focusing on cognates, more explicit grammar, bilingual vocabulary lists, and extension activities.

- ❑ Another important tool that we implemented is using more Spanish in common areas outside the classrooms. We have put signs in entrances, on classroom doors, and in corridors, reminding people to maintain the target language in each class-room and to primarily speak Spanish in common areas.

As we approach our tenth anniversary, the tremendous dedica-tion and effort shown by Spanish teachers at DIA have allowed our school to take the necessary steps toward advancing and elevating the status of Spanish.

—Patricia Corduban
Second-grade Spanish Teacher
Dual Immersion Academy—Escuela DIA
K–8, 50-50 Model, founded in 2002
Grand Junction, Colorado

It is important to adhere to some foundational principles during this long-term instructional process. We recommend the following five principles as the basis for instruction in DL programs.

Principles That Guide the Development of Two Languages in a DL Program

1. *The Status Principle: The two languages in a DL program must have equal status to ensure that students attain full proficiency in both.* As discussed in Chapter 2, languages other than English rarely enjoy equal status with English. If students get the message, whether subtle or explicit, that the non-English language is not very important, this may affect their motivation to learn the lan-guage and can lead to reluctance to use that language both in and out of school. It is critical for the success of DL programs to equal-ize the status of the two languages, at least within the school com-munity. Regardless of prevailing attitudes toward bilingualism and the non-English language and its speakers outside of school, it should be clear in every way that the two languages are highly valued within the school walls.

   The high value that is attached to both languages in a DL program must be clear from the first day of school. It is much easier to establish equal value for both from the beginning, or at least dur-ing the first year of the program, than to change the social envi-ronment of the class after one language has become superior to the other. At the school level, consider the suggestions given in

Myth ⊘

MYTH: *Treating each language of a dual language program the same is the best way to respect the equality of both languages.*

FACT: Because of the tremendous power of English, it is often necessary to raise the status of the non-English language above that of English to balance the value of the two languages (e.g., Valdes, 1997).

the Teacher Tip entitled "Equalizing the Value of the Two Languages in the Classroom" to equalize the value of the two languages explicitly within the school from the very beginning of the program (for new programs) or during the school year (for established programs). At the classroom level, consider the suggestions presented in the Teacher Tip, "How to Indicate the Switch in Language of Instruction When the Same Teacher Uses Both Languages During the Day" in Chapter 2.

2. *The Bridge Principle: Students need to access what they know in their two languages at all times.* Students who are developing proficiency in two languages can benefit greatly from the cross-linguistic transfer that occurs between languages. Strategies that are known in one language can be used to figure out new meanings in the other language; words that sound alike can be borrowed from one language and used in the other; and grammatical rules in one language can be applied in the other. Sometimes this cross-linguistic transfer leads to correct usage and sometimes it leads to inaccuracies that are perceived as mistakes. Regardless of the outcome, encourage students to engage in cross-linguistic transfer. Not all students may be able to do this readily, so you need to create opportunities for students to use what they know in one language to help them develop higher levels of proficiency in the other language (Beeman & Urow, 2012).

Doing this may involve the active teaching of cognates, not only during LA, but also when every subject is taught. (See http://velazquezpress.com for bilingual glossaries and other cross-lingual reference tools for mathematics, social studies, and science.) It could also involve transferring background information and literacy strategies learned in one language—in, for example, science—to completing an activity in the other language. For

TEACHER TIP

Equalizing the Value of the Two Languages in the Classroom

❖ Try to be aware whenever the language of instruction or communication switches away from the non-English language.

❖ Keep track of the selective use of one language for certain functions, such as comforting or joking in one language while reprimanding in the other language.

❖ Keep a balance of visuals in the two languages across the classrooms.

❖ Check your classroom library to make sure that it does not showcase books in English (which are usually more readily available) over books in the non-English language.

❖ Watch how many professionals of each language work in the classroom; ensure that the language other than English does not become dwarfed by staff imbalances, such as special educators delivering interventions, reading specialists, or paraprofessionals who speak only English.

❖ Watch literacy outreach efforts to parents and the presence of parent volunteers in the classroom to ensure equal representation of the two languages.

❖ Ensure that all publications, websites, and blogs created by the program present the two languages with equal status.

example, if students learn the different names given to storms in their science class in Spanish (e.g., *huracán, ciclón, tifón*), they can apply synonyms learned during English LA class as they write a memoir following the model shown in *Hurricanes!* (London & Sorensen, 1998). These bridging activities can occur in either classroom and in either language. In the example just mentioned, the bridge between *hurricane, cyclone*, and *typhoon* and *huracán, ciclón*, and *tifón* could be done in either the English LA class or the Spanish science class, making the bridge between knowledge and strategy complete in both subject areas. In fact, as you saw in Chapter 4, time dedicated to bridging between the two languages should be incorporated into each content area unit. The same needs to be done during LA instruction across the two languages.

3. *The Balanced Literacy Principle: To develop literacy in two languages, use instructional strategies that begin with authentic and interesting text, and then focus on specific aspects of written language.* Five areas have been identified as critical for effective reading instruction: phonemic awareness, phonics, fluency, vocabulary, and comprehension (National Reading Panel, 2000). Although it is essential that literacy instruction include direct teaching of these explicit skills, it is also essential that such instruction be embedded in authentic language that is both meaningful and interesting to students. This is true for all children learning to read and write, and it is indispensable for students who are becoming literate in two languages. For many students in DL programs, their introduction to literacy is through a language in which they are not fully proficient; thus, it is critical that meaning and relevance be at the forefront of literacy instruction to motivate and drive learning. The use of a wide range of strategies that include direct and indirect as well as holistic and specific instruction has been referred to as the balanced literacy approach (Fountas & Pinnell, 2001). Using various modalities, the teacher begins by keeping control during teaching and learning, but gradually releases control, uses more open-ended tasks, and gradually shifts the responsibility of completing a given activity from the teacher to the students, and always within a meaningful context.

4. *The Integrated Instruction Principle: It is easiest to learn language and to learn about language through another content area.* As we have discussed in earlier chapters, the integration of language and content instruction is key to the success of DL programs. It is essential that all teachers, regardless of their specialty or language of instruction, establish both language and content objectives for all their lessons. The implication of this principle for the LA block is that students can learn about language by focusing on a topic that comes from another content area. Science is a good content area for planning LA instruction because many schools are now mandated to have students focus not only on reading literature, but also on reading informational or disciplinary text. Thus, using science, or another content area, as a context for LA instruction

allows teachers to do both (National Governors Association Center for Best Practices and the Council of Chief State School Officers, 2010). Another advantage of this principle is that it involves use of concrete objects or activities for teaching language, for which manipulatives, illustrations, and other realia are usually readily available. It is important to remember that LA is a content area in and of itself and, therefore, has its own content objectives (in the case of our example, knowledge and skills related to genres), yet it also has language objectives to be considered (the language that students need to learn about language.) To model this, for our sample lesson we use *Hurricanes* as a topic that comes from science.

5. *The Oral Language Foundation Principle: Literacy is developed on a foundation that is set in oral language.* Creating links between the skills of language is especially valuable for developing literacy since oral language forms an essential foundation for reading and writing. At the beginning stages of young children's literacy development, an oral language base is essential. Children can read more easily what they can say. Similarly, for L2 learners, reading a text that the students can understand orally is easier than reading text that is unfamiliar. This does not mean that we need to wait until a high level of oral proficiency is developed; it can be done in a graduated fashion.

Myth

MYTH: *You have to wait until students have a solid base in oral language before beginning formal instruction in literacy.*

FACT: You can start to teach reading and writing explicitly to children by the time they reach first grade and, in fact, literacy instruction can begin from the very beginning—as soon as children are exposed to their new language—if it is done in developmentally appropriate and meaningful ways. However, since students can more easily read what they can talk or think about, our lesson framework always begins with a concrete activity that becomes the source of meaningful oral language use which is, in turn, linked to reading and writing instruction (e.g., Genesee & Geva, 2006).

To make sure that students are not reading text for which they do not have an oral base, it is essential that we begin literacy tasks with pre-reading activities in which oral language is built and existing knowledge about a topic is activated. To do this effectively, teachers must identify key language that is necessary for processing written text.

We illustrate the importance of these five principles as we devise instructional strategies for developing bilingual oral proficiency and biliteracy. Before we describe teaching strategies for developing proficiency in two languages, we discuss programmatic issues regarding language instruction.

Programmatic Issues in Language Instruction

Three questions are frequently asked about the best programmatic setup for teaching LA while developing proficiency in two languages. The first question addresses the distinction between LA and second-language (L2) instruction. The second question, which pertains to TWI programs, is whether to provide language instruction in language-specific groups; that is, should students be grouped according to home language to teach language-oriented classes? The third question is whether to start literacy instruction in both languages simultaneously or sequentially; if sequentially, which language should be introduced first?

Question 1: Do we include second language instruction as well as language arts instruction in our program?

LA and L2 instruction are distinct components of instruction. LA is a content area in its own right and focuses on oral language, reading, literature, and composition. It aims to develop students' comprehension and capacity to use oral and written language. L2 instruction is provided to students who have little or no proficiency in the language of instruction. For ELLs who enter English medium schools above second grade, for example, content area instruction is usually at a level that is beyond their language proficiency. Thus, they are given specialized support in English-as-a-second language to help them become proficient enough to learn content in English as quickly as possible. In many such schools, ELLs are given instruction in English-as-a-second language during the LA period and are gradually integrated into the mainstream classroom for the entire school day as their proficiency in English increases.

Providing L2 instruction as a separate component is not necessary for most students in DL programs. Most DL students begin learning English-as-a-second language in pre-kindergarten, or kindergarten, and they develop language proficiency through academic content, including LA. Some programs find it necessary to add a period called English-as-a-second language (ESL) or Spanish-as-a-second language (SSL) in the case of Spanish-English TWI or IMM programs (or whatever the non-English language happens to be: Japanese-, Arabic-, or Korean-as-a-second language). This is done when teachers feel that a student, or a group of students, needs extra support developing proficiency in their second language. L2 instruction may also be necessary if the program accepts students who enter above second grade and do not have enough proficiency in one of the languages of instruction. If students are to be given specialized L2 instruction for support, it is highly recommended that it be as an additional component of the school day rather than as a replacement for LA or any other content area. L2 instruction could take place after school, on Saturdays, or during vacation.

Question 2: Do we group students in TWI programs according to their home or dominant language for language instruction?

Unless students have been identified as needing additional L2 instruction, there is no reason to separate them on the basis of their home language for any kind of instruction. Even if one wanted to group students according to their home or dominant language, it might not be possible because it may be difficult to identify a common home or dominant language for many students. Separating students according to their home language is not recommended for another reason: It can create an affective division in the school or classroom between the two language groups. Even in the best school environments, students tend to interact socially in language-specific groups, in the lunchroom as well as outside of school. Having a formal arrangement whereby the two groups are separated for instruction does not help students from different language backgrounds mix together. Since there is no compelling pedagogical reason to separate the language groups, except for special L2 instruction, instruction can take place at all times with all students together.

However, this does not mean that all students are taught in the same way, using the same strategies, when they are together. Instruction needs to be differentiated according to students' proficiency in the language of instruction and other individual student needs and interests. This can be done during whole-group instruction as well as by grouping students according to a pre-planned criterion or characteristic. Strategies for differentiating content-area instruction are described in Chapter 4 and can serve as models for differentiation during LA instruction. For example, communicative objectives can be differentiated by proficiency level in this order: *identifying* and *naming* (for the lowest levels of proficiency), *describing*, *explaining*, and *summarizing* (for the highest level). To tailor instruction according to students' literacy level, locating leveled materials or, in cases where the level of instructional material is unknown, computing the reading levels of texts can be helpful in matching students' proficiency level with the books they are reading. See the Resources note, "How to Compute the Reading Levels of Texts." You can also vary how much support to provide to students as they complete tasks, be it verbal or visual.

RESOURCES

How to Compute the Reading Levels of Texts

For English, use the Fry (1968) graph:

- www.readabilityformulas.com/fry-graph-readability-formula.php

For Spanish, use the modified Fry that appears in Crawford (1984):

- www.eric.ed.gov:80/ERICWebPortal/search/detailmini.jsp?_nfpb=true&_&ERICExtSearch_SearchValue_0=ED273119&ERICExtSearch_SearchType_0=no&accno=ED273119

TEACHER TIP

Language Enrichment Strategies for Native Speakers

❖ Expand students' vocabularies using a thesaurus to find more exact or precise terms for overused nouns and verbs.

❖ Teach descriptive vocabulary (adjectives and adverbs) that is appropriate to grade level and proficiency level.

❖ Revise first drafts to add descriptive details or to provide greater support of main ideas.

❖ Create a table with transition words and phrases that can be used to create logical relationships among ideas or to compare and contrast statements in the text.

❖ Use sections of mentor texts to study the authors' craft—how various authors gain power, convey ideas, and/or establish mood.

❖ After reading, support inferences made using information gathered from the text.

❖ Compare two texts on the same theme and analyze which is more effective with respect to the essential characteristics of a particular genre; or, compare two texts designed for two different audiences and purposes and show how they were crafted to meet the needs of each situation.

❖ Watch oral presentations on topics related to the main theme of a unit and "unpack" the strategies used by the speaker to gain the audience's attention and maintain interest.

Question 3: Do we begin literacy instruction in the students' home language or do we teach literacy simultaneously in the two languages?

There is great pressure—mostly from parents of English-speaking children and from a society where English has great political power and an educational system that places great importance on standardized testing in English—to begin literacy instruction in English to native

English-speaking students to ensure that they do not lag behind their monolingual peers in reading and writing in English and that they score well on mandated tests administered only in English. Programs with a 50/50 language allocation model are more likely to succumb to this pressure because there is more flexibility in scheduling. It is much more difficult to begin literacy instruction for English-speaking students in their home language in 90/10 or even 80/20 programs because of the limited time spent in English. However, as described in Chapter 1, research indicates clearly that it is not necessary to teach beginning literacy in English to English-speaking students. In fact, it may not even be advisable to do so for several reasons. First, English-speaking students are less likely to reach sufficient levels of proficiency in the non-English language to process new concepts if literacy instruction in the other language is delayed. Thus, English-speaking students need as much time in the non-English language as possible. Second, it is easier to learn decoding skills in Spanish, which is a more transparent language than English, so that initial literacy in Spanish is often easier than in English (Bear et al., 2007, p. 13). Moreover, reading skills acquired in Spanish readily transfer to reading in English. Nevertheless, many DL programs opt for simultaneous literacy instruction for all students, starting literacy in both languages right from the beginning.

If a sequential model is chosen, it is the non-English language that should be used for teaching initial literacy to all students. To ensure valid assessment, local assessment policies must be established to mirror the language of literacy instruction decisions so that testing of literacy skills matches the language used to teach literacy.

Implications for Scheduling

Taking account of answers to these three questions, we come up with the following scenario, which is illustrated graphically in Table 5.1. For simultaneous introduction to literacy, all students take LA in both languages during a long LA block. If there is a 150-minute block, for example, half of it can be in English and the other half in the non-English language. This would allow for fluid bridging between the two languages, exploring and pointing out similarities and differences between the languages. For sequential introduction to literacy, all students, regardless of their home language, are given initial LA instruction in the non-English language. After two years, English LA and literacy are introduced and continue in

Table 5.1

Language Arts and Second Language Instruction Models			
SIMULTANEOUS INTRODUCTION TO LITERACY			
All Grades	**Language Arts Block**		
	All Students		
	Literacy in the non-English language	Literacy in English	Bridge
	Second-Language Instruction (if necessary)		
	Instruction in students' L2, offered outside of school time and to each language group separately		Bridge
SEQUENTIAL INTRODUCTION TO LITERACY			
Kindergarten and Grade 1	**Language Arts Block**		
	All Students		
	Literacy in the non-English language		Bridge
	Second-Language Instruction (if necessary)		
	Instruction in students' L2, offered outside of school time and to each language group separately		Bridge
Grade 2 and Above	Same as simultaneous introduction to literacy		

subsequent years along with continued literacy instruction in the other language. In both scenarios, students who need support in developing L2 proficiency might be given a period of L2 instruction, as mentioned earlier, as an additional component outside of the regular school time (see Table 5.1).

Planning for Language Instruction

Planning for language instruction in a DL program is most effective when it is organized around a framework, preferably the same one that is used to teach other academic content.

> "If students speak two languages, they should receive instruction that uses both languages strategically and in a way that makes pedagogical sense. Thus, we prefer the term two-language learners (Escamilla, 2000) to describe our bilingual students because it captures their two-language background. Instead of looking for one language that is dominant, we need to view students who speak two languages as having strengths in both languages (de Jong, 2011).
> —Beeman and Urow, 2012

Using the Thematic Unit Planning Tool

We use the Thematic Planning tool introduced in Chapter 4 for planning LA instruction. Using the same planning tools in LA and other content areas makes it easier for teachers to plan all their lessons and, in the case of different teachers teaching different content areas, coordination is easier as well. When planning the LA unit or lesson, the focus is on LA topics (such as reading/writing strategies; character, setting, plot; genre studies; figurative language) rather than on science, mathematics, or social studies. However, the big idea or theme for the LA unit can and should be related to a grade-level content area to provide a context or a vehicle for teaching LA concepts. Each part of the planning tool is presented separately in the following sections.

Establishing a Focus for the Theme and Linking to Standards

Using our unit template, we chose *genre* as the main LA concept for our unit, with the following "big idea" and guiding questions for LA shown in Figure 5.2. In this case, we also used an upper-grade theme of "hurricanes," which crosses all major text genres as the context for the LA concepts to be taught. We have used the categories of genre from Systemic Functional Linguistics (SFL) (Knapp & Watkins, 2005; Schleppegrell, 2004), namely: *personal genre* (recount, narrative, memoir, and reader response), *factual genre* (procedural writing, directions, retelling of events, summaries, and research reports), and *analytic*

Unit Theme/Topic (Big Idea): People write about natural events for many reasons: to inform, to analyze natural phenomena, or to share life experiences with others.

Guiding Questions:
- What are the different genres of written language, and how do we use each in our lives?
- How do these genres differ from each other, and how are they similar?
- What strategies do good readers use when all the information is not provided in a given text in order to draw reasonable inferences?
- What language conventions do we use to write in these different genres?

Time Frame for the Unit: 2–3 weeks

Figure 5.2 Thematic Unit Planning Tool: Theme

genre (personal accounts, persuasive essays, expositions, explanations, and comparisons). As suggested in SFL, poems, journals, newspaper articles, and letters are formats that writers may use to accomplish the functions or purposes of these three major genres.

The first section of our planning tool is presented in Figure 5.2.

Note that the time frame for the LA unit is dictated to some extent by the time frame that has been designated for the content area unit (in this case, science). This happens because it is the non-LA content area that guides what happens in the language-focused part of LA instruction rather than the other way around. Ideally, the major concepts for the content-area topics, whether drawn from science or social studies, that serve as a context for LA instruction will have been covered extensively by the time they are used for LA instruction. Remember, content areas other than language are chosen to provide context to ensure that language is learned in a meaningful way, one that is relevant to the students' daily lives, at least within the school curriculum. This is especially important when students are learning about language in a language in which they are not highly proficient, that is, their L2. By choosing a content area other than language to be the hook for our LA lesson planning, we also ensure a strong connection among the various topics that students are expected to learn about and the different skills that they are expected to master. This kind of linkage is also important to ensure that both literature and disciplinary literacy are integrated into the LA block, as urged by the Common Core and other standards (National Governors Association Center for Best Practices and the Council of Chief State School Officers, 2010).

The standards that are met through this unit are also listed in this first part of our lesson planning guide. We have included L2 standards for Spanish because they are available and because Spanish is the most commonly taught language in DL programs in the U.S. See Figure 5.3.

LA Standards (National or State)	L2 Standards: English	L2 Standards: Spanish
COMMON CORE:	*WIDA Consortium English Language Development Standards* (2007; 2012):	*WIDA Consortium Spanish Language Arts Standards (2005):*
Reading: Key Ideas and Details		*Primaria Avanzada*
Quote accurately from a text when explaining what the text says explicitly and when drawing inferences from text (RL.5.1).	Standard 2: The Language of Language Arts; L, S, R, W	1. Lectura y Literatura: Leer y responder a la literatura y otras obras representativas de las sociedades hispanohablantes.
Writing: Text Types and Purposes		C. Leer, interpretar y analizar críticamente materiales literarios y no literarios de países y comunidades hispanohablantes. (Específicamente: I.C.2a: Hacer y apoyar inferencias y formar interpretaciones sobre temas y tópicos principales.)
Write opinion pieces on topics of texts, supporting a point of view with reasons and information (W.5.1).		
Write informative/explanatory texts to examine a topic and convey ideas and information clearly (W.5.2).		2. Escritura: Escribir para comunicarse eficazmente en español.
Write narratives to develop real or imagined experiences or events using effective technique, descriptive details, and clear event sequences (W.5.3).		A. Producir texto escrito en español para comunicarse con distintas audiencias con propósitos diversos.
Language: Vocabulary Acquisition and Use		(Específicamente 2.A.2d: Escribir de forma diversa, incluidos escritos narrativos (p. ej., ficción, autobiografía), enunciativos (p. ej. informes, ensayos), y persuasivos (p. ej. editoriales, anuncios publicitarios).
Acquire and use accurate, grade-appropriate general academic and domain-specific words and phrases, including those that signal contrast, addition, and other logical relationships (e.g., however, although, nevertheless, similarly, moreover, in addition) (W.5.6).		3. Lenguaje oral: Escuchar y hablar eficazmente en español en situaciones diversas.
Speaking and Listening: Presentation of Knowledge and Ideas		B. Comunicar oralmente información, opiniones e ideas usando lenguaje apropiado según la situación, el propósito y la audiencia. (Específicamente 3.B.2f. Diferenciar entre el estilo formal e informal de hablar el español y utilizar el estilo apropiado de acuerdo con la audiencia y el propósito.)
Report on a topic of text or present an opinion, sequencing ideas logically and using appropriate facts and relevant, descriptive details to support main ideas or themes; speak clearly at an understandable pace (SL.5.4).		4. Uso y estructura del Lenguaje: Aplicar conocimientos de la función y estructura de la lengua

Figure 5.3 Thematic Unit Planning Tool: Standards

		española para comunicarse eficaz-mente.
		B. Reconocer y usar la forma y estilo linguisticos apropiados para comunicarse con audiencias diferentes, para propósitos difer-entes, en lugares diferentes
		(Específicamente: 4.B.2c Identificar, seleccionar y usar cor-rectamente la selección de pal-abras, expresiones y estilo, teniendo en cuenta el propósito y contexto de la comunicación.)

Note to reader: The same standards could have been illustrated using any set of upper-grade-level standards (5–8) of the Common Core. Fifth grade was selected because this theme is frequently taught at that level.

Figure 5.3 *(continued)*

Setting the Primary Objectives for the Unit

The two primary types of objectives, content and language, are most explicitly connected with the curriculum and need to be set first. However, it may be easier to keep in mind all five objectives as you begin to write content and language objectives for each lesson or unit. When an extension into the three secondary objectives becomes apparent, it can be added to the lesson plan.

▶ CONTENT OBJECTIVES

As with any other content area, such as science or mathematics, LA has its own content objectives that are specified in the curriculum. In the case of LA, these objectives refer to the language-related skills and knowledge that students are expected to learn each year, and they include skills related to reading and writing, knowledge of fictional and nonfictional writing, and so forth. The language-related content objectives of LA differ from the language objectives to be discussed in the next section in that they refer to the language skills needed to acquire and talk about the language objectives that are part of the content of the LA curriculum. In this sense, they are like the obliga-tory language skills students need to acquire other content, like math-ematics or science, but in the case of LA they refer to the language skills needed to talk about language learning. The content objectives of LA are based on grade-level expectations and, therefore, they must be the same whether the language of instruction is the student's L1 or L2. For that reason, an appropriate level of academic rigor must be applied, hence the need to link your unit to applicable fifth-grade standards. Also, as suggested in the preceding chapter, these objectives should be set according to what you expect of native speakers of the language, with scaffolding provided for students who lack native-like proficiency.

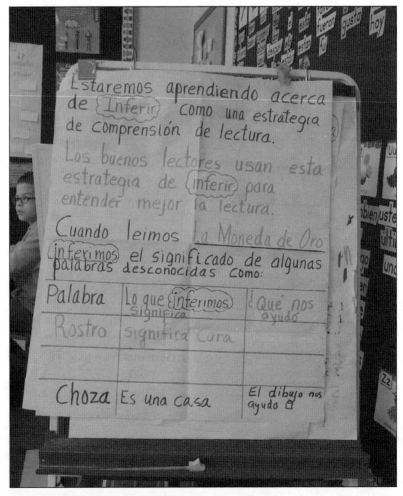

Clear language objectives advance language and literacy development.

Instruction must be differentiated in order to make these objectives attainable even for students whose proficiency level is not native-like. Instruction (and assessment) can be differentiated by varying the language demands of tasks given to students, either individually or in small groups. You can also differentiate instruction by giving students texts that are at an attainable level (i.e., leveled text). At the lower grade levels, when most students are still at the early stages of proficiency in their L2, instruction must be sheltered, using L2 instructional strategies (Echevarria, Vogt & Short, 2008). This is demonstrated by our choice of teaching activities and strategies, presented later in the planning tool for our lesson or unit.

It is also important to tap into students' "funds of knowledge" regarding the topic of instruction and to create new relevant knowledge where none exists. Identify which students have experience with different genres of language—because they come from homes where storytelling is common, or where poetry is recited at family gatherings, or where adults discuss newspaper articles and movies they have seen. Through these experiences, some students will have become aware of the different ways in which one can write or talk about a topic.

▶ LANGUAGE OBJECTIVES

Language objectives for LA, like the language objectives for any other content area, refer to the language needed to master the content. Because our unit will focus on genres, the language objectives have to do with the correct use of words and language structures to narrate stories about hurricanes or describe and explain hurricanes in personal, factual, and analytic writing. Because we are using a topic that comes from another content area—science, in this case—we want to coordinate the delivery of the LA unit with the science unit so that students are prepared to talk about storms and characteristics and experiences related to hurricanes in the LA classroom as they read and write across the different genres.

We also must be aware of how well students have mastered the content objectives for the unit on hurricanes because it will affect how readily they understand the different ways of talking or writing about hurricanes. This means that some of our LA objectives will overlap with both the language and content objectives set for the particular content area that is being used as the hook for LA instruction. The greatest overlap would occur as students read and produce factual and analytic genres. Coordination of instruction is an easier task to accomplish for the lower grade levels, where it is likely that the same teacher is responsible for all the academic content areas. In upper grade levels, or when different teachers are assigned to each language (and, consequently, to different content areas), close coordination between teachers is essential. This is why the use of a unit template, whether on paper or in digital format, makes it easier for different teachers to make the connections among the various content areas.

It is in the selected content area—science (where students learn primarily about hurricanes), in our case—that students acquire an explicit awareness that different genres call on different discourse structures and language conventions to accomplish their distinct purposes, such as level of formality, vocabulary, transition words, how to write dialogue, use quotations, provide references, and so forth. During LA instruction, you would model how language works across the different genres: *personal*, *factual*, and *analytic*; and you help students to become skilled in the use of language for these distinct purposes. In sum, your goal is to ensure that all students have the language skills needed to talk and write about hurricanes using different genres in which hurricanes might be described or discussed or serve as the background for narratives. The language skills and knowledge students need to accomplish this constitute your language objectives during LA instruction.

In addition, for our unit, students for whom Spanish is an L2 may need to learn words such as newspaper (*diario*), information (*información*), to *express* (*comunicar*), and so on. They may also need to learn the gender of words that are likely to be used when talking about hurricanes (**los** *huracanes*) using different genres, such as *report* (**el** *informe*), *poem* (**el** *poema*), so they can choose the correct article and make subjects and adjectives agree by number and gender. It is likely that native speakers will know these things about Spanish, but they may not be familiar to L2 learners. In TWI programs, it may be necessary to have language objectives that all students are expected to

TEACHER TIP

Practicing Target Language Objectives

To ensure sufficient practice with target language objectives, the following strategies and tools can be useful:

❖ Cooperative learning tasks, where partners or small groups have specific roles and tasks, during which they must communicate with one another using specific vocabulary, phrases, and grammatical structures, are useful for students.

❖ Language (vocabulary) notebooks, in which students list the words and phrases they are learning along with images or self-constructed explanations that remind them of the meanings of new words, are helpful to students.

❖ Special templates for word study, such as the Explicit Vocabulary Instruction Procedure developed by Kate Kinsella, are useful. Refer to the following websites:

  • http://teacher.scholastic.com/products/authors/pdfs/Narrowing_the_Gap.pdf

  • www.scoe.org/docs/ah/AH_kinsella2.pdf; and associated products, and

  • www.longmanhomeusa.com/products.php?mid=24&pid=F-0EH-10

❖ Consider making student-constructed glossaries with student-friendly definitions. Research shows that students remember these definitions better than those they copy from dictionaries or thesauruses. These can be kept electronically or in hard-copy journals and notebooks established for that purpose.

❖ And, related to the above, do not be tempted to begin and end vocabulary instruction with dictionary definitions. Research shows that student-friendly definitions support learning (Bolger, Balass, Landen, & Perfetti, 2008), whereas copying dictionary definitions does not (Scott & Nagy, 1997); rather, it causes many misunderstandings and difficulty in using terms correctly.

attain and additional objectives for students for whom the lesson is in their L2 (see the example in Figure 5.4).

Using our unit template, Figure 5.4 indicates examples of the primary objectives just discussed as well as the secondary objectives that we will talk about next.

Content Objectives (Language Arts):	Language Objectives:
1. To identify the three genres: personal, factual, and analytic.	1. To acquire writing conventions common in different genres of writing; vary writing expectations and transition words taught by proficiency level of students: e.g., *because, however, eventually; after . . . , on . . . , by . . . (a certain time)*; *one reason, another reason; first, second, third, next, last.*
2. To identify characteristics that these four genres share and that are different.	
3. To produce writing in these three genres focusing on conventions used to write each genre.	
4. To acquire the strategy of making reasonable inferences from information provided in a text.	2. To learn Tier 2 verbs like *forecast, rise, measure, strike, destroy, form, swirl.*
	3. To use synonyms for frequently used words in order to vary word choice when writing to make the piece more interesting to readers.
	For L2 Learners of Each Language:
	Spanish: Teach the gender of key words and which article to use (*el/la; los/las*).
	English: Active participle modifiers/-ing verb forms as adjectives (*swirling, spinning, rising*, etc.) to modify *winds, storms*, etc.

Figure 5.4 Thematic Unit Planning Tool: Objectives

Setting the Secondary Objectives for the Unit

The cross-linguistic, cross-cultural, and general learning objectives you select when teaching LA will necessarily have a language focus, but they should intersect with and expand upon the same objectives that are set in the content unit on which LA instruction is based—in this case, hurricanes.

▶ CROSS-LINGUISTIC OBJECTIVES

Cross-linguistic objectives focus on making the link between the student's two languages. These objectives ensure that students are given the opportunities and skills they need to transfer what they know in one language to the other. As you will recall from Chapter 4, this is the time that is called "the bridge" (Beeman & Urow, 2012), when students investigate similarities and differences between their two languages. For example, they might discover ways of figuring out the meaning of unknown words or phrases in one language based on what they know in the other language. Since the focus of this part of the school day is on language, planning for and dedicating special time to bridging is essential. This is a crucial element of LA instruction also because it is a suitable time for shifting between the two parts of the LA or literacy block where half of the time is spent in one language and the other half in the other language. For example, Table 5.2 shows what a 150-minute block might look like.

According to this plan, the LA or literacy block would begin with about 70 minutes of instruction in one language. Then the teacher would shift the students' attention to make connections between what they have just learned in one language with the other language, for about 10 minutes; this activity would serve to intro-duce the lesson in the other language. It is also possible to leave the bridge until the end of this long period and use it as a wrap-up or review activity, as was shown in Table 5.1. For our unit on genres, students can compare and contrast the structure of each genre they are studying in the two languages. For example, how is a newspaper article in Spanish about a storm (a factual genre) similar to, and dif-ferent from, one in an English medium newspaper (also a factual genre)?

▶ CROSS-CULTURAL OBJECTIVES

Cross-cultural explorations during LA instruction expand students' awareness of the social and cultural factors that shape language use. Cross-cultural objectives for LA instruction also refer to the exploration of literature in the two languages of the program and

Table 5.2

Example of the Bridge		
70 minutes of language arts in one language	10 minutes of the bridge • If two teachers are involved in deliver-ing LA instruction, determine which teacher is responsible for the bridge segment.	70 minutes of lan-guage arts in the other language

DUAL LANGUAGE VOICE: FOUR-LEVEL SPANISH LANGUAGE ARTS FOR HIGH SCHOOL

Secondary teachers participate in many conversations about content development and student achievement. However, much of the time these conversations are all related to English and how students can perform better in English.

At Albuquerque High School this is not the case. My colleagues and I are also concerned with Spanish performance and how the two are interrelated. We believe that Spanish language arts (SLA) is a vehicle for giving Spanish the attention it deserves as students continue through the secondary years in our Dual Language program. We want our students to take four years of SLA in order to provide them with the same linguistic development as they receive in English; it's what we call "linguistic equality."

Developing our Spanish language arts program has been a struggle at times due to the lack of a culturally appropriate curriculum; a lack of challenging, grade-level materials; and sometimes the misunderstanding that SLA is just another Spanish World Language class. This has slowly changed over the course of the last few years. Finally, our greater school community now perceives SLA as a tool to help students in their bilingual development, by reinforcing language arts skills at advanced levels as well as literary and cultural understanding and appreciation. The curriculum at each grade level is consistent with that of the English language arts, but definitely not a translation of ELA curriculum. ELA and SLA are two separate avenues for language and literacy development, as well as literary appreciation for our students.

Many Spanish teachers have also started to work more closely in collaboration with ELA teachers to develop a deeper understanding of how bilingual students acquire and deepen their academic and social language across languages.

For many years at Albuquerque High, students did not pursue all four years of SLA. This has stopped, as now we require students to take all four years of SLA to attain their Bilingual Seal at graduation. Previously, the Bilingual Seal lacked a more structured and rigorous Spanish language arts sequence, but we have now made these changes, as we noted that our students' academic Spanish was weaker by comparison than English.

By no measure are we finished; rather, we are just beginning to educate ourselves about the importance of language and literacy development in Spanish. Our colleagues have definitely lost the perception that Spanish language arts is just another World Language offering at our school. Instead, we have elevated its status to the same enjoyed by ELA.

—Mishelle L. Jurado
Spanish Language Arts II Tenth-Grade
Teacher and Bilingual Coordinator
Albuquerque High School; Two-Way 50/50
Albuquerque, New Mexico

reflect the customs, norms, and values that stories represent. This is why it is so important to expose students to a wide range of literature that reflects the many cultures represented by the two languages used in the program. Cross-cultural exploration of literature in different languages is a way for students to learn not only about the values (acceptance of natural phenomena) and customs (such as how people prepare for a hurricane in different cultural contexts) associated with different languages, but also to learn to critically examine the authenticity of characters in the literature of those languages in trade books (see the checklist entitled "Checklist for Checking the Quality of Books in Languages Other than English" in Chapter 3). Engaging in these kinds of activities not only broadens students' perspectives, but also raises their awareness of the social norms that dictate how their own language is used in the community they live in.

In our unit, we model how to introduce myths from the Hispanic world—in our case, a Puerto Rican myth explaining the origin of hurricanes. We also introduce a variety of terms used around the world to refer to the same weather phenomena (*typhoon, cyclone,* and *hurricane*). In our LA unit, we also sought to expose students to literature that spans the Hispanic world, sometimes drawing on Mexican or Salvadorian literature, other times Dominican or Puerto Rican literature, and even other parts of Latin America. We also wanted to

> **MYTH:** *Translated books are best because they are familiar stories and easy to find.*
>
> **FACT:** Translated books may not depict the language in a truly authentic cultural fashion. While high-quality translated bilingual books can lend themselves to the exploration of many cross-linguistic and cross-cultural activities, it is important for students to have firsthand experiences understanding both languages and cultures in literature written by bona fide members of those language communities (Barrera et al., 2003; Hudelson et al., 1994).

represent the life experiences and perspectives of U.S.-born Latinos. Another avenue to explore during LA instruction as part of the unit's cross-cultural objectives could be values and attitudes toward different genres: How much do people rely on or trust news reports on television, in newspapers, and on the Internet? What roles do poetry and fables play in families' lives?

▶ GENERAL LEARNING OBJECTIVES

These objectives allow students to learn the skills and strategies that help them navigate through all types of written material. Learning that academic texts in many Spanish-speaking countries have the table of contents (*índice*) at the end of the book rather than at the beginning, as is the case in English, is an example. General learning objectives also might include note taking, using reference materials, or using the library or Internet to research an author.

The three secondary objectives are related to one another given that they overlap to a certain extent. When we engage students in cross-linguistic activities, they are also learning about cultural similarities and differences and are developing general learning strategies and skills.

Locating Materials for Language-Focused Instruction

For LA instruction to go as smoothly as possible, two kinds of published materials are necessary: (1) texts that represent personal, factual, and analytic genres related to the various topics covered in all the content areas, and (2) texts that reflect the cultures represented by the two languages of the DL program. Materials must be at different readability levels (refer to the Resources note earlier in this chapter for ways of determining readability levels for English and Spanish when the levels of materials are unknown). Remember that readability formulas can never account for other factors that affect readability, such as learner background knowledge or interest level. Therefore, always consider readability indices as just one piece of information that must be considered along with knowledge of your learners to really determine what can be used successfully in your classroom. Texts should be available in a relatively balanced proportion in the two languages. This can be a challenge in languages other than English and Spanish, although children's and adolescents' books representing many cultures have become more readily available in many languages in the last two decades. The following Resources note lists sources for books in languages other than English and Spanish.

It is also important to have a good selection of bilingual books because they can be useful in promoting cross-linguistic awareness and transfer. Bilingual books can also help prepare students for learning new content; they can preview new information in their stronger language before it appears in a lesson in the other language. Teachers can also use bilingual books to engage students in self-assessment—for example, to gauge their comprehension of concepts presented in different content areas. For more ideas on how to use bilingual books, see Cloud, Genesee, and Hamayan (2009).

Some websites are helpful for locating materials in both languages that can be useful in meeting cross-cultural objectives. For example, the website Colorín Colorado (www.colorincolorado.org) maintains lists of books that reflect students' different cultural worlds (see "Books and Authors" in the site). There are also websites with webcasts of authors that can be useful during LA instruction for author studies and for inspiring students to become writers themselves. The Rhode Island Teachers of English Language Learners (RITELL) website, called "The Booklist Project," includes lists of books designed by teachers that are useful because they depict various cultural experiences and profile authors from diverse cultural and linguistic backgrounds.

Many books listed on sites like these are available in bilingual versions. There are many other such resources on the web that teachers can tap into when teaching LA in a DL program.

Another valuable source of materials for language-focused instruction is books produced by students themselves. The LA instructional block is the perfect time for students to prepare their own books. They can write books in either of their languages, produce bilingual books, or write a version of an existing book in the other language—not just translating the book but rewriting it to reflect the culture of the target language group. Students can also record their own or others' books

RESOURCES

Publishing Houses for Languages Other than Spanish

Chinese:
- www.nihaobooks.com/?gclid=CKCTgKLqi6oCFQzHKgod7Xmlyw
- www.chinesebooksforchildren.com/
- www.asianparent.com/?gclid=CMjByOvqi6oCFQp75Qodd0Ga1w

Korean:
- www.hanbooks.com/
- www.littleseouls.com/category_28/Childrens-Bilingual-Books.htm

Portuguese:
- www.semfronteiraspress.com

Various Asian Languages:
- www.afk.com/

Book Companies for Books in a Variety of Languages:
- www.multilingualbooks.com
- www.mantralingua.com/usa/home.php
- http://en.childrenslibrary.org/
- www.internationalchildbook.com/languages/1120134
- www.mothertonguebooks.co.uk/shop/
- www.languagelizard.com

on MP3 or MP4 files or upload them to YouTube for others to enjoy. Just as it is important for published books in any language to be of high quality, books produced by students should be of high quality as well. Producing high-quality student books creates opportunities for students to engage in text editing where they focus explicitly on specific and discrete aspects of language. Such books are also excellent opportunities for noticing and discussing cross-linguistic and cross-cultural issues. High-quality student books that are made of durable material and are visually attractive can be catalogued and placed in the school library or the classroom so that other students can enjoy them. Examples of student-produced books that focus on bilingual/bicultural identity issues can be found at www.multiliteracies.ca.

> **Materials:**
> For our unit on hurricanes, see Appendix H for a partial list of materials that could be used in Spanish and English. We list multimedia and Internet-based literacy materials as well as text-based sources to better reflect the diversity of texts that students should experience to prepare them for literacy of all types.

Teaching Strategies and Activities— Planning for Active Learning

So that the teaching strategies you choose are the most effective, you should have a sense of the background knowledge that students need in order to learn the new concepts you have planned for them. This knowledge base serves as the lower planks of the scaffolding they can use to build new concepts. For our LA lesson, which is embedded in a unit linked to science, students need to be aware that they can write about a topic in different ways to attain different goals. In their science lessons, students would have encountered information about hurricanes, primarily in the form of summaries (factual) or explanations and comparisons (analytic). The LA block is a time when you can focus on the medium in which this information is given: informational texts, television reporting, newspaper articles, myths and fables, stories, and/or personal accounts.

In Figure 5.5, we return to our Unit Planning tool that lists the background knowledge students need to participate in the lesson about different genres of writing, assuming that the topic of hurricanes has already been introduced to students during their science class.

Background Knowledge Needed:
Awareness that we can write about a single topic in different ways.
Awareness that different ways of writing serve different purposes.

Figure 5.5 Thematic Unit Planning Tool: Background Knowledge Needed

A Three-Phase Plan for Instruction

As was demonstrated in Chapter 4, a lesson or unit framework is just as important for planning and delivering LA instruction as it is for planning instruction in content areas. We use the same three-phase framework presented in Chapter 4 to teach our LA or literacy block. Lessons begin with a Preview phase, followed by a Focused Learning phase, and end with an Extension phase (Gordon, 2000). By using the same framework in LA and the other content areas, you can ensure predictability and make it possible for students to establish the same routines for learning in different content areas.

Throughout our lesson, we planned activities that would encourage students to be actively involved in language use, both orally and in writing. It is especially important to get students talking, otherwise they will spend an inordinate amount of time in school being silent. Reluctance to talk is magnified in classes where students are called on to use their second and less-proficient language. Students may remain silent in class, even when given the opportunity to talk, because they lack the linguistic competence to express themselves. In these cases, giving students phrases that they might need for everyday school communication is helpful. These phrases can be used for classroom transactions; for example, "Can I have . . . ?" or "Are you finished with . . . ?" or "How do I say . . . ?"

It is also useful to give students phrases and wording to facilitate oral communication specific to the theme or unit under study; for example, in the case of our unit on genres, "I enjoyed the part about . . ." or "This text gives a more accurate and complete explanation than this text." These phrases for oral use can be written on a poster and placed on the wall to help those students who need a reminder of how to say something, thus reinforcing the link between written and oral language. This type of preparation to help students participate orally can take place in the first phase of our lesson, the Preview phase, which we turn to now.

▶ THE PREVIEW PHASE

Three things happen during the Preview phase:

1. Daily or weekly routines

2. A concrete activity that sets the foundation for new concepts to be learned

3. Finding out what the students know about the topic.

To begin, each lesson starts with the routines that belong to the block of time devoted to language study. These routines can be general classroom routines, such as the calendar if the LA block is first in the day. Or, for example, a student can give a news report of an event that happened the day before or predict the weather for the following day (good contexts for practicing the past tense and the future tense, respectively). Daily routines can also be specific to language issues. A fun routine for the LA block is to start each lesson with a "language tidbit" that students or the teacher share with the classroom. For example, *agua* is a feminine noun, but we say "el agua." And idioms that have a funny literal interpretation, such as "I have my eye on you" or "costar un ojo," can be turned into art projects. Students can illustrate the literal interpretation of the idiom, posting their illustrations in the hallways and then having a competition to see who can guess the idiom.

RESOURCES

For a source of remarkable language tidbits, go to www.merriam-webster.com and click on a feature called "Ask the Editor." This shows brief videos of their editors talking about noteworthy language phenomena.

For Spanish idioms, see *The Big Red Book of Spanish Idioms* (Weibel, 2004) or go to www.languagerealm.com/spanish/spanishidioms.php.

The Preview phase is also the time to gather information about background knowledge that students are bringing with them to the lesson. Because hurricanes are the context for teaching genres, you would first want to determine whether students are familiar with hurricanes. If the topic of hurricanes has not been covered in science prior to this LA lesson, you would want to make sure that students know what hurricanes are before you move to the concept of genres. For this reason, it is advisable to wait until the topic of hurricanes is taught in science so that you can use it effectively as the context for the LA lesson on genres. Here is one way of determining whether students know enough about hurricanes: Show several photographs of hurricanes and observe your students as they try to describe what is going on in the pictures. Or, you could ask students who have experienced a hurricane to share their experience with their classmates. This lets you form a general idea of what students know about the topic, as well as their level of interest in it.

Once you have established students' familiarity with the content domain of the lesson, you can focus on previewing the LA part of the lesson. For this part of the lesson, you could play a game that we will call "Find My Genre." Each student gets a short text on hurricanes. Some of these texts will be a piece of fiction; others will be a poem, a newspaper article about a hurricane, or a short text taken from an academic nonfiction book. All texts should be printed on the same type and size of paper, rather than the original or copied from the original. Make sure there are equal numbers of examples for each genre. For beginning level or very young children, texts of the same genre could be identical; for students with higher levels of proficiency, the texts of the same genre could be different. Distribute the texts randomly among the students and have them find the other students with the same genres.

For either activity, you can give students phrases that will help them accomplish the task. For example, for the "Find My Genre" game, students will need to say "How does your piece look?," "Show me your piece," "Let me see," or "Does your paragraph start with . . . ?" Giving students these phrases will help them complete the game. The purpose of the Preview phase is to find out what students know about the different types of text as well as to ensure that they have the language needed to talk about them. By beginning with a concrete activity, teachers can reinforce or introduce the background knowledge that students need in order to develop the target concept further at the same time that they build the funds of oral language necessary to understand text about that concept.

Our Planning tool for this part of the lesson would look like what is shown in Figure 5.6.

TEACHER TIP

Activities That Can Be Used in the Preview Phase

All of the following activities are accompanied by oral language, with the teacher eliciting statements, responses, and reactions from students during and after the activity is completed.

❖ Watch a video (of an author, of a myth).

❖ Share an experience related to the theme.

❖ Make models or find examples of something.

❖ Guess what a hidden object is, or any other guessing game.

❖ Take a field trip, and then invite a speaker to talk on the topic.

❖ Interview a peer or a parent to gather information.

❖ Play a game that revolves around the big idea of the lesson.

While engaged in each activity, be sure to do the following:

❖ Build speaking skills.

❖ Build word knowledge.

❖ Offer scripts and help students learn phrases as "chunks" of useful language.

❖ Ask stage-specific questions.

Such oral language development will, of course, continue across the phases of the lesson, but it begins in the Preview stage.

Activities for the Preview Phase	Grouping Arrangements
1. Show pictures of hurricane; ask students to describe them.	1. Whole class
2. Play the "Find My Genre" game.	2. Individual and small group
3. Interview a classmate or adult who has experienced a hurricane; find out as much as you can about a hurricane by interviewing the informant. If more than one person has experienced a hurricane, compare their experiences and make a list of common events that occurred.	3. Teams form questions and take turns asking

Figure 5.6 Thematic Unit Planning Tool: Preview Phase

▶ THE FOCUSED LEARNING PHASE

To move into the Focused Learning phase of the lesson on genres, you can extend the "Find My Genre" activity. This will make for a smooth transition and will build on the language that the students have just learned or that was just reinforced. One extension of the activity would be for students to stay in their genre-specific groups throughout the lesson so they become experts in that genre by the end of the unit.

Many of the strategies mentioned in Chapter 4 could be used in this phase of the lesson and could be expanded to have a language

DUAL LANGUAGE VOICE:
THE USE OF LITERATURE TO HELP YOUNG LEARNERS NAVIGATE THROUGH THEIR SECOND LANGUAGE EDUCATION

Growing up as the only French kid on the block was not easy. It meant learning another language (English) if I wanted to have friends. It did, however, also mean that I grew up fully bilingual without needing to study my second language. It was a hard lesson to learn, but a lesson well learned.

In my French immersion classroom, I've tried to replicate these optimal second language learning conditions as closely as possible by creating a space where my students need to communicate in their L2; by giving them plenty of opportunity to practice it with other adults and peers; and by flooding them with rich, meaningful input in fun social and educational contexts. I immerse my students in French just as I was immersed in English. One of the most precious tools at my disposal to do this meaningfully is books. Every day, we read and discuss books they can relate to so that they can better understand their world. My students look forward to the moment I will sit in my rocking chair and prepare them for the next reading. In kindergarten, as they begin their voyage of self-discovery, we explore books that help them build their identities and express, in their new language, their emerging selves and growing awareness of their environment. At first, when they do not have enough vocabulary to form full sentences, I encourage them to respond in English, replacing certain words with the vocabulary they have in their L2. As their vocabulary, repertoire of formulaic expressions, and grammatical knowledge grow, I expect them to incorporate new features when they communicate. Then, in grades 1 and 2, after they are comfortable in their L2 environment, the books I choose to enhance my teaching help them further expand their vocabulary and understand the subject matter we are studying in a language that is not theirs. My oral language production expectations also change. With the support of both myself and peers, I expect them to put sentences together with the help of metalinguistic clues, visuals, and some translation from L1 to L2. Consequently, my students experiment with their new language in a safe environment, with books providing the right context to help them navigate successfully through their immersion experience.

—France Bourassa
Kindergarten/Elementary Cycle 1 French Immersion Teacher
St. John Fisher Junior Elementary School
Lester B. Pearson School Board
Pointe-Claire, Quebec

focus. During this phase, students should be actively using language. However, getting students to actively use language in class is not always an easy task. In most classrooms, students spend very little time using oral language to discuss instructionally relevant things.

You should aim to have every student participate in listening and speaking during as much of the class as possible. In this way, you will encourage students to try out their language as much as possible so their language skills will develop. It can be especially challenging to make students active listeners. Himmele and Himmele (2009, 2011)

Strategies for Active Listening Comprehension

- ❖ Do focused viewing, listening for specific information.

- ❖ Provide cooperative learning activities (Turn and Talk; Share a Line, etc.).

- ❖ Have students participate by raising their hands (or thumbs up, down, sideways) when they hear key words or phrases, holding up response cards, and so forth.

- ❖ Have children find pictures that correspond to the part of the story being told.

- ❖ Have students preview and predict, and then later check their predictions.

- ❖ Have students retell the story or parts of the story to each other.

- ❖ Have them complete story maps or graphic organizers as the story is read.

- ❖ Read part of the story, and then read it again to see what additional information they get on a second reading.

- ❖ Have pairs of students act out parts of the story, and have other students tell them what was missing from their performances

- ❖ Give word cards to pairs of students for words that are new to them, and see whether they can figure out the meaning of the words from the story.

- ❖ Hold up response cards (yes/no, true/false, or specific answers), or write their responses on whiteboards to hold up for the teacher to see.

- ❖ Have students share charts or note-taking templates completed in pairs.

- ❖ Use quick draws/writes, chalkboard splashes (where all the students write their responses on assigned spots on the classroom whiteboard/blackboard or on chart paper, and then students respond to similarities, differences, and surprises), ranking activities, and so forth (see Himmele & Himmele, 2011).

suggest a range of active response formats during listening activities (see the Teacher Tip entitled "Strategies for Active Listening Comprehension") to create what they call a "language-rich classroom."

You can encourage students to listen actively by reading characteristics of each genre, and then ask each expert group to figure out which characteristics belong to their genre and claim it as their own. Students can add to their list during the whole lesson. By the end of the lesson or unit, each group will justify the list of characteristics that they have included in their genre and produce a poster showing the similarities and differences among the three genres.

When planning instructional activities, make sure you use a variety of strategies to ensure a balanced approach to the development of literacy. In the section of the Focused Learning phase of our Planning tool (see Figure 5.7), strategies that are part of balanced literacy practice are noted in parentheses. You also want to be sure to use culturally responsive and authentic reading materials to prompt students' writing. You can see in our unit that we have used culturally responsive myths (*Por que soplan los vientos salvajes*), community-literacy sources (e.g., newspaper accounts), and culturally situated narrative texts (*Sergio and the Hurricane*) even when working in English (see Appendix I. The Caribbean nations experience frequent hurricanes, making this is an excellent setting around which to situate the literature you use. We have also integrated multimedia in both languages (video, audio, etc.).

With the main part of the lesson completed, we now turn to the third phase of the unit, the Extension phase.

▶ THE EXTENSION PHASE

This phase of instruction is important in order to demonstrate to students that what they are learning about their two languages is useful in their daily lives. In our unit on genres, for example, students need to see how the different types of oral and written text about storms are actually represented in their communities. To accomplish this, have students do such activities as investigating myths about storms or weather-related phenomena in their families, or examining reports in newspapers, television newscasts, and scientific reports about storms that their community experienced. The Extension phase is also a time when students can produce something useful for their community,

Focused Learning Phase (with balanced literacy practice noted in parentheses)	Grouping Arrangement
During the whole lesson, expert genre groups continue to add to their descriptions of their genre.	
1. Front-load key words that will be used in the Read-aloud. Conduct a follow-up activity with a word sort for practice (word work; front-loading of oral language).	1. Whole class; partners practice.
2. Expert groups begin to identify characteristics of their genre and continue to refine their list during the whole unit.	2. Small groups
3. Introduce the specific Puerto Rican myth *¿Por que soplan los vientos salvajes?*, and use it to point out specific features of myths. Discuss character, setting, and plots; text structures used; and style of writing (**narrative; personal genre**). (direct teaching; Read-aloud)	3. Whole class
4. Answer factual and inferential questions about the myth. Discuss how to make reasonable inferences based on the information provided in the text for questions left unanswered by the text (guided reading).	4. In partners; follow-up discussion with the whole class.
5. Discuss the author's craft: Use of descriptive language ("Los tainos vivían en casidas llamadas bohíos, construidas con madera y tablas de palma y techo de paja"), or figurative language ("El mar brillaba como una joya y tenía el color de una turquesa").	5. Whole-class discussion of whatever device has been taught. Small groups report in.
6. Write a summary/retelling (**factual genre**) of the myth and create an illustration that reflects the theme of the myth. Share the summaries from the author's chair (Writer's Workshop).	6. Individuals
7. Use a newspaper account of a hurricane (e.g., from *El Nuevo Día*) as a mentor text for writing a newspaper account (**factual genre**); teach the five WH questions and how reporters use this schema to write an account of a natural event; have students notice the features of newspaper articles; show how photographs are used to complement the information provided in the text (guided writing); practice writing a newspaper article for a hurricane that a child experienced or has read about (partner write); compare the features of the newspaper account to the features of the myth.	7. Whole class, with each child having an individual copy of the article; partner write.
8. Join guided reading groups to review the conditions that cause hurricanes to form by reading supplemental informational texts, preferably after this information is presented in their science class; have each group reporter give an oral report about the causes of hurricanes (an explanation of how hurricanes form based on the guided reading book assigned to each group; **analytic genre**), while the illustrator points out what the reporter is sharing on a visual designed by the team (guided reading).	8. Cooperative learning groups

Figure 5.7 Thematic Unit Planning Tool: Focused Learning Phase

9. Expert genre groups produce a poster that shows characteristics of the genre, with sample excerpts from the genre to demonstrate its key features.	9. Small groups
For sample activities for English language arts, see Appendix I.	

Figure 5.7 *(continued)*

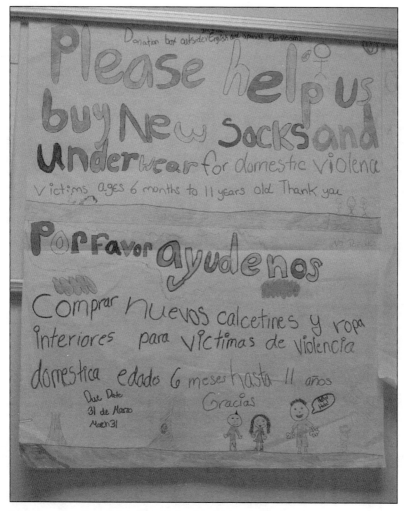

Engage in community projects to extend student learning opportunities.

Extension Phase	
1. Ask students to interview two people about a storm they have experienced. Then have students present the information in two forms: as a news report and as a first-person account.	1. Small groups or pairs
2. Produce a public service poster on how to prepare for a snow storm, hurricane, or heat wave, whichever is typical in the region. Parents can be invited to serve as judges during a contest for the best poster.	2. Small groups or pairs
3. Create a dramatic version of the myth, "¿Por que soplan los vientos salvajes?" Visit another class to present the student-produced play.	3. Class project

Figure 5.8 Thematic Unit Planning Tool: Extension Phase

such as a poster that has suggestions on how to prepare for snow storms, hurricanes, or heat waves (depending on the school location).

The Unit Planning tool in Figure 5.8 lists some of the activities that can be used during the Extension phase, and the Teacher Tip entitled "Possible Field Trips/Class Visitors from the Community" suggesting possible field trips has ideas for making links with the local community.

Assessment

It is important to continuously monitor: (1) each student's literacy development, (2) how effective your instruction is and what needs to be done differently to improve it, and (3) which texts work well and which do not so that you differentiate each student's experiences during the unit effectively. You can do this using formal assessment tools or informal teacher-based assessments.

▶ INFORMAL ASSESSMENT METHODS

Here are some informal assessment methods that you could use.

Running Records. This type of assessment is conducted by choosing leveled materials for the student to read and then observing how well students read the text. Running records focus on error types, accuracy, and self-correction rates. The rate with which students make errors helps determine a student's reading level. An easy text would be one for which the student's accuracy is between 96 and 100 percent; an appropriate instruction text would be between 93 and 95 percent; a challenging text would be between 90 and 92 percent; and a difficult text would be below 90 percent (Scholastic, 2002). In addition to observing the types of errors students make (substitution, omission, insertion,

TEACHER TIP

Possible Field Trips/Class Visitors from the Community

❖ Visit a weather station, or invite a Spanish-speaking weather reporter from a local news channel.

❖ Visit a local hardware store or supermarket in the Latino community and ask what most people buy to prepare for a storm.

❖ Invite a local scientist (preferably who speaks the language of instruction for this unit) to come to class to talk about the effect that storms have on the environment.

❖ Invite parents to visit the class and tell myths they know about hurricanes or other strong storms.

❖ Hold a contest and invite several parents to see the carousel of public service posters. Have them judge the top three posters against established criteria.

❖ Interview a "storm chaser," and view the photographs taken up close of various storms that person has followed.

❖ Invite a public safety official to talk to students and parents about the precautions they take and the services they provide in advance of a serious storm. Follow up by investigating the EPA website (in Spanish and English):
- www.epa.gov/espanol/eventosnaturales/huracanes.html
- www.epa.gov/hurricane/

❖ Hold a poetry contest writing *cinquain* and other formulaic poems about storms.

attempt, repetition, appeal for help, self-correction), teachers can also note whether the student uses meaning and structural and visual cues to help her/him read. As well, pay attention to students' fluency, intonation, and phrasing. For those reading in their L2, teachers should make a distinction between inter-language production (using native language speech sounds to read an English or Spanish word, which is natural for L2 learners) and a true mispronunciation of a word that cannot be explained by transfer from the native language. (For more information about running records, see www.scholastic.ca/education/movingup withliteracyplace/pdfs/grade4/runningrecords.pdf.)

RESOURCES

For Formal Assessment (see Appendix J for descriptions)

Benchmark Assessment Systems:

❖ *Developmental Reading Assessments/Evaluación del desarollo de la lectura* (DRA2/EDL2) for Grades K–8

❖ *Fountas and Pinnell Benchmark Assessment System (BAS)* in English

❖ *Sistema de evaluación de la lectura (SEL)* in Spanish for K–2

Other Assessment Systems:

❖ *Flynt-Cooter English-Español Reading Inventory for the Classroom*

❖ *Brigance Inventory of Basic Skills–Spanish Edition*

Reading and Writing Conferences. During reading conferences, teachers observe students while reading a story or text and engage them in a conversation about their reading and writing strategies. Teachers ask what strategies students use to figure out the meaning of words they are struggling with, how they decide whether what they are reading makes sense, how they organize information if they are writing a science report or how they organize a story if they are writing a narrative, and so on. During reading conferences, teachers can also see whether the learner understands the major story events and plot of the story, details about characters, sequence of events, and so forth; for other ideas on assessing reading behavior, see the strategies recommended at www.readinglady.com/mosaic/tools/tools.htm#1.

Writing conferences are conducted in a similar way. They help teachers understand how students approach writing and the strategies they employ (such as using an outline or graphic organizer to plan their writing), what tools they use to support themselves when writing (thesaurus, writer's notebook, word wall, etc.), and which self-checking tools they are familiar with.

Writing Samples Scored with Rubrics. Holistic and analytic scoring tools can be used to look at writing development in both languages over time. The WIDA rubric in English is one such tool (see Download

Products, WIDA ELP 2007 Edition, at www.wida.us.) The "6 + 1 Traits" is another useful tool. It focuses on the following aspects of writing: ideas, organization, voice, word choice, sentence fluency, conventions, and presentation. They assess writing in Spanish www.eric.ed.gov/ERICWebPortal/contentdelivery/servlet/ERICServlet?accno=ED 464493) and in English (http://educationnorthwest.org/resource/464).

Writer's Notebook. This can be used as a formative assessment tool that focuses on vocabulary and sentence patterns in students' writing, providing information that teachers can use to guide students to notice other words and patterns that would help move their writing forward.

The Unit Planning tool in Figure 5.9 lists some of the activities that can be used for assessment as well as performance indicators

---

Planning Assessments

Formative

Evaluate students' writer's notebooks to see what they are noticing about newspaper articles and how to craft them. In their glossary sections, look for terms students are noting that may be useful to them when writing their own articles when reporting on natural events for a newspaper.

Summative

Evaluate the articles written by students for a newspaper on selected natural events using a six-traits rubric. Give the students' scores in all six areas so they can understand their strengths and weaknesses as writers.

Performance Indicators for Evaluating Student Performance

ELD Standard 2: The Language of Language Arts	Topic: Newspaper Article Writing (Factual Genre)

Connection: *Common Core Standards for English Language Arts and for Literacy in History/Social Studies, Science, and Technical Subjects*

Writing: Text Types and Purposes
Write informative/explanatory texts to examine a topic and convey ideas (W.5.2).

Speaking and Listening: Presentation of Knowledge and Ideas
Report on a topic or text or present an opinion, sequencing ideas logically and using appropriate facts and relevant, descriptive details to support main ideas or themes; speak clearly at an understandable pace (SL.5.4).

Context for Language Use: Students assume the position of a news reporter who interviews those affected to create a factual account of a natural weather event, such as a hurricane.

(continues)

Figure 5.9 Thematic Unit Planning Tool: Planning Assessments and Outreach to Families and Community

Cognitive Function: Students at all levels of English language proficiency create an article for a newspaper to convey a factual account of a natural event based on first-person accounts.

Listening:

Entering: Underline facts in the oral statements given by witnesses to the weather event that are read aloud, working with a partner.

Emerging: After listening to witness statements read by the teacher or a peer, classify the oral statements as facts or opinions.

Developing: After listening to witness statements read by the teacher or a peer, determine which includes more facts about the storm that would be useful when writing a newspaper account.

Expanding: After listening to two accounts of the same event, compare them to determine which contains more accurate factual information.

Bridging: After listening to two accounts of the same event, interpret the emotional state of each person during the storm.

Speaking:

Entering: Working with a peer, name major events that transpired during the storm using illustrations, according to first-person accounts.

Emerging: Describe major storm events and their impact on the community using illustrations.

Developing: Explain major events that transpired during the storm from the viewpoint of various people who witnessed them (e.g., first responders, elderly adults, children).

Expanding: Discuss the impact of the storm on various neighborhoods in the community using photographs taken by residents right after the storm.

Bridging: Interpret the significance of the storm events for particular segments of the population who experienced the storm (e.g., children, elderly adults, first responders).

Reading:

Entering: After reading a simple account of the storm with photographs that tell the story, work with a partner to identify the five WHs—*Who? What? When? Where? Why?*

Emerging: After reading a short account of the storm with several photographs with captions, list the five WHs.

Developing: After reading an short article from a community paper, work with a partner to identify key language that provides the major details about the storm and write it into a graphic organizer of the five WHs and an H (*How?*).

Expanding: Read and compare two articles from two separate sources to determine the most important facts about the weather event.

Bridging: After reading a newspaper article written at grade level, summarize the major details about a weather event in sequence.

Figure 5.9 *(continued)*

Writing:

Entering: Write captions for several photographs taken after the storm, using a word box.

Emerging: Working with a partner, write a short paragraph of several sentences that describes the main events that transpired during the storm.

Developing: Describe the events of the storm according to two first-person accounts using notes from a reporter's notebook.

Expanding: Organize information gathered from three first-person accounts into an article about the storm for a community newspaper.

Bridging: Write a feature article for a local newspaper. The article should be illustrated with photographs, draw upon first-person accounts of at least three people who witnessed the storm, and use a quotation from at least one source interviewed for the article.

Topic-Related Language: Students at all levels of English language proficiency interact with grade-level words and expressions, such as *scoop, reporter, spread, feature article, fact, opinion, bias, column, editor, human interest, interview, lead, caption, by-line, layout.*

Note to reader: These performance indicators are based on 2012 WIDA English Language Development Standards. You should check for updates to WIDA ELD standards and use the ones that are most recently approved.

Planning for Meaningful Involvement of Families/Outreach to the Community:

Ask students to interview two people about a storm they have experienced. Have the students present the information in two forms: as a news report and as a first-person account.

Produce a public service poster on how to prepare for snow storm, hurricane, or heat wave, whichever is typical in the region. Parents can be invited to serve as judges during a contest for the best poster.

Figure 5.9 *(continued)*

for evaluating student performance for the language of language arts. It also describes some activities that reach out to the community.

Summary: Language Teaching in Dual Language Programs

In this chapter, we discussed principles that can guide the development of oral language proficiency as well as reading and writing in two languages. We discussed how to plan for instruction, set objectives, and prepare to teach. We modeled and discussed in detail how to use our template to plan Spanish and English LA units to promote proficiency in both languages and build bridges between the two languages. We discussed the major phases of a lesson to consider in order to ensure maximal language and literacy development. We demonstrated ways to include the family and community as partners in the learning process, and how to tap the cultural and linguistic "funds of knowledge" students and families can bring to enrich instruction.

▶ Putting It All Together

IN THIS FINAL CHAPTER, we summarize and integrate the most important information we have presented in the preceding five chapters. Developing, implementing, and monitoring the success of DL programs is challenging. To facilitate your work, we provide two comprehensive checklists that touch on the most important recommendations and issues that need to be considered when setting up new programs and revising existing programs. There are two checklists: one covers the selection, design, and planning of a program; the other covers instructional planning. These checklists were the focal topics of Chapters 2 through 5. Before we discuss them, we want to return to the foundations of DL education.

DL programs have existed since the mid-1960s in the U.S. and Canada. We have gained much insight about what makes for a successful program during the more than 45 years that these programs have existed. Our understanding of effective programs is based to a great extent on the extensive research that has been undertaken to evaluate alternative program models in the U.S. and in Canada. Thus, we are very fortunate that there is a great deal of scientific evidence to guide our thinking about and planning for DL programs. We do not need to rely on our hunches and intuitions. This is most fortunate because, in fact, people have many intuitions about DL learning and teaching that are not supported by scientific evidence and, therefore, they are misleading. Throughout this book, we have identified the most salient of these myths and refuted them in light of the scientific evidence. We also provided a very brief discussion of key research findings in Chapter 1 so that you can make decisions that are compatible with key evidence from evaluations of DL education. The important point here is that if you are working in a district that is beginning to develop a new DL program, the important first step is to familiarize yourself with relevant research. By doing so, you will not be misled by the many common myths and misunderstandings that surround DL learning. If you work in a district with existing programs, it is useful to revisit research on DL education to make sure that you are not misguided by myths that have emerged in your community since the inception of the program and to ensure that you are up-to-date on what research has to say.

We are not recommending that you become professional researchers or totally expert in the research. However, to make responsible and appropriate decisions, you must be familiar with the basic research in this field. While this might seem like a daunting task, many high-quality nontechnical reviews of this research are available. Creating study groups, attending well-regarded professional conferences where this research is discussed, and inviting researchers to speak to you and your colleagues are all ways of familiarizing yourself with relevant research with relatively little effort and pain. The nearby Resources note provides some user-friendly references, along with brief synopses of each.

RESOURCES
_____

User-Friendly Research References

Genesee (journal article, 2004)

❖ Provides a comprehensive summary of research on immersion for majority language students.

❖ Research reviewed was done primarily in Canada and the U.S. on the outcomes of English-speaking students in L2 immersion programs.

❖ Findings are from different program models, and they concern the suitability of immersion for all students and alternative instructional approaches to promoting L2 development.

Genesee and Lindholm-Leary (book chapter, 2012)

❖ Reviews research on the education of ELLs in the U.S, focusing on educational outcomes in DL programs.

❖ Summarizes decades of research on ELLs with respect to their oral language (L1 and L2), reading, and academic development.

❖ Examines factors that affect the achievement of ELLs, including the type of educational program they are in; home, school, and community factors; background factors; and disability.

Howard, Sugarman, and Christian et al. (online document, 2007)

❖ Designed to be used by dual language programs as a tool for planning, self-reflection, and growth.

❖ Guiding principles are based in large part on the Dual Language Program Standards developed by Dual Language Education of New Mexico (www.dlenm.org). Guiding principles are organized into seven strands: assessment and accountability, curriculum, instruction, staff quality and professional development, program structure, family and community, and support.

Howard and Sugarman (book, 2011)

❖ Examines the role of program and classroom cultures in the development of bilingualism and biliteracy in two-way immersion students.

❖ Describes effective programs that foster a school culture of intellectualism, equity, and leadership.

❖ Provides evidence of how these three cultures function as organizing principles for program and classroom practices as exemplified in four exemplary TWI programs.

Lindholm-Leary and Genesee (book chapter, 2010)

❖ Provides brief descriptions of alternative forms of education for ELLs in the U.S., including transitional bilingual, developmental bilingual, and two-way immersion programs.

❖ Reviews research evidence concerning the oral language, literacy, and academic achievement of ELLs in alternative DL programs.

❖ Identifies characteristics of effective DL programs, including curriculum, instructional, and personnel factors.

DUAL LANGUAGE VOICE: NETWORKING WITH DUAL LANGUAGE COLLEAGUES AND EXPERTS

Using the resources and expertise found within your own school community to ensure the fidelity of your dual language model implementation is, of course, the ideal. However, building and maintaining the staff's capacity for that support requires "being connected" to the greater professional community. Maintaining a network with colleagues and experts in the field is crucial to identifying and sharing best practices. Learning from one another is what we expect from our students, and learning from other's mistakes strengthens our practices and our capacity to support our own programs.

A number of organizations are helping to facilitate this networking by hosting annual conferences that bring together experts from our larger community, including researchers, practitioners, and community supporters. Dual Language Education of New Mexico (www.dlenm.org) is part of this effort. La Cosecha Dual Language conference (www.dlenm.org/lacosecha) is one of the ways that DLeNM supports and advocates for high-quality dual language education. This premier networking event is organized primarily by teachers and for teachers, and it brings together 1,500 members of our larger community from around the country that are willing to share their experience and knowledge to "harvest" the best of our multilingual/multicultural communities. Attendance at conferences like La Cosecha provides individuals and school teams with access to presentations and workshops that focus on the essential features of a program's implementation and/or classroom instruction. Whether a school community is planning a new program or a veteran program is interested in improving their instruction, conferences like La Cosecha have valuable information and resources to offer.

In addition, networking events like La Cosecha offer the opportunity to connect with our larger community. And, with a unified voice, these events educate, inspire, and invite our policy makers, board of education members, educational administrators, families, and the business community to join us in preparing our students for the future.

The excitement around dual language education enrichment has reached all corners of our educational community. Dual language education holds the promise of ensuring high academic achievement, bilingual/biliteracy skills, and cross-cultural competency for all students. What's more, it will take commitment to a larger unified voice and community to ensure that every school community implementing dual language education has the resources and guidance needed to ensure our success.

Other annual events that provide opportunities to connect and continue to build capacity in the support of our programs include the following:

1. State conferences (NMABE, Oregon AMME, WABE, MABE, IIAME, SAAABE, CABE [CO & CA])
2. National conferences (AMME, NABE, Two-Way CABE, ACTFL)

—David Rogers
Executive Director, Dual Language
Education of New Mexico
www.dlenm.org

The following Resources note includes websites with connections to lists of DL programs across the U.S., newsletters, conference listings, materials, and other resources that DL educators will find useful.

RESOURCES

Websites of Useful Organizations

CAL (Center for Applied Linguistics):

- www.cal.org/twi/

The CAL Two-Way Immersion site provides a directory of two-way programs, guiding principles for dual language education, frequently asked questions, and a variety of tools for practitioners (including standards and benchmarks, assessments, evaluator's toolkit, TWI program toolkit, and a description of SIOP [Sheltered Instruction Observation Protocol] modified for TWI programs [TWIOP]). New programs may be especially interested in the TWI toolkit:

- www.cal.org/twi/toolkit/

(continues)

CARLA (Center for Advanced Research on Language Acquisition):

• www.carla.umn.edu/immersion/index.html

CARLA provides immersion education programs with a newsletter, conferences and summer institutes, bibliographies, information on research projects, directories to programs, immersion resources, and frequently asked questions (FAQ) about immersion programs.

DLENM (Dual Language Education of New Mexico):

• www.dlenm.org/

This site provides information on new developments in DL education, conferences, as well as links to information on program development, professional development, advocacy, family and community, instruction and assessment, and research and development. They publish a DL newsletter, Soleado, as well.

IRC (Illinois Resource Center):

• www.thecenterweb.org/irc/pages/f_duallanguage-dir.html

The IRC has a directory of DL programs in Illinois, as well as a newsletter, Dual Language on Demand. They frequently offer specialized training for DL programs, both new and continuing. They have produced DualU: A Teacher Training Curriculum, which is an online resource available by subscription. It contains resources, lesson plans, and activities that address all areas of dual language instruction.

NDLC (National Dual Language Consortium):

• www.dual-language.org/index.htm

This is the home page for a consortium of five non-profit organizations and several dual language researchers. On this site you will find descriptions of different types of DL programs and links to resources.

ATDLE (Association of Two-Way and Dual Language Educators):

• www.atdle.org

Largely dedicated to professional development, ATDLE holds an annual conference and provides resources to programs in the form of videos and articles that promote DL education. They also produce a newsletter for two-way and other dual language programs.

Planning New Programs and Revising Existing Programs

The first checklist that follows focuses on planning new programs and reviewing existing programs. It is organized according to the topics discussed in Chapter 2. You may need to reword specific items to make it more appropriate for your needs, depending on whether you are working on a new program or in an existing program. You may also want to add items that are relevant to your particular setting. After viewing this checklist, it should be clear that devising a new program is challenging, and that meeting these challenges takes time. So, if at all possible, it is critical that your school, in collaboration with the school district, allocate time to take account of the multiple items in this checklist. We recommend that at least one year be spent planning before implementing a new program. It may be that some items will require immediate attention and while others can be considered in a more progressive manner, as the program is implemented. But attention needs to be given to all of these issues within a year or two of starting up a program. We recommend that you consider identifying individuals or subgroups of individuals who will take responsibility for specific topics or sets of topics in order to facilitate planning. If you adopt this strategy, make sure that you make provisions for all individuals and subgroups to meet periodically so that they are informed of one another's work. If such meetings are not planned, you run the risk that decisions will be made by different groups and individuals that are not compatible with one another.

We highly recommend that programs that have existed for some time use this checklist as part of an ongoing assessment process. Many practical considerations in schools can shift programs away from their original formats, and it is important to make sure that these changes have not compromised the program model that you selected. Alternatively, you may find that a revision in the program model is called for because of changes in the school, the school district, or the community at large. The checklist can facilitate realigning your program to better reflect these changes.

✓ Planning a New DL Program and Reviewing an Existing DL Program

Setting the Foundation

❑ Has a cohesive team (no more than four or five members) been formed to plan or revise and oversee the foundation work for the DL program?

❑ Has a clear and succinct message been prepared describing the mission of the program?

❑ Has up-to-date research that shows positive results for DL education been reviewed? And has a one- or two-page summary of the research, written in clear and easy-to-understand language, been prepared and disseminated?

❑ Have testimonials from different constituents been collected?

❑ Have concerns and criticisms of DL programs been identified and responses prepared?

❑ Has an outside expert who can serve as a neutral voice for the school been identified, and has that person become part of the team?

❑ Are team members confident and comfortable explaining the "why" of DL programs?

Preparing the Groundwork

At School

❑ Is there a dissemination plan to let everyone in the school know about the DL program?

❑ Has an information packet for school and district staff been prepared?

❑ Have arrangements been made with one or two other DL programs for site visits?

❑ Have professional development sessions been prepared for all school staff and DL program teachers?

In the Community

❑ Have key community people been identified?

❑ Have the concerns of the community regarding DL education been identified?

❑ Are there spokespersons who can talk to different constituents (parents, school board members, high-level administrators, principals, teachers) in their preferred language?

✓ **Planning a New DL Program and Reviewing an Existing DL Program** (continued)

❑ Are there student voices (in person or recorded) showing how well students can learn both languages?

❑ Have community meetings been held to inform new parents about the program?

❑ Has an information packet that addresses parent and community issues regarding the program been prepared in both languages?

❑ Have local media featured the program?

The Goals of the Program

❑ Have the goals of the program been determined or revisited?

❑ Do these goals address language, academic content, and cross-cultural learning?

❑ Do the goals extend over at least five years or the entire length of the planned program?

❑ Is it clear how the DL program coordinates with the rest of the school and district?

The Program Model

❑ Are you familiar with the various DL program models?

❑ Have people in other DL programs been consulted to get their recommendations and advice regarding the current or planned program model?

❑ Have advantages and disadvantages of the various DL models been considered for your context—for example, with respect to human and educational resources, teacher and community preferences, and space?

❑ Have steps necessary to raise the status of the non-English language in the community been taken? Are plans in place to take action?

❑ Have the languages of instruction been allocated to different content areas with the necessary time allocations?

❑ Is there a lesson framework to be used consistently across the program?

❑ Has a schedule been developed?

❑ Does the schedule stay true to the model at each grade level?

❑ Are teachers in agreement as to how the two languages are to be used for classroom instruction?

(continues)

✓ **Planning a New DL Program and Reviewing an Existing DL Program** *(continued)*

❑ Have the teachers agreed on how to indicate a switch of language of instruction?

Preparing for Teaching

❑ Has the curriculum, and how it is to be delivered, been determined?

❑ Have decisions been made regarding how students are to be assessed?

❑ Have plans been made to avoid or minimize the impact of standardized testing in English during the early grades in the event that DL students do not meet district or state cutoffs?

❑ Do in-house assessments yield enough information about student progress to counteract the possible negative impact of standardized testing?

❑ Does the evaluation plan yield information needed by teachers, administrators, parents, legislators, and students to advocate for the program and review it periodically?

❑ Have materials been ordered for all content areas?

❑ Does the physical space (school and classrooms) reflect the bilingual-bicultural character and goals of the DL program?

❑ Does the classroom arrangement encourage interaction among students?

❑ Is a professional development plan in place for the whole academic year

  ❑ for DL teachers?

  ❑ for other teachers in the school?

  ❑ for paraprofessionals and other support personnel?

  ❑ for administrators?

❑ Do teachers have enough classroom support?

Recruiting Teachers and Students

❑ Have all necessary teachers been recruited?

❑ Do teachers who are new to DL teaching have the time they need to prepare for instruction?

❑ Have all the necessary resource teachers and other support personnel—paraprofessionals, curriculum writers, parent liaisons—been recruited?

❑ Is the recruitment and admission of students into the program satisfactory?

Planning for Instruction

In the next checklist, entitled "Planning for Instruction," we identify issues to think about when planning for instruction, whether it is content or language instruction. The success of a DL program ultimately depends on the quality of instruction, so this aspect of planning is of utmost importance. DL programs are value-added, enriched forms of education. They aim to provide students with all of the advantages of a regular education along with competence in two languages, cross-linguistic awareness, and cross-cultural competence. To achieve these ambitious goals, effort must be expended to plan instruction carefully and thoroughly. Since time is a premium in DL programs, a key feature of DL programs is integration. This involves integration of:

- content and language learning,
- cross-linguistic, cross-cultural, and general learning objectives with language and content objectives,
- DL teachers when planning instruction for DL students at the same and consecutive grades,
- DL and general classroom teachers, and
- the DL program with other programs in the school and with district priorities.

It will not be possible to achieve all of your instructional goals in one year. Therefore, we recommend that you take a long-term approach. Identify those instructional issues that must be dealt with the first year, and devise a plan and strategies to tackle other instruction issues in successive years. Be realistic, but also be ambitious so that you address the multiple aspects of instruction that are critical for achieving the enriched learning outcomes you have set for your students.

DL educators who have been working in other programs can be a valuable source of inspiration and insight about how to plan for instruction. Moreover, there are multiple sources of information on the web that can inform your decisions and your selection of materials. We recommend that classroom teachers and district personnel work in teams to develop curriculum, unit plans, and materials. This will not only facilitate instructional planning, but will also ensure higher quality outcomes because, to paraphrase the old saying, "two heads are better than one."

Teachers plan together to promote learning across languages.

Planning for Instruction

Overview of the Unit
- ☐ Can the unit be linked or tied to several content areas?
- ☐ Has an anchor content area been chosen?
- ☐ Does the unit allow you to draw on a rich array of supportive texts and activities?

Objectives
- ☐ Have content objectives been set?
- ☐ Have language objectives been set?
- ☐ Have cross-linguistic objectives been set?
- ☐ Have cross-cultural objectives been set?
- ☐ Have general learning skills and strategies objectives been set?

Selecting Materials
- ☐ Do the materials you have selected match the objectives set for this unit?
- ☐ Are there materials at different levels of literacy so that you can differentiate instruction and meet students' diverse needs?

  Do you have materials in different media?
- ☐ Have you included literacy materials from the academic content domains that relate directly to the theme of the unit?

Planning for Instruction *(continued)*

Teaching Strategies and Activities for Active Learning

A. Preview Phase

❑ Have you determined the background knowledge that students need in order to benefit from this unit?

❑ Do you have a clear preview phase in which that background knowledge is acquired or reinforced?

❑ Have you identified the key language skills that you want to reinforce during the Preview phase?

B. Focused Learning Phase

❑ Have you identified ways for students to know what they will learn and be able to do at the end of the unit?

❑ Have you identified strategies for teaching the focal concept(s) in the unit with clarity while making necessary linguistic modifications?

❑ Have you planned for ways to reinforce student learning?

C. Extension Phase

❑ Do you have activities that apply what students have learned to their daily lives at home or in their neighborhood?

❑ Have you found ways to connect to other themes or topics?

❑ Have you planned for ways to bring family and community resources into the classroom to support learning objectives?

Planning Assessment

❑ Have you identified ways to monitor student progress toward attainment of the unit objectives while instruction is taking place?

❑ Do you have ways of providing useful feedback to students?

❑ Do you have ways to monitor the progress of struggling learners and to provide additional support as needed?

❑ Do you have formal and informal ways of assessing learning at the end of the unit?

Outreach to the Community

❑ Do you know how you will make connections with the community using the concepts covered in this unit?

Conclusion

Dual language programs have a long and successful history in the U.S. and in Canada. Educators developing new programs or reviewing the effectiveness of existing programs can rest assured that over forty-five years of scientific evidence confirms that school-age children are able to mature and thrive in these programs. More specifically, they are able to acquire advanced levels of competence in two languages and, at the same time, achieve grade-appropriate levels of achievement in academic domains. In short, they are enriched programs that work. Moreover, they work for students with a variety of learner characteristics, including students who are often at risk for academic difficulty in school. Whether students attain these remarkable achievements depends on the quality of the program and this, in turn, depends on the quality of planning and monitoring that goes into the implementation of these programs. In this book, we have sought to provide state-of-the-art guidance on how to implement a quality program. A great deal of effort goes into creating a quality DL program. However, there is tremendous satisfaction in knowing that DL students have what it takes to be successful in the globalized communities in which they will be living. It is education for the future.

Prepare children for life in a global community.

Appendix A

A Thematic Unit Planning Tool

Unit Theme/Topic:

Guiding Questions:

Time Frame for the Unit:

Content Standards (national or state):	Second Language Standards (target language or English depending on language of instruction):
Content Objectives:	Language Objectives: Content Obligatory: Content Compatible: Language Functions:

Cross-Linguistic Objectives (bridging):

Cross-Cultural Objectives:

General Learning Skills and Strategies Objectives:

Materials:

Background Knowledge Needed:

(continues)

© 2013 by Else Hamayan, Fred Genesee, and Nancy Cloud from *Dual Language Instruction from A to Z* (Portsmouth, NH: Heinemann)

Major Teaching Activities:	Grouping Arrangements:
Preview Phase:	
Focused Learning Phase:	
Extension Phase:	

Extensions to Language Arts:

Bridging to Other Subjects (art, music, dance, and movement):

Planning Assessments:

Formative:

Summative:

Performance Indicators for Evaluating Student Performance:

ELD Standard: _____ The Language of: _____ Topic: _____

Connection (list the relevant standards here):

Context for Language Use:

Cognitive Function:

Listening:

Speaking:

Reading:

Writing:

Topic-Related Language:

Planning for Meaningful Involvement of Families and Outreach to the Community:

© 2013 by Else Hamayan, Fred Genesee, and Nancy Cloud from *Dual Language Instruction from A to Z* (Portsmouth, NH: Heinemann)

Appendix B

Resources Related to Metamorphosis (in English and in Spanish)

LADYBUGS

Trade Books:

Hall, M. 2007. *Mariquitas/Ladybugs* (Pebble Plus Bilingual, Spanish Edition). Mankato, MN: Capstone Press. (ATOS level 1.5; Reading level K–1; Interest level P–2; Guided reading level D)

Marsico, K. 2008. *Cómo crece una mariquita.* New York: Children's Press, an imprint of Scholastic, Inc. (Lexile 580L; Reading level 3.2; Guided reading level I, Interest level K–3)

Rau, D. M. [Spanish translation and text composition by Victory Productions]. 2008. *¡Trepa mariquita, trepa! Parte de la serie ¡Vamos criaturita, vamos!* Tarrytown, NY: Marshall Cavendish Benchmark. (Emergent literacy; Interest level K–1)

Schwartz, D. M. [Spanish translation Guillermo Gutiérrez and Tatiana Acosta]. 2001. *La catarina (parte de la collección ciclos de vida en la serie Trampolín a la ciencia).* Milwaukee: Gareth Stevens Publishing. (Reading level 2; Interest level ages pre-K–2)

Books That Can Be Extended to Other Subject Areas:
Mathematics Counting Backwards:

Gerth, M. 2000. *Diez pequeñas mariquitas.* Atlanta, GA: Piggy Toes Press. (Pre-K–K; limited reading level information but appears to be emergent level)

Language Arts:

Carle, E. 1996. *La mariquita malhumorada.* Translated by Teresa Mlawer (Revised Translation). New York: Harper Arco Iris, an imprint of Harper Collins Publishers. (Reading level 2.5–2.8; Interest level pre-K–3; English version GLE 3.3; Lexile 560L; DRA 18–20; Guided reading level J)

Sátiro, A. 2004. *La mariquita Juanita.* Barcelona, Spain: Ediciones Octaedro. (Second grade; Interest level pre-K–2)

Arts:

Como hacer una mariquita o catarina de papel: www.youtube.com/watch?v=qfN73_W7_4E

Poetry:

- www.mundopoesia.com/foros/poesia-infantil/172153-la-curiosa-mariquita.html
- www.mundopoesia.com/foros/poesia-infantil/339605-la-mariquita.html
- www.menudospeques.net/recursos-educativos/poesias/poesias-animales/Page-215

Other Print Resources:

Echols, J. C. 1993. *Ladybugs Teacher's Guide Preschool–1.* Berkeley, CA: Lawrence Hall of Science, University of California at Berkeley, part of the GEMS (Great Explorations in Math and Science) Project. Filled with great activities for young children: visuals, patterns; teaches life cycles, among other topics.

© 2013 by Else Hamayan, Fred Genesee, and Nancy Cloud from *Dual Language Instruction from A to Z* (Portsmouth, NH: Heinemann)

Websites (adapt for use in Spanish):

- Ladybug Lady: www.ladybuglady.com

- How to Make a Ladybug Habitat: www.ehow.com/how_5057186_make-ladybug-habitat.html

- National Wildlife Federation: Insects and Anthropods: www.nwf.org/Kids/Ranger-Rick/Animals/Insects
  -and-Arthropods/Ladybugs.aspx

- The ladybug is the official New York State and New Hampshire insect; see resources collected at www.net
  state.com/states/symb/insects/ny_ladybug.htm and www.netstate.com/states/symb/insects/nh_
  ladybug.htm.

BUTTERFLIES

Children's Trade Books:

Rau, D. M. [Spanish translation and text composition by Victory Productions]. 2007. *¡Vuela mariposa, vuela!*
Parte de la serie ¡Vamos criaturita, vamos! Tarrytown, NY: Marshall Cavendish Benchmark. (Emergent
literacy; Interest level K–1)

Rice, D. H. 2004. *La vida de una mariposa* (part of *Time for Kids Nonfiction Readers:* level 1.5). Huntington
Beach, CA: Teacher Created Materials. (Reading level 1.5; Guided reading level E, DRA level 8: Lexile
190)

Royston, A. [traducción de Patricia Abello]. 2012. *Ciclo de vida de la mariposa.* Chicago: Heinemann Library.
(Guided reading level K, Accelerated reader level 3.6; Interest level grades 1–3). Also available in a
more scaffolded version as *La mariposa/Butterfly*, also by A. Royston. 2011. Chicago:
Heinemann/Raintree (a division of Capstone Publishers)

Books That Can Be Extended to Other Subject Areas:

Language Arts:

Carle, E. 1994. *La oruga muy hambrienta.* New York: Philomel. (Reading level J; Interest level pre-K–2)

Poetry:

- www.mundopoesia.com/foros/poesia-infantil/389232-mariposas-rimado.html

- www.mundopoesia.com/foros/poesia-infantil/353256-mariposa-de-oro.html

- Canción (en YouTube) *La mariposa monarca*, www.youtube.com/watch?v=4Br_YLgj8YE

Websites:

- Globes and maps showing North America (for geography part of the unit related to migration patterns)
  with all wording in Spanish.

- *La metamorfosis de la mariposa*; por Angélica Baride Ruiz www.youtube.com/watch?v=Al6P3kLQsWo

- The Children's Butterfly site: www.kidsbutterfly.org/

- Missouri Botanical Garden Butterfly School site: www.butterflyschool.org/student/index.html

- How to Make Butterfly Gardens: www.ca.uky.edu/entomology/entfacts/ef006.asp

- Ayudas gráficas en español: www.eduplace.com/graphicorganizer/spanish/

© 2013 by Else Hamayan, Fred Genesee, and Nancy Cloud from *Dual Language Instruction from A to Z* (Portsmouth, NH:
Heinemann)

Appendix C

Sample Activities for the Preview Phase of Our Model Lesson

- Visit a museum of natural history, concentrating on an exhibit that shows metamorphosis or different stages of growth in animals. Engage in guided exploration at a nature preserve or natural history museum—see, for example, www.flmnh.ufl.edu//butterflies/neotropica/default.htm; en español, www.flmnh.ufl.edu/butterflies/neotropica/index_sp.html. (Florida Museum of Natural History)

- Read well-illustrated books—fiction or nonfiction—on growth in animals; for example, *Cómo crece una mariquita*. (Book reference given in Appendix B.)

- View videos that show growth in animals; for example, *La oruga muy hambrienta*. (YouTube version: www.youtube.com/watch?v=DC2qSWEjD28)

- Do a demonstration about the changing life cycles of other insects that undergo complete metamorphosis using examples that are already familiar to the students (beetles, mosquitos, flies, bees, ants).

- Have the students participate in an activity related to the topic (such as a WebQuest), again, using examples or objects that are familiar.

© 2013 by Else Hamayan, Fred Genesee, and Nancy Cloud from *Dual Language Instruction from A to Z* (Portsmouth, NH: Heinemann)

Appendix D

Sample Activities for the Metamorphosis Unit (to be Conducted in Spanish)

- *El ciclo vital de la mariquita en imágenes*: http://refugioantiaereo.com/2011/02/el-ciclo-vital-de-la -mariquita-en-imagenes
- Early-grade activities: www.slideshare.net/patyrs82/proyecto-los-insectos-1601426. Includes experiments, art projects, literacy-oriented activities.
- Third-grade activities: www.pnwboces.org/Science21/Resources_In_Spanish.html (go to Grade 3, Unit 4, on this page). See only the activities on stages of growth in a butterfly, including *Mi Diario de Una Mariposa (para anotar observaciones acerca de los cambios de forma)*.
- Free printable writing paper: http://printstationary.net/stationaryletterhead/kids/paperBug.php
- Experiments: http://old.dentonisd.org/pecancreek/lattaya/ladybugs.htm (conducted in Spanish)

© 2013 by Else Hamayan, Fred Genesee, and Nancy Cloud from *Dual Language Instruction from A to Z* (Portsmouth, NH: Heinemann)

Appendix E

Scientific Processes Rubric (for Content Objectives)

NOMBRE _____ FECHA _____

MIEMBROS DEL GRUPO _____

Destreza	Logrado 4	Proficiente 3	Desarrollando 2	Comenzando 1	Comentario del Maestro
Escucha y Sigue Direcciones	No solo escucha cuidadosamente y sigue direcciones, pero también ayuda a otros a entender las direcciones	Siempre escucha y sigue direcciones	Casi todo el tiempo escucha y sigue direcciones	Raramente escucha las direcciones, o solo capta parte de las direcciones	
Predice con Reflexión	Hace predicciones basadas en información pertinente y es capaz de dar razones soportadas con evidencia	Siempre hace predicciones cuidadosas basadas en información relevante	A veces hace predicciones basadas en información relevante	Hace predicciones con poca frecuencia o hace predicciones sin basarlas en información relevante	
Observa con Exactitud	Es capaz de hacer 4 o mas observaciones con precisión y hacer deducciones basadas en ellas	Es capaz de hacer 2–3 observaciones relevantes sobre un fenómeno o organismo	Es capaz de hacer una observación; pero es una observación obvia	Tiene dificultad en hacer predicciones pertinentes acerca del fenómeno o organismo	
Trabaja Cooperativamente	Siempre muestra conducta sumamente cooperativa	Usualmente demuestra conducta cooperativa	Algunas veces demuestra conducta cooperativa	Demuestra dificultad en trabajar cooperativamente	
Respeta los Materiales	Respeta los materiales todo el tiempo independientemente e anima a los otros a hacer lo mismo	Usualmente respeta los materiales	A veces respeta los materiales, pero otras veces el maestro tiene que hacerle recordar como se trata los materiales	Solo respeta los materiales con mucha supervisión del maestro	

Based on a rubric developed by *Science 21: Science for the 21st Century*, Putnam Northern Westchester BOCES, see www.pnwboces.org/science21/About_Science_21.html. Originally appeared as part of the third-grade Spanish resources for teachers, September 2007, www.pnwboces.org/science21/pdf/spanish_resources/Spanish_Assessment_GR3.pdf. Adapted with permission from Science 21.

© 2013 by Else Hamayan, Fred Genesee, and Nancy Cloud from *Dual Language Instruction from A to Z* (Portsmouth, NH: Heinemann)

Appendix F

Resources for the Mathematics Component of the Unit (for Delivery in English)

MEASUREMENT

Lead Books:

A. To introduce the topic of linear measurement, choose among the following titles (listed with related activities or teacher guides):

Murphy, S. J. 1996. *The Best Bug Parade* (part of the MathStart Series). New York: Harper Collins. Title focuses on comparing sizes with *-er; -est*; has extension activities at the back of the book for parents and children). (Level 1; ages 3 and up; Reading level 1.2; Lexile 200). Teacher guides at www .klandskills.ca/famlit/resources/math/BestBugParade.pdf; http://mathstart.net/activities; Chalk Talk Blog: http://larremoreteachertips.blogspot.com/2010/03/best-bug-parade.html; Teacher Vision: www .teachervision.fen.com/childrens-book/printable/61580.html

Lionni, L. 1960. *Inch by Inch*. New York: Scholastic. (Also available in hardcover from Alfred A. Knopf, 2010, New York.) (Reading level 2.1; Guided reading level: K). Title focuses on an inchworm that can measure inches of various birds' body parts. Teacher guides at: http://www.theteachersguide.com/lesson% 20plans/Math/MEA0016.html, http://www.teachertime123.com/2011/01/inch-by-inch-lesson-plan/

There are many more of these types of materials on the web; search by your grade level and the name of the book + measurement.

B. To deepen the knowledge of measurement:

Cleary, B. P. 2007. *How Long or How Wide? A Measuring Guide*. Minneapolis: Millbrook Press. [ATOS level 3.1; Lexile 730]

Pluckrose, H. 1995. *Length* (part of the Math Counts series). Chicago: Children's Press. Also includes the concept of *height*. [Guided reading level K, Grade 2]

Salzmann, M. E. 2009. *What in the World Is an Inch?* Edina, MN: ABDO Publishing Company. [Second grade; Guided reading level K–M; ATOS level 2.0–2.5]

For Pre-K–K:

Rauen, A. 2008. *Finding Shortest and Longest*. ("Getting Started with Math" series). Pleasantville, NY: Weekly Reader Publishing. [Guided reading level: C; DRA: 3; EI 3–4; Lexile 20) Focuses on -er, -est.

C. To introduce time measurement for recording the time elapsed in different stages of growth in days/weeks (seasons):

Royston, A. 2009. *Life Cycle of a Butterfly*. Second Edition. Chicago, IL: Heinemann-Raintree. (Now part of Capstone Press). [Guided reading level: L; Lexile 670L; ATOS 3.7]

Crewe, S. 1997. *The Ladybug*. Austin, TX: Raintree; Steck-Vaughn. [Lexile 600; Grade level 2.5; Guided reading level pre-K]

© 2013 by Else Hamayan, Fred Genesee, and Nancy Cloud from *Dual Language Instruction from A to Z* (Portsmouth, NH: Heinemann)

D. For counting forward and backward; cardinal numbers to 10 (early grades):

Gerth, M. (2000). *Ten Little Ladybugs.* Atlanta, GA: Piggy Toes Press. (Interest level pre-K and up)

Mathematics Activity Sheets:

Matching ladybugs with same number of dots, counting and adding to 20: simple mathematics problems with ladybugs

Mathematics Games/Projects:

• Grouchy Ladybug clock. Has hour and minute hand for practicing telling time: www.vickiblackwell.com/ladybugclock.pdf

• Ladybug board game with dice. (Source: uca.edu/steminstitute/files/2011/07/ladybugs.pdf)

• Ladybug mat and recording sheet. (Source: http://mathwire.com/themes/themelb.html)

• Vicki Blackwell site: www.vickiblackwell.com/lit/ladybug.html (see clock, accordion book)

• Ladybug number line (for counting forward and backward): www.abcteach.com/documents/number-line -ladybugs-1-10-2448

• Counting and recording numbers of butterflies activity in Big Butterfly Count project: www.bigbutterfly count.org/; www.naba.org/butter_counts.html

© 2013 by Else Hamayan, Fred Genesee, and Nancy Cloud from *Dual Language Instruction from A to Z* (Portsmouth, NH: Heinemann)

Appendix G

Activities for Outreach to the Community

PLANNING FOR MEANINGFUL INVOLVEMENT OF FAMILIES/OUTREACH TO THE COMMUNITY:

Measurement Activities:

• Have students take home tape measures with inches marked on one side and centimeters on the other. Have them measure a certain number of small items in their home with a family member. Have them report back on which was shorter/longer, wider, and taller (-est).

• Have students make a timeline showing the weeks and days until an important family event occurs (within the two to three weeks of the unit). With a family member, have them record how many days/weeks are left each day until the event occurs.

• Invite family or community members into the classroom to say how they use measurement every day in their jobs (biologist [entomologist, if possible], seamstress, carpenter, bricklayer, biologist, architect, and so forth).

• Take students on a field trip to a place where a butterfly collection is housed. Have them estimate, if under glass (or if not, carefully measure) the size of the butterflies and report back in class.

Literacy:

The Grouchy Ladybug Telling Time Family Literacy Bag (book available in Spanish): www.colorincolorado .org/article/31252/

The Very Hungry Caterpillar Family Literacy Bag (book available in Spanish): www.colorincolorado.org/ article/31255

© 2013 by Else Hamayan, Fred Genesee, and Nancy Cloud from *Dual Language Instruction from A to Z* (Portsmouth, NH: Heinemann)

Appendix H

A List of Selected Materials to Use in Spanish and English for a Unit on Hurricanes

Genre	Spanish	English
Personal	Ambert, A. 1997. *¿Por qué soplan los vientos salvajes?* Crystal Lake, IL: Rigby. Puerto Rican/Taino myth. (Saludos/Greetings Red Level/Grade Level 3). Also available in English version.	Wallner, A. 2000. *Sergio and the Hurricane.* New York: Henry Holt and Co. A tale set in San Juan, Puerto Rico. (Grade level 3.2; Lexile 700; Guided reading level L) London, J. 1998. *Hurricane!* Carmel, CA: Hampton-Brown. Takes place in Puerto Rico. (Guided reading level P and up)
Factual	Article on Hurricane Irene (or any hurricane) from Periodico *El Nuevo Día* (daily newspaper in San Juan) Anuncio Para el Público: *Medidas de Seguridad/Lista de Suministros Para Un Huracán* (on page 20 of Mezzanotte titles below)	*Time for Kids:* Hurricane Katrina (or other similar story) *FEMA for Kids:* • www.ready.gov/kids/know-facts • www.ready.gov/kids/make-plan-kids
Analytic	Mezzanotte, J. 2007. *Huracanes.* (Serie Tormentas). Milwaukee, WI: Weekly Reader Early Learning Library (Grade level 3.3; Guided reading level N) *Second version is available at a lower reading level:* Mezzanotte, J. 2010. *Huracanes.* (Serie Tiempo extremo). Pleasantville, NY: Weekly Reader books, an Imprint of Gareth Stevens Publishing (Beginning Reader version) Rice, W. B. 2010. *Los huracanes.* [translation of the *Hurricanes* book in the series "Forces in Nature; Earth and Space Science (Science Readers: A Closter Look)"]. Huntington Beach, CA: Teacher Created	Multimedia: Discovery Channel Discovery Education Streaming. 2001. *Weather Smart: Hurricanes* ("The Stages of Hurricane Development" segment from a streaming video for Earth/space science, Grade level 3–5, 4.17 minutes). • www.discoveryeducation.com Chambers, C. 2007. *Hurricane* (part of the Wild Weather Series). Chicago: Heinemann Raintree, a division of Reed Elsevier, Inc. (now distributed by Capstone). (Grade 2; Guided reading level M). First Library Books offer a straightforward introduction to a topic; limit text to three to four sentences per page; use fonts

(continues)

© 2013 by Else Hamayan, Fred Genesee, and Nancy Cloud from *Dual Language Instruction from A to Z* (Portsmouth, NH: Heinemann)

Genre	Spanish	English
	Materials. (Lexile 660; Guided reading level K)	of 18 points or larger for readability; feature large, colorful photos and illustrations that truly support the text; provide helpful nonfiction features, including a glossary, index, and list of appropriately leveled books for further reading.
	Schuh, M. 2011. *Huracanes/Hurricanes.* Pebble Plus Bilingual Book. Mankato, MN: Capstone Press. (Guided reading level N; Lexile 450)	Green, J. 2005. *Hurricanes* (part of the Extreme Weather theme set, Level D; Grade level 6.0–6.5). Washington, DC: National Geographic Society
		Lauber, P. 1996. *Hurricanes: Earth's Mightiest Storms.* New York: Scholastic. (Reading level 5.5; Lexile 900)

© 2013 by Else Hamayan, Fred Genesee, and Nancy Cloud from *Dual Language Instruction from A to Z* (Portsmouth, NH: Heinemann)

Appendix I

Sample Activities for the Focused Learning Phase in English

ENGLISH LANGUAGE ARTS:	GROUPING ARRANGEMENT:
1. Introduce Discovery Channel video: *Weather Smart: The Stages of Hurricane Development* (4.16 minutes in length). [Subscription needed to view the entire video set; see excerpts at http://dsc.discovery.com/news/video/hurricanegallery.html.] (Focused viewing; frontloading of key vocabulary)	1. Whole class, with teacher-guided discussion after the viewing
2. Read aloud *Sergio and the Hurricane* (listed in Appendix H). The story is set in San Juan, Puerto Rico, and the author recounts the experiences of Sergio and his family as they weather a strong hurricane (in English). Focus on use of *descriptive language* ("bright windsurfing boats on the turquoise water") or figurative language ("the wind was rattling the shutters like it wanted to break in," "utility poles are snapping like matchsticks"). You could also reinforce the concepts of *character*, *setting*, and *plot*. After reading, use the book and its visuals to elicit hurricane memoirs from the students. Placing students in groups of two or three, have them tell where it took place, where they were when it hit land, how old they were, who else was there with them, how they felt, and how it ended. Review the concepts of *character*, *setting*, and *plot*, and use of descriptive or figurative language as the memoirs are shared. (Read-aloud; oral practice of recounts)	2. Whole class, followed by partner or triad activity
3. Hurricane song (with actions). Sponsored by Time4Learning.com available on YouTube, (www.youtube.com/watch?v=SpJi0tcSExs), with music by Tom Glazer from Weather Songs, (also available at http://www.youtube.com/watch?v=Lkqoc9IFrcl). Assign lines of the song to different sets of students according to their proficiency levels and have them sing their part along with the music. All of the students sing the chorus. (Front-loading of content and vocabulary)	3. Whole class, partners

(continues)

© 2013 by Else Hamayan, Fred Genesee, and Nancy Cloud from *Dual Language Instruction from A to Z* (Portsmouth, NH: Heinemann)

4. Use the book *Hurricane!* (listed in Appendix H) as a mentor text to model ideas, sentence fluency, and/or conventions. Model how the text shows, rather than tells, where the story takes place, and how it tells how the day began and who was there (ideas). Then, show how the transitions and connectors that the writer uses link one sentence or paragraph to the next (e.g., use of conjunctions *and* and *but*, time clauses with *then*, *after*, *as*, *while*). [Sentence fluency]. Show how the author uses conventions (in this case, quotation marks), exclamation points, commas, hyphens, apostrophes, and/or periods. (Writer's Workshop)	4. Whole class, individual
5. Report back: Convince people why they should evacuate if they live near the coast and a hurricane is predicted to strike land. Give at least two arguments for why evacuation is the best option, and refute the reasons why people stay in a hurricane zone despite the warnings. (Oral Practice; front-loading of persuasive arguments in preparation for future writing)	5. Teams
6. Bridging segment: Use the maps and visuals from the books read, and others the teacher selects, to show the location and stages in hurricane development, bridging from Spanish to English. This activity builds the language needed to give explanations about hurricane development also in English. (Visual literacy; assessment of language and content objectives)	6. Direct teaching, followed by partner practice

© 2013 by Else Hamayan, Fred Genesee, and Nancy Cloud from *Dual Language Instruction from A to Z* (Portsmouth, NH: Heinemann)

Appendix J

Reading Assessment Tools

Developmental Reading Assessments/Evaluacion del de saroollo de la lectura (DRA2/EDL2), Grades K–8. The DRA2/EDL2 is a series of benchmark books used to establish the reading level of the student and to learn about reading abilities and habits. It is designed to pinpoint strengths and needs of students in reading engagement, fluency and accuracy, comprehension, and reading habits and interests. It is used for progress monitoring as well. Test-use tutorials are available for both systems at the publisher's website, www.pearson school.com/index.cfm (search for DRA).

Fountas and Pinnell Benchmark Assessment System (English) and in Spanish for Grades K–2 as Sistema de evaluacíon de la lectura (SEL). This benchmark assessment measures the instructional and independent reading abilities of students. The system provides a one-to-one, comprehensive assessment to determine independent and instructional reading levels for placing students on the Fountas and Pinnell A–Z Text Gradient, and connecting assessment to instruction with the Continuum of Literacy Learning. Teachers can use the system to determine students' independent and instructional reading levels, and to determine reading placement levels, instructional groups, and assess the outcomes of teaching. See: www.heinemann.com/fountasandpinnell.

The Flynt-Cooter English-Español Reading Inventory for the Classroom (1999) includes placement sentences, paragraph reading assessments in both Spanish and English for fiction and nonfiction texts around which running records are conducted, and comprehension is checked. It also includes interest inventories for both younger and older learners.

The Brigance Inventory of Basic Skills–Spanish Edition includes an IRI in Spanish and English consisting of graded word lists and graded passages for grades PP–5 to assess oral reading. There are also reading vocabulary comprehension grade placement tests for grades P–6 and comprehension passages for P–6 in Spanish and English. Additionally, there are helpful functional word recognition assessments of basic vocabulary, signs and labels and number words, as well as diagnostic assessments to assess word analysis skills such as phonics, suffixes/prefixes, syllables, and word stress. Another useful area assessed is that of listening comprehension for grades pre-K–8. Finally, there are a few writing assessments designed to evaluate manuscript and cursive handwriting, mechanics, and alphabetization skills. This assessment, first developed in the 1980s, may be most useful for direct diagnostic assessments, as there are other, more current measures developed to directly assess reading levels using current benchmarking systems. See: www.curriculum associates.com/products/detail.aspx?title=brigabsr.

© 2013 by Else Hamayan, Fred Genesee, and Nancy Cloud from *Dual Language Instruction from A to Z* (Portsmouth, NH: Heinemann)

References

Abedi, J., & Dietel, R. 2004. "Challenges in the No Child Left Behind Act for English Language Learners." *Phi Delta Kappan* 8: 782–785.

The Academy of Natural Sciences of Drexel University. (2013). *Butterfly Life Cycle.* Available at: www.ansp.org/museum/butterflies/life_cycle.php

Alarcon, F. X. 2008. *Animal Poems of the Iguazu/Animalrio del Iguazu.* San Francisco: Children's Book Press.

Au, K., & Jordan, C. 1981. "Teaching Reading to Hawaiian Children: Finding a Culturally Appropriate Solution." In H. T. Trueba, G. P. Guthrie, & K. H. Au (Eds.), *Culture and the Bilingual Classroom: Studies in Classroom Ethnography* (pp. 139–152). Rowley, MA: Newbury House.

August, D., & Shanahan, T. (Eds.). 2006. *Developing Literacy in Second Language Learners. Report of the National Literacy Panel on Minority-Language Children and Youth.* Mahwah, NJ: Lawrence Erlbaum.

Bailey, A. L., & Butler, F. A. 2002. *An Evidentiary Framework for Operationalizing Academic Language for Broad Application to K–12 Education: A Design Document.* Los Angeles, CA: University of California (National Center for Research on Evaluation, Standards, and Student Testing).

Barrera, R. B., Quiroa, R. E., & Valdivia, R. 2003. "Spanish in Latino Picture Storybooks in English: Its Use and Textual Effects." In A. Ingram Willis, G. E. Garcia, R. B. Barrera, & V. J. Harris (Eds.), *Multicultural Issues in Literacy Research and Practice* (pp. 11–27). Mahwah, NJ: Erlbaum.

Bear, D. R., Helman, L., Templeton, S., Invernizzi, M., & Johnston, F. 2007. *Words Their Way with English Learners: Word Study for Phonics, Vocabulary, and Spelling Instruction.* Upper Saddle River, NJ: Pearson/Merrill Prentice Hall.

Beeman, K., & Urow, C. 2012. *Teaching for Biliteracy: Strengthening Bridges Between Languages.* Philadelphia: Caslon.

Bialystok, E. 2006. "The Impact of Bilingualism on Language and Literacy Development." In T. K. Bhatia & W. E. Ritchie (Eds.), *The Handbook of Bilingualism* (pp. 577–601). Malden, MA: Blackwell Publishing.

Bialystok, E. 2007. "Cognitive Effects of Bilingualism: How Linguistic Experience Leads to Cognitive Change." *International Journal of Bilingual Education and Bilingualism* 10(3): 210–223.

Block, N. 2007. "Dual Immersion Programs in Predominantly Latino Schools." Unpublished doctoral dissertation. Claremont Graduate University, Claremont, CA.

Bolger, D. J., Balass, M., Landen, E., & Perfetti, C. A. 2008. "Context Variation and Definitions in Learning the Meanings of Words: An Instance-Based Learning Approach." *Discourse Processes* 45: 122–159.

Bostwick, M. 2001. "English Immersion in a Japanese School." In D. Christian, & F. Genesee (Eds.), *Case Studies in Bilingual Education* (pp. 125–138). Alexandria, VA: TESOL.

Bruck, M. 1978. "The Suitability of Early French Immersion Programs for the Language Disabled Child." *Canadian Journal of Education* 3: 51–72.

Bruck, M. 1982. "Language Disabled Children: Performance in an Additive Bilingual Education Program." *Applied Psycholinguistics* 3: 45–60.

Bruck, M., Tucker, G. R., & Jakimik, J. 1975. "Are French Immersion Programs Suitable for Working Class Children?" *Word* 27: 311–341.

Bushong, R. W. 2010. "The Academic Word List Reorganized for Spanish Speaking English Language Learners." Master's thesis for the degree of Master of Arts in TESOL. University of Central Florida, College of Graduate Studies, Orlando, FL.

Calderon, M., & Minaya-Rowe, L. 2003. *Designing and Implementing Two-Way Bilingual Programs.* Thousand Oaks, CA: Sage.

Cazabon, M., Nicoladis, E., & Lambert, W. 1998. "Becoming Bilingual in the Amigos Two-Way Immersion Program" (Research Report 3). Santa Cruz, CA, and Washington, DC: Center for Research on Education, Diversity, & Excellence.

Cenoz, J. 2009. *Towards Multilingual Education: Basque Educational Research from an Educational Perspective.* Bristol, UK: Multilingual Matters.

Chamot, A. U., & O'Malley, J. M. 1994. *The CALLA Handbook: Implementing the Cognitive Academic Language Learning Approach.* White Plains, NY: Addison Wesley Longman.

Christian, D., Genesee, F., Lindholm-Leary, K., & Howard, E. 2008. *Final Progress Report: CAL/CREDE Study of Two-Way Immersion Education.* www.cal.org/twi/CREDEfinal.doc.

Cloud, N., Genesee, F., & Hamayan, E. 2000. *Dual Language Instruction: A Handbook for Enriched Education.* Portsmouth, NH: Heinle & Heinle.

Cloud, N., Genesee, F., & Hamayan, E. 2009. *Literacy Instruction for English Language Learners.* Portsmouth, NH: Heinemann.

Collier, V. P., & Thomas, W. P. 2009. *Educating English Learners for a Transformed World.* Albuquerque, NM: Fuente Press.

Collins, L., Halter, R. H., Lightbown, P. M., & Spada, N. 1999. "Time and the Distribution of Time in L2 Instruction." *TESOL Quarterly* 33(4): 655–680.

Coxhead, A. 2000. "A New Academic Word List." *TESOL Quarterly* 34, 213–238. www.vuw.ac.nz/lals/research/awl/index.html.

Crandall, J., Stein, H., & Nelson, J. 2012. "What Kinds of Knowledge and Skills Do Mainstream Teachers, English as a Second Language Teachers, Bilingual Teachers, and Support Staff Need to Implement an Effective Program for English Language Learners?" In E. Hamayan & R. Freeman (Eds.), *English Language Learners at School: A Guide for Administrators* (pp. 9–17). Philadelphia: Caslon.

Crawford, A. N. 1984. "A Spanish Language Fry-Type Readability Procedure: Elementary Level." *Bilingual Education Paper Series* 7(8).

Crystal, D. 2003. *English as a Global Language* (2nd edition). Cambridge, UK: Cambridge University Press.

Cummins, J. 1981. "The Role of Primary Language Development in Promoting Educational Success for Language Minority Students." In *Schooling and Language Minority Students: An Educational Framework* (1st edition, 3–49). Los Angeles: Evaluation, Dissemination and Assessment Center, California State University.

Cummins, J. 2007. "Rethinking Monolingual Instructional Strategies in Multilingual Classrooms." *Canadian Journal of Applied Linguistics* 10: 221–241.

Cummins, J., Bismilla, V., Chow, P., Cohen, S., Giampapa, F., Leoni, L., Sandhu, P., & Sastri, P. 2005. "Affirming Identity in Multilingual Classrooms." *Educational Leadership* 63(1): 38–43.

D' Ambrósio, U. 1985. "Ethno-Mathematics and Its Place in the History and Pedagogy of Mathematics." *For the Learning of Mathematics* 5(1): 44–48.

D' Ambrósio, U. 2000. "Ethno-Science and Ethno-Mathematics. A Historiographical Proposal for Non-Western Mathematics." Downloaded 7/5/11 from: http://iascud.univalle.edu.co/libro/libro_pdf/Ethnoscience%20and%20ethnomathematics.pdf

de Jong, E. J. 2002. "Effective Bilingual Education: From Theory to Academic Achievement in a Two-Way Bilingual Program." *Bilingual Research Journal* 26 (1): 65–84.

de Jong, E. J. 2011. *Foundations for Multilingualism in Education: From Principles to Practice.* Philadelphia: Caslon.

Dijkstra, A. F. J., & van Heuven, W. J. B. 2002. "The Architecture of the Bilingual Word Recognition System: From Identification to Decision." *Bilingualism: Language and Cognition* 5(3): 175–197.

Directory of Foreign Language Immersion Programs in U.S. Schools. 2012. Washington, DC: Center for Applied Linguistics. Available at: www.cal.org/resources/immersion/

Directory of Two-Way Bilingual Immersion Programs in the U.S. 2012. Washington, DC: Center for Applied Linguistics. Available at: www.cal.org/twi/directory

Echevarria, J., & Short, D. 2010. "Programs and Practices for Effective Sheltered Content Instruction." In *Improving Education for English Language Learners: Research-Based Approaches* (pp. 251–323). Sacramento, CA: California Department of Education.

Echevarria, J., Vogt, E., & Short, D. 2008. *Making Content Comprehensible for English Language Learners: The SIOP Model* (3rd Edition). Boston: Allyn & Bacon.

Erdos, C., Genesee, F., Savage, R., & Haigh, C. 2011. "Individual Differences in Second Language Reading Outcomes." *International Journal of Bilingualism* 15(1): 3–25.

Escamilla, K. 2000. "Bilingual Means Two: Assessment issues, Early Literacy and Spanish-speaking Children." *Proceedings of the Research Symposium on High Standards in Reading for Students from Diverse Language Groups: Research, Practice & Policy.* Held in Washington, DC: April 19–20, 2000, Office of Bilingual Education and Minority Languages Affairs, U.S. Department of Education.

Fisher, D., & Frey, N. 2010. "Unpacking the Language Purpose: Vocabulary, Structure, and Function." *TESOL Journal* 1(3): 315–337.

Fortune, T. (with M. R. Menke). 2010. *Struggling Learners and Language Immersion Education.* Minneapolis: University of Minnesota, The Center for Advanced Research on Language Acquisition.

Fountas, I., & Pinnell, G. S. 2001. *Guiding Readers and Writers/Grades 3–6.* Portsmouth, NH: Heinemann.

Francis, D. J., Lesaux, N. K., & August, D. 2006. "Language of Instruction for Language Minority Learners." In D. August & T. Shanahan (Eds.), *Developing Literacy in a Second Language: Report of the National Literacy Panel* (pp. 365–414). Mahwah, NJ: Lawrence Erlbaum.

Freeman, Y., Freeman, D., & Mercuri, S. 2004. *Dual Language Essentials for Teachers and Administrators.* Portsmouth, NH: Heinemann.

Fry, R. 1968. "A Readability Formula That Saves Time." *Journal of Reading* 11: 513–516.

Fry, R. 2007. *How Far Behind in Mathematics and Reading Are English Language Learners?* Washington, DC: Pew Hispanic Center.

Garcia, O. 2011. "The Translanguaging of Latino Kindergartners." In K. Potkowski & J. Rothman (Eds.), *Bilingual Youth: Spanish in English-Speaking Societies* (pp. 35–55). Amsterdam: John Benjamins.

Garcia, Y. 2003. "Korean/English Two-Way Immersion at Cahuenga Elementary School." *NABE News* 26: 8–11.

Genesee, F. (Ed.). 1999. "Program Alternatives for Linguistically Diverse Students." *Educational Practice Report No. 1.* Washington, DC: Center for Research on Education, Diversity & Excellence. Available at: www.cal.org/crede/pubs/edpractice/EPR1.htm

Genesee, F. 2003. "Rethinking Bilingual Acquisition." In J. M. deWaele (Ed.), *Bilingualism: Challenges and Directions for Future Research* (pp. 158–182). Clevedon, UK: Multilingual Matters.

Genesee, F. 2004. "What Do We Know About Bilingual Education for Majority Language Students?" In T. K. Bhatia, & W. Ritchie (Eds.), *Handbook of Bilingualism and Multiculturalism* (pp. 547–576). Malden, MA: Blackwell.

Genesee, F. 2007. "French Immersion and At-Risk Students: A Review of Research Findings." *Canadian Modern Language Review* 63: 655–688.

Genesee, F., & Gándara, P. 1999. "Bilingual Education Programs: A Cross-National Perspective." *Journal of Social Issues* 55(4): 665–685.

Genesee, F., & Geva, E. 2006. "Cross-Linguistic Relationships in Working Memory, Phonological Processes, and Oral Language" (Chapter 7). In D. August, & T. Shanahan (Eds.), *Developing Literacy in Second Language Learners. Report of the National Literacy Panel on Minority-Language Children and Youth,* pp. 175–184. Mahwah, NJ: Lawrence Erlbaum.

Genesee, F., & Lindholm-Leary, K. 2012. "The Education of English Language Learners." In K. Harris, S. Graham, & T. Urdan (Eds.), *APA Handbook of Educational Psychology,* pp. 499–526. Washington DC: APA Books.

Genesee, F., Lindholm-Leary, K., Saunders, W., & Christian, D. 2006. *Educating English Language Learners: A Synthesis of Research Evidence*. NY: Cambridge University Press.

Genesee, F., Savage, R., Erdos, E., & Haigh, C. (in press). "Identification of Reading Difficulties in Students Schooled in a Second Language." In V. Gathercole (Ed.), *Bilinguals and Assessment: State of the Art Guide to Issues and Solutions from Around the World*. Clevedon, UK: Multilingual Matters.

Goldenberg, C. 2008 (Summer). "Teaching English Language Learners: What the Research Does—And Does Not—Say." *American Educator*, 8–44.

Gomez, L., Freeman, D., & Freeman, Y. 2005. "Dual Language Education: A Promising 50-50 Model." *Bilingual Research Journal* 29: 145–164.

González, N., Moll, L. C., & Amanti, C. 2005. *Funds of Knowledge: Theorizing Practices in Households, Communities and Classrooms*. Mahwah, NJ: Lawrence Erlbaum.

Gordon, J. 2000. "The Lesson Cycle." In N. Cloud, F. Genesee, and E. Hamayan, *Dual Language Instruction: A Handbook for Enriched Education* (pp. 177–183). Boston: Heinle & Heinle.

Greenfield, P. M., Quiroz, B., & Raeff, C. 2000. "Cross-Cultural Conflict and Harmony in the Social Construction of the Child." In S. Harkness, C. Raeff, & C. M. Super (Eds.), *New Directions for Child and Adolescent Development* (93–108). San Francisco: Jossey-Bass.

Guiding Principles for Dual Language Education, Second Edition. 2007. Washington, DC: Center for Applied Linguistics.

Ha, J. H. 2001. "Elementary Students' Written Language Development in a Korean/English Two-Way Immersion Program." Unpublished master's thesis, California State University, Long Beach, CA.

Hall, M. 2007. *Mariquitas Mariquitas/Ladybugs* (Pebble Plus Bilingual, Spanish Edition). Mankato, MN: Capstone Press.

Hamayan, E. 2010. "Separado o Together? Reflecting on the Separation of Languages of Instruction." *Soleado* (winter) 1: 8–9.

Hamayan, E., & Freeman, R. 2012. *English Language Learners at School: A Guide for Administrators*. Philadelphia, PA: Carlson.

Hamayan, E., Marler, B., Sanchez Lopez, C., & Damico, J. 2013. *Special Education Considerations for English Language Learners: Delivering a Continuum of Services* (Second Edition). Philadelphia, PA: Carlson Press.

Hiebert, E. H. 2005. "In Pursuit of an Effective, Efficient Vocabulary Curriculum for Elementary Students." In E. H. Hiebert and M. L. Kamil, M. L. (Eds.), *Teaching and Learning Vocabulary: Bringing Research to Practice* (pp. 243–263). Mahwah, NJ: Lawrence Erlbaum Associates.

Hilliard, J., & Hamayan, E. 2012. "How Do You Plan for Language Development?" In E. Hamayan & R. Freeman (Eds.), *English Language Learners at School: A Guide for Administrators*. Philadelphia: Caslon.

Himmele, P., & Himmele, W. 2009. *The Language-Rich Classroom: A Research-Based Framework for Teaching English Language Learners*. Alexandria, VA: ASCD.

Himmele, P., & Himmele, W. 2011. *Total Participation Techniques: Making Every Student an Active Learner*. Alexandria, VA: ASCD.

Howard, E., & Loeb, M. 1998. "In Their Own Words: Two-Way Immersion Teachers Talk About Their Professional Experiences." *ERIC Digest*. Washington, DC: Center for Applied Linguistics.

Howard, E., & Sugarman, J. 2011. *Realizing the Vision of Two-Way Immersion: Fostering Effective Programs and Classrooms*. Washington, DC: Center for Applied Linguistics.

Howard, E., Sugarman, J., & Christian, D. 2003. *Trends in Two-Way Immersion Education: A Review of the Research*. Retrieved August 2011 from: www.csos.jhu.edu/crespar/techReports/report63.pdf

Howard, E., Sugarman, J., Christian, D., Lindholm-Leary, K., & Rogers, D. 2007. *Guiding Principles for Dual Language Education*. Washington, DC: Center for Applied Linguistics. Available at: www.cal.org/twi/guiding_principles.pdf

Howard, E., Sugarman, J., Perdomo, M., & Adger, C. 2005. *The Two-Way Immersion Toolkit*. Providence, RI: The Education Alliance at Brown University.

Howard, E. R., & Christian, D. 2002. *Two-Way Immersion 101: Designing and Implementing a Two-Way Immersion Education Program at the Elementary School Level*. (Educational Practice Report No. 9). Santa Cruz, CA, and Washington, DC: Center for Research on Education, Diversity & Excellence.

Howard, E. R., Olague, N., & Rogers, D. 2003. *The Dual Language Program Planner: A Guide for Designing and Implementing Dual Language Programs*. Santa Cruz, CA, and Washington, DC: Center for Research on Education, Diversity & Excellence.

Howard, E. R., & Sugarman, J. 2007. *Realizing the Vision of Two-Way Immersion: Fostering Effective Programs and Classrooms*. Washington, DC: Delta Systems and ERIC Clearinghouse on Languages and Linguistics.

Hudelson, S., Fournier, J., Espinosa, C., & Bachman, R. 1994. "Chasing Windmills: Confronting the Obstacles to Literature-Based Programs in Spanish. *Language Arts* 71: 164–171.

Improving Education for English Learners: Research-Based Approaches. 2010. Sacramento, CA: California Department of Education.

Jacobs, H. H. 1997. *Mapping the Big Picture: Integrating Curriculum and Assessment K–12*. Alexandria, VA: Association for Supervision and Curriculum Development.

Jiménez, R. G., Garcia, G. E., & Pearson, P. D. 1996. "The Reading Strategies of Bilingual Latina/o Students Who Are Successful English Readers: Opportunities and Obstacles." *Reading Research Quarterly* 31: 90–112.

Kagan, S. 1995. "We Can Talk: Cooperative Learning in the Elementary ESL Classroom." *TESOL Elementary Education Newsletter* 17(2): 3–4.

Kallick, B. O., Jacobs, H. H., Holt, M. A., Johnson, A. W., Truesdale, V., Lachowicz, J., Thompson, C., Johnson, J. L., Lucas, M., O'Neil, S., & Wilson, J. M. 2004. *Getting Results with Curriculum Mapping*. Alexandria, VA: Association for Supervision and Curriculum Development.

Knapp, P., & Watkins, M. 2005. *Genre, Text, Grammar: Technologies for Teaching and Assessing Writing*. Sydney: University of New South Wales Press, Ltd.

Lantolf, J. P. 2005. "Sociocultural Theory and L2 Learning: An Exegesis." In E. Hinkel. (Ed.), *Handbook of Second Language Research* (pp. 335–354). Mahwah, NJ: Erlbaum.

Lindholm-Leary, K. 2011. "Student Outcomes in Chinese Two-Way Immersion Programs: Language Proficiency, Academic Achievement, and Student Attitudes." In D. Tedick, Christian, D., & Fortune, T. (Eds.), *Immersion Education: Practices, Policies, Possibilities* (pp. 81–103). Avon, UK: Multilingual Matters.

Lindholm-Leary, K., & Genesee, F. 2010. "Alternative Educational Programs for English Learners." In *Improving Education for English Learners: Research-Based Approaches*. Sacramento, CA: California Department of Education.

Lindholm-Leary, K., & Genesee, F., 2010. "Alternative Educational Programs for English Learners." In *Improving Education for English Learners: Research-Based Approaches* (pp. 323–382). Sacramento, CA: California Department of Education.

Lindholm-Leary, K., & Hargett, G. 2007. *Evaluator's Toolkit for Dual Language Programs*. Download from: www.cal.org/twi/EvalToolkit/

Lindholm-Leary, K., & Hernandez, A. 2011. "Achievement and Language Proficiency of Latino Students in Dual Language Programmes: Native English Speakers, Fluent English/Previous Ells, and Current Ells." *Journal of Multilingual and Multicultural Development*, DOI:10.1080/01434632.2011.611596.

Lindholm-Leary, K. J. 2001. *Dual Language Education*. Avon, UK: Multilingual Matters.

Lindholm-Leary, K. J. 2008. "Language Development and Academic Achievement in Two-Way Immersion Programs." In T. Fortune, & D. Tedick (Eds.), *Pathways to Bilingualism: Evolving Perspectives on Immersion Education*. Clevedon, UK: Multilingual Matters.

Lindholm-Leary, K. J. 2010. *PROMISE Initiative Student Outcomes*. San Bernardino, CA: PROMISE Design Center.

Lindholm, K. J., & Aclan, Z. 1991. "Bilingual Proficiency as a Bridge to Academic Achievement: Results from Bilingual/Immersion Programs." *Journal of Education* 173: 99–113.

Lindholm-Leary, K. J., & Borsato, G. 2006. "Academic Achievement." In F. Genesee, K. Lindholm-Leary, W. Saunders, & D. Christian (Eds.), *Educating English Language Learners* (pp. 176–222). New York: Cambridge University Press.

Lindholm-Leary, K. J., & Howard, E. 2008. "Language Development and Academic Achievement in Two-Way Immersion Programs." In T. W. Fortune, & D. J. Tedick (Eds.), *Pathways to Multilingualism: Evolving Perspectives on Immersion Education* (pp. 177–200). Oxford, UK: Blackwell.

Linguistics: www.cal.org/resources/immersion/

Linguistics: www.cal.org/twi/directory

London, J., & Sorensen, H. 1998. *Hurricane!* Carmel, CA: Hampton Brown.

Lubliner, S., & Hiebert, E. H. 2011. "An Analysis of English-Spanish Cognates as a Source of General Academic Learning." *Bilingual Research Journal* 34: 76–93.

Lyster, R. 2007. *Learning and Teaching Languages Through Content: A Counterbalanced Approach.* Amsterdam: John Benjamins.

Lyster, R., Collins, L., & Ballinger, S. 2009. "Linking Languages Through a Bilingual Read-Aloud Project." *Language Awareness* 18: 366–383.

Marian, V., & Shook, A. 2012. "The Cognitive Benefits of Being Biliingual." Available at: www.dana.org/news/cerebrum/detail.aspx?id=39638

Marsico, K. 2008. *Como crece una mariquita.* New York: Children's Press (an imprint of Scholastic, Inc.).

Mehisto, P., & Asser, H. 2007. "Stakeholder Perspectives: CLIL Programme Management in Estonia." *International Journal of Bilingual Education and Bilingualism* 10(5): 683–701.

Met, M. 1998. "Curriculum Decision-Making in Content-Based Language Teaching." In J. Cenoz & F. Genesee (Eds.), *Beyond Bilingualism: Multilingualism and Multilingual Education* (pp. 35–63). Clevedon, UK: Multilingual Matters.

Met, M., & Stewart, V. (Eds.). 2012. *Chinese Language Learning in the Early Grades: A Handbook of Resources and Best Practices for Mandarin Immersion.* Asia Society. Download at: http://asiasociety.org/files/chinese-earlylanguage.pdf

Moll, L., Amanti, C. A., Neff, D., & González, N. 1992. "Funds of Knowledge for Teaching: Using a Qualitative Approach to Connect Homes and Classrooms." *Theory Into* Practice 31(2): 132–141.

Montone, C., & Loeb, M. I. 2000. *Implementing Two-Way Immersion Programs in Secondary Schools* (Educational Practice Report No. 5). Santa Cruz, CA, and Washington, DC: Center for Research on Education, Diversity & Excellence. Available at: www.cal.org/crede/pubs/edpractice/EPR5.htm.

Moreira, D. 2008. *Explorations Between Ethnomathematics and Anthropology in Relation to Mathematics Education.* Available at: http://dg.icme11.org/document/get/324

Moreira, D. 2008. *Explorations Between Ethnomathematics and Anthropology in Relation to Mathematics Education.* 11th International Congress on Mathematical Education, Monterrey, Mexico, July 6–12, 2008. Downloaded on 7/5/11 from: http://dg.icme11.org/tsg/show/19

Myers, M. 2009. "Achievement of Children Identified with Special Needs in Two-Way Spanish Immersion Programs." Unpublished doctoral dissertation. Washington, DC: The George Washington University.

National Center for Education Statistics. 2003. "Societal Support for Learning: Family Support (Indicator 37)." In *The Condition of Education, 2003.* Available at: http://nces.ed.gov/pubs2003/2003067_6.pdf

National Governors Association Center for Best Practices and the Council of Chief State School Officers. 2010. *Common Core State Standards for English Language Arts and Literacy in History/Social Studies, Science, and Technical Subjects.* Washington, DC: National Governors Association.

National Governors Association Center for Best Practices and the Council of Chief State School Officers. 2010. *Common Core State Standards for Mathematics.* Washington, DC: National Governors Association.

National Governors Association Center for Best Practices and the Council of Chief State School Officers. 2010. *Common Core State Standards for English Language Arts & Literacy in History/Social Studies, Science, and Technical Subjects.* Washington, DC: National Governors Association.

National Reading Panel. 2000. *Teaching Children to Read: An Evidence-Based Assessment of the Scientific Research Literature on Reading and Its Implications for Reading Instruction* (Executive Summary). Washington, DC: National Institute of Child Health and Human Development (NICHD) and U.S. Department of Education.

National Research Council. 2012. *A Framework for K–12 Science Education: Practices, Crosscutting Concepts, and Core Ideas.* Washington, DC: The National Academies Press. Available at: www.nap.edu/catalog.php?record_id=13165

National Research Council of the National Academy of Sciences, National Science Teachers Association, American Association for the Advancement of Science, and Achieve (January 2013). *Next Generation Science Standards (Second Public Draft Version).* Washington, DC: Achieve, Inc. Downloaded on January 10, 2013 at: www.nextgenscience.org/next-generation-science-standards.

Paradis, J. 2006. "Second Language Acquisition in Childhood." In E. Hoff, & M. Shatz (Eds.), *Handbook of Language Development* (pp. 387–405). Oxford, UK: Blackwell.

Paradis, J., Genesee, F., & Crago, M. 2011. *Dual Language Development and Disorders: A Handbook on Bilingualism and Second Language Learning.* Baltimore, MD: Brookes.

Porter, K. 1986. *Discovering Butterflies and Moths.* New York: The Bookwright Press.

Rau, D. M. [Spanish translation and text composition by Victory Productions]. 2007. *¡Vuela mariposa, vuela!* (part of the series ¡Vamos criaturita, vamos!). Tarrytown, NY: Marshall Cavendish Benchmark.

Rice, D. H. 2012. *La vida de una mariposa* (part of Time for Kids Nonfiction Readers). Huntington Beach, CA: Teacher Created Materials.

Richards, H. V., Brown, A. F., & Forde, T. B. 2006. *Addressing Diversity in Schools: Culturally Responsive Education.* National Center for Culturally Responsive Educational Systems. Available at: www.nccrest .org/Briefs/Diversity_Brief.pdf

Riches, C., & Genesee, F. 2006. "Cross-Linguistic and Cross-Modal Aspects of Literacy Development." In F. Genesee, K. Lindholm-Leary, W. Saunders, & D. Christian, *Educating English Language Learners: A Synthesis of Research Evidence* (pp. 64–108). New York: Cambridge University Press.

Rogoff, B. 2003. *The Cultural Nature of Human Development.* Oxford: Oxford University Press.

Scarcella, R. 2003. *Accelerating Academic English: A Focus on the English Learner.* Oakland, CA: Regents of the University of California.

Schleppegrell, M. J. 2004. *The Language of Schooling: A Functional Linguistics Perspective.* Mahwah, NJ: Lawrence Erlbaum.

Schleppegrell, M. J., & O'Hallaron, C. L. 2011. "Teaching Academic Language in L2 Secondary Settings." *Annual Review of Applied Linguistics* 31: 3–18.

Scholastic Canada Ltd. 2002. "How to Take Running Records." Adapted from *Alphakids Assessment Teacher's Guide.* Available at: www.scholastic.ca/education/.../pdfs/grade4/runningrecords.pdf

Scott, J. A., & Nagy, W. E. 1997. "Understanding the Definitions of Unfamiliar Words." *Reading Research Quarterly* 32: 184–200.

Shannon, S. M. 2002. "Parents Choose Dual Language Programs in Colorado: A Survey." *Bilingual Research Journal* 26(3): 681–696.

Snow, C. E., Burns, M. S., & Griffin, P. 1998. *Preventing Reading Difficulties in Young Children.* Washington, DC: National Academy Press.

Snow, M. A., Met, M., & Genesee, F. 1989. "A Conceptual Framework for the Integration of Language and Content in Second/Foreign Language Instruction." *TESOL Quarterly* 23: 201–217.

Thomas, W., & Collier, V. 2002. *A National Study of School Effectiveness for Language Minority Students' Long-Term Academic Achievement.* Santa Cruz, CA: Center for Research on Education, Diversity and Excellence.

Urow, C., & Beeman, K. 2011. "El Puente: Crando Conexiones Metalinguisticas." *Soleado: Promising Practices from the Field* 4(1): 2–3, 13 (a publication of Dual Language Education of New Mexico).

Valdes, G. 1997. "Dual-Language Immersion Programs: A Cautionary Note Concerning the Education of Language-Minority Students." *Harvard Educational Review* 67: 391–429.

Weibel. P. 2004. *The Big Red Book of Spanish Idioms.* New York: McGraw-Hill.

West, M. 1953. *A General Service List of English Words, 1953.* London: Longman, Green, & Co. Available at: http://jbauman.com/aboutgsl.html

WIDA Consortium. 2005. *Normas WIDA del Español (WIDA Spanish Language Arts Standards).* Madison, WI: Board of Regents of the University of Wisconsin System on behalf of the WIDA Consortium, Wisconsin Center for Education Research, University of Wisconsin-Madison. Available at: www.wida.us/standards/slaspanish.pdf

WIDA Consortium. 2007. *WIDA English Language Proficiency (ELP) Standards, 2007 Edition.* Madison, WI: Board of Regents of the University of Wisconsin System on behalf of the WIDA Consortium, Wisconsin Center for Education Research, University of Wisconsin-Madison.

WIDA Consortium. 2012. *2012 Amplification of the English Language Development Standards; Kindergarten–Grade 12.* Madison, WI: Board of Regents of the University of Wisconsin System on behalf of the WIDA Consortium, Wisconsin Center for Education Research, University of Wisconsin-Madison.

Wiggins, G., & McTighe, J. 2005. *Understanding by Design, Second Edition.* Alexandria, VA: Association for Supervision and Curriculum Development.

Wrubel, R. M. 2002. *Great Grouping Strategies.* New York: Scholastic.

Index

continuous professional development, 37–38

curricular connections with community, 109–110

developing community support, 57–58

elevating Spanish status, 160–161

embedding Web 2.0 tools, 129–130

Four-level Spanish Language Arts for High School, 182–183

helping schools choose a DBE program, 66–67

importance of planning and monitoring, 65, 67

importance of yearlong planning, 44–45

networking with dual language colleagues and experts, 208–209

special needs students, 106–107

dual-language immersion, 19. *See also* Two-Way Immersion (TWI)

E

early immersion, 12–13

English Language Learners, 2, 62–63. *See also* special needs students
  academic outcomes, 30–33
  English outcomes, 25–26, 28–30

English language outcomes, explaining, 28–30

English-speaking students, 2. *See also* special needs students
  academic outcomes, 33
  English outcome, 27–30
  socioeconomic status and academic success, 35–36

special education academic success, 35

equalizing the two languages, 160–163

ethnomathematics, 97, 127

ethnoscience, 97, 127

evaluation. *See* assessment

Evaluator's Toolkit for Dual Language Programs, 24, 39

executive control functions, 7, 8, 30

Explicit Vocabulary Instruction Procedure, 179

F

families and community
  checklist for program key features, 41
  extension phase, 138
  unit planning—outreach, 148

figurative language, 139, 172, 196, 231

first-language models, 19–20

fluency, 72, 164, 199, 201, 232, 233

Flynt-Cooter English-Español Reading Inventory for the Classroom, 200

Foreign/Second Language Immersion
  academic success, 27–28
  alternative forms of, 12–13
  characteristics of, 8
  checklist of key features, 39–41
  content objectives, 89
  delayed 12–13
  defined, 5
  early total 12–13
  90/10 vs. 50/50 13–14
  parental choice, 10–11
  program model comparisons, 22–23
  rationale for, 15

lesson-planning framework,
Appendix A
Lima, Francisca Silva, 129
Lindholm-Leary, Kathryn, 21,
26, 27, 31, 34, 207
literacy
academic success and, 91,
105
developing, 19, 29, 30, 108
early literacy practices, 112
foundation, 111–112
home literacy index, 106
reading and writing, 124–125
sequencing instruction in L1
and L2, 169–171
longitudinal data, 81
low-incidence languages, 102
Lyster, Roy, 77

M

Madrigal-Hopes, Diana L., 67
mainstream, 2, 5–7, 19, 106, 111,
112, 167
maintenance bilingual
education, 17. *See also*
Developmental Bilingual
Education (DBE)
maps, 126, 130, 142
materials, 127–130, 184–187,
216
mathematics instruction, model
unit, 149–155
Met, Myriam, 90
metalinguistic awareness, 30
Mexican literature, 183
models of dual language
education, 8–21
Moll, Luis, 6
multiculturalism, 37
multimedia materials, 128
music, 74, 80, 139, 142
Myers, Marjorie L., 107
myths
bilingual code-mixing, 96
children are linguistic
sponges, 10

conversational fluency means
proficiency, 158
equality for both languages,
162
exposure is sufficient, 91
minority parents should use
English at home, 110
minority parents want
English education, 59
more English, increased
achievement, 28
oral language proficiency
before instruction in
literacy, 165
limited L2 exposure is
sufficient to yield benefits,
63
translated books are best, 184
young children acquire
second language quickly,
10

N

National Center for Education
Statistics, 106
National Council for Social
Studies (NCSS), 110
National Council of Teachers of
Mathematics (NCTM),
149–150
National Dual Language
Consortium (NDLC), 210
NDLC. *See* National Dual
Language Consortium
(NDLC)
Networking with colleagues and
experts, 208–209
neurocognitive advantages,
7–8
newspaper
community involvement
through, 61, 82
instruction using, 173, 177,
178, 181, 184, 187, 195
nonfiction books, 128
Nora, Julie, 110

technology tools for, 129
visuals for, 135
vocabulary and, 70
word problems, 155
reading and writing conferences, 200
recruiting
  teachers, 84–85
  students, 85
research notes
  addressing incongruity, 47
  definition of, 2
  intensive exposure, 71
  strategies, 95
  successful L2 readers, 94
  value of family literacy, 106
  vocabulary, 121
research findings, dual
    language programs
  academic outcomes, 30–33
  English learning outcomes, 24–30
  outcomes for ELLs, 34–35
  outcomes for English-
    speaking students, 35–36
  suitability for special needs, 33–34
research references, 206–207
resources
  About DL Education in
    General, 42
  Academic Word Lists, 122
  Formal Assessment, 200
  How to Compute the Reading
    Levels of Texts, 168
  Language Tidbits, 189
  A List of Selected Videos on
    DL Education, 49
  Lost Ladybug Project, 138
  Publishing Houses for
    Languages Other than
    Spanish, 186
  Some Excellent Conferences
    for Administrators and
    Teams of Teachers, 83
  Sources for Evaluating Dual
    Language Programs, 39

Spanish idioms, 189
User-Friendly Research
  References, 206–207
Websites of Useful
  Organizations, 209–210
Working with Students with
  Special Learning Needs, 36
Riches, Caroline, 29, 111
Rogers, David, 209
running records, 198–199

S

Salvadorian literature, 183
Sátiro, Angelica, 139
scaffolding, 6–7, 12, 38, 77, 89, 124, 177, 187
scheduling, 52, 58, 69, 74, 170–171
secondary objectives, 88, 125–126, 175, 179, 180–184
SEI. *See* Structured English
  Immersion (SEI)
self-assessment, 143, 185
sentence fluency, 201, 232
sequential model of literacy
  instruction, 170
sequential participation
  structures, 131
Shanahan, Timothy, 111
Sheltered Instruction
  Observation Protocol, 209
sheltered instructional
  strategies, 80, 98
Simé, Cynthia, 129
simultaneous participation
  structures, 137
Sistema de evaluación de la
  lectura, 200
"6 + 1 Traits," 201
Snow, Marguerite Ann, 90
social interaction, importance
  of, 9–10
sociocultural, communication
  differences, 6–7

V

value-added learning, 45
Vázquez, Dania, 45
videos, program promotion, 49–50
virtual field trips, 138
visuals
    bridging, 23, 68, 140, 147
    general learning objectives, 98
    graphic organizers, 135
    multimedia, 128
    vocabulary, 121
vocabulary
    academic, 92
    acquisition, 174
    assessment of, 144
    balanced literacy, 164
    from books, 193
    bridging, 140
    communication using, 134
    content-obligatory language, 90, 121–123
    cross-linguistic, 94
    descriptive, 169
    learning, 111, 121, 133
    by proficiency level, 126
    strategies, 38
    technical, 92, 93
    transition words, 169
    using visuals for, 121
    word study, 179
    in writing, 121

W

Web 2.0 tools, 129, 142
webquests, 136, 223

Weibel, Peter, 189
WIDA Consortium English Language Development Standards, 145–147, 155, 174, 200–201
wikis, 130, 163
word choice, 201
word walls, 133, 139, 200
writer's notebook, 201, 203
Writer's Workshop, 196
writing. *See also* Language Arts and literacy instruction and literacy skills
    "6 + 1 Traits," 201
    academic, 29, 91–94, 93
    assessment, 81, 200
    community-literacy sources, 195
    conferences for teachers, 201
    cross-linguistic, 95–96
    genre, 180, 187–188
    holistic, 200–201
    letters, 112
    literacy skills, 124–125
    narrative texts, 200
    notebook, 201
    oral language development and, 165
    outside of school, 112
    poetry, 112, 139, 177
    projects, 139
    samples scored with rubrics, 200–201
    sources to prompt student, 195
    text structure, 151
    text types, 174

Nancy Cloud ■ Fred Genesee ■ Else Hamayan

LITERACY INSTRUCTION *for* ENGLISH LANGUAGE LEARNERS
A Teacher's Guide to Research-Based Practices

LITERACY INSTRUCTION FOR ENGLISH LANGUAGE LEARNERS
is for everyone who teaches English language learners
to read and write. It turns important research findings
about ELL students into evidence-based, effective
classroom practice. It helps teachers:

- learn more about the ELL students in their classroom

- support the emergence and early development of
  English literacy skills in nonnative speakers

- help English learners reach their full potential as
  readers and writers

- promote biliteracy in English and students' home
  languages

- guide ELL students as they develop academic
  language and literacy in English

- connect reading and writing strongly to promote
  growth in each

K–8 / 978-0-325-02264-2 / 2009 / 256pp / $25.00

- assess the literacy skills of English language
  learners and use that information to plan
  responsive instruction.

**Ideal for
Book Study Groups**
Book Study Bundle
978-0-325-03093-7
15 copies / $318.75
SAVE $56.25!

Heinemann
DEDICATED TO TEACHERS

Visit **www.heinemann.com** *to read Sample Chapters of our books and order online.*

To order by phone call **800.225.5800** or fax **877.231.6980.**

@HeinemannPub